Food, Nutrition, and You

FERGUS M. CLYDESDALE

University of Massachusetts

FREDERICK J. FRANCIS

University of Massachusetts

PRENTICE-HALL, INC., Englewood Cliffs, New Jersey 07632

Library of Congress Cataloging in Publication Data

Clydesdale, F   M
   Food, nutrition, and you.

   Includes bibliographies.
   1. Food. 2. Food Supply. 3. Nutrition.
I. Francis, F. J., 1921– joint author. II. Title.
TX354.C58   641.1   76-40097
ISBN 0-13-323048-1
ISBN 0-13-323030-9 pbk.

Printed in the United States of America.

10 9 8 7 6 5 4 3 2

PRENTICE-HALL INTERNATIONAL, INC., *London*
PRENTICE-HALL OF AUSTRALIA PTY. LIMITED, *Sydney*
PRENTICE-HALL OF CANADA, LTD., *Toronto*
PRENTICE-HALL OF INDIA PRIVATE LIMITED, *New Delhi*
PRENTICE-HALL OF JAPAN, INC., *Tokyo*
PRENTICE-HALL OF SOUTHEAST ASIA PTE. LTD., *Singapore*
WHITEHALL BOOKS LIMITED, *Wellington, New Zealand*

Contents

part ▌▌

Food Supply   143

Preface

In the late sixties there was a great upheaval and questioning on University campuses across the entire nation. The dramatic, violent, and sometimes sad results of this movement were apparent nationally. However, there was also a questioning of "relevancy" in education which did not make headlines but certainly aroused some academicians to take a new and perhaps different perspective of what was being taught. Coupled with this awareness was the increasing demand by students for information on nutrition, food, and health. This demand was initially satisfied by those who prescribed food for cure-alls and magic, and led to a very lucrative market for those in the business of selling or promoting quick-weight-loss, cures for any disorder, and ultimate happiness from certain foods. Unfortunately, the majority of scientists did not respond constructively at that time but merely stated their disapproval to one another and not to consumers or to students.

The early seventies brought into view another parameter which further complicated the situation. This of course was the dramatic increase in food prices and unavailability caused by an overburdened world trying to produce food for an overpopulated planet with limited energy resources.

This book, in part, arose from our attempt to meet these demands.

In the years 1968 to 1970, the authors were involved with curriculum changes and a reevaluation of student needs on the University of Massachusetts, Amherst, Campus. It was our opinion that we, in the sciences, had been shortchanging the nonscience majors by not providing them with enough information to judge the critical issues, which were arising in the food-population-health-energy area. It was also our opinion that perhaps we had been attempting to make a scientist out of a poet in one semester—an impossible task. Certainly the reverse is equally impossible—the creation of a poet from a scientist in one semester.

However, it seems this inescapable logic had been largely overlooked in the academic community.

Therefore, we decided to begin a science course in the area of Food and Nutrition aimed specifically at nonscience majors. This course began with an enrollment of 260 students and within two semesters had a preregistration of some 3,000 students. Unfortunately, we were only able to teach 1,300, but by teaching the course each semester we could handle 2,600 students per year. As a result of some five years of teaching this course we decided that a book covering certain aspects of the course that the students were most interested in, might serve an appropriate service to the public.

It is the intent of this book to provide an insight into the realities of nutrition and food supply as well as the benefits of a varied diet, which of course is sound nutrition. For instance it must be realized that with the current population of the world we must utilize technology to produce, distribute, and ultimately feed this population. Fresh food cannot be distributed over great distances nor can a tomato be grown in two feet of snow. Technology allows the year-round availability of food and its subsequent distribution.

Certainly "fresh" foods are excellent sources of nutrients but care must be used in defining "fresh." If "fresh" is defined as grown close by, picked, rushed to the kitchen and eaten, then fresh foods are probably the best tasting and most nutritious. However if "fresh" is defined as sitting in a truck or a store for a week, then "fresh" is not always best.

It is our hope that the reader will realize that food is not magic —it allows one to achieve one's genetic potential, no more; that foods are simply chemicals and that the only scientific reason for eating is to replace the chemicals in the body with chemicals from food; that we live in an overpopulated, underenergized world and that the rational, sane use of technology will help, not hinder.

The secret to good health through food is to eat a varied diet and, in America, to probably eat a little less of everything.

There must be more communication of these facts to the public from scientists.

We hope that this book will provide some of this communication. No one book can have all the answers. However, perhaps a beginning can be achieved so that consumers will be less confused— less frightened—and will be able to learn to eat a healthy diet which fits their lifestyle and provides them with a healthier, happier, and more satisfying way of life on our crowded planet.

F. M. Clydesdale

F. J. Francis

part **I**

Food Safety, Preservation, and Nutrition in the United States

In a book on food and nutrition it is necessary to consider the food situation of the world as well as of the United States because availability and price of food are determined by world demand as well as the level of technology in a particular part of the world. As certain commodities achieve world demand, prices rise and the consumer cuts back on purchases of high-priced food. This trend has been evident in the United States with many commodities such as wheat, sugar and beef. Therefore, the authors have deemed it advisable to treat this book in two parts.

The first part of the book deals with the overall food picture as it exists in the United States. It deals with a marketplace which has thousands of items for sale to fit every lifestyle. Superimposed upon this array of plenty is an underlying concern of the consumer about safety and nutrition—about the way food is handled, grown, processed, and prepared. It is the intent of Part I of this book to attempt to place today's food in perspective.

The authors, along with most scientists, would agree that food grown to the peak of maturity in the backyard and rushed to the kitchen to be eaten is probably the most tasty and nutritious food. However, in a vast country and a vaster overpopulated world containing many different lifestyles, such a situation is not common or practical. Therefore, it is the author's contention that we must learn about the foods that are available today, take advantage of their convenience for our lifestyle, and utilize them in a diet which is varied and healthy.

Unfortunately, the consumer today is not being presented with all the facts about food. It is a terrible disservice to consumers to destroy their confidence in the safety and nutritive value of their food without presenting them with a balanced picture giving both the positive and negative aspects of today's food.

Certainly many criticisms can be leveled at our food supply today, but these fade into oblivion as we perceive the disappearance of all the gross nutritional deficiency diseases. Scurvy, rickets, beri-beri, pellagra—all are unknown in the United States today.

3

The processing of food is essential to avoid the syndrome of lean years and fat years. Preservation of food is necessary to extend crop life and avoid starvation.

Government agencies now test food and food additives for safety. In ancient times men tried food, and if it was tasty and harmless, they continued to eat it. If it was poisonous, they died.

We have the potential of being the best-fed nation in the history of the world. Education, with all the facts, is essential to achieve this potential goal. Instilling paranoia and suspicion is negative. Education should utilize positive, concrete, practical suggestions for leading a happier and healthier life. A varied diet consistent with your lifestyle can achieve this goal.

chapter **1**

Food: A Basic Problem

It is an interesting commentary on our present way of life that a tremendous amount of antifood literature is appearing daily in all the popular journals and newspapers. Such literature would have us return to the good old days. However, do we want to return to the good old days? Myriad cranks, quacks, and faddists are now promoting the idea that our nutritional past was a glory of "natural" healthful eating to which we must return for food salvation. However, in general one must admit that the "good old days" of nutrition are merely a myth.

Just before World War I, for example, rickets, beriberi, pellagra, and goiter—all extremely serious nutrition-deficiency diseases—were, according to American Medical Association conclusions, "common

5

diseases in the United States." These maladies are no longer even tabulated as causes of death in this country, but they were a couple of generations ago. In 1900, the infant death rate was over 162 per 1,000. Today it is less than 25 per 1,000. An even better indicator of nutrition is the mortality rate. In 1900 it was about 20 per 1,000. That rate has now been reduced by more than 95 percent! Moreover, children reach their mature height five years sooner than they did in 1900, and grow three to six inches taller.

Of course, our longer life span is due in large part to infectious-disease control and modern drugs. Faddists, however, say that drugs would be less necessary if children ate better, but this is an idiotic approach to good nutrition.

We have the potential to be the best fed people in history, but in our human frailty we sometimes abuse this potential. We do tend to ingest too many fun foods, too much fat, too much animal protein, and in general we eat too much. However, this is not due to the food industry, nor to the food-service industry, and certainly not to the advances in food technology.

We must be aware of change if we are to deal with what Alvin Toffler has written about in *Future Shock*. We must be aware of what is being produced, why it is being produced, and how it is being tested. We cannot just read a book because it is in print and assume that the writers are always correct when they tell us that everything we are eating is an illegitimate child of technology and is being produced only for the almighty dollar.

In addition to such nonsensical utterances, we have another misconception: millions of people are starving today, yet we are led to believe that if we went back to the ways of nature this problem could be solved. Those who live the organic way are deluding themselves if they believe this approach will ease the suffering of the human race. The organic way will never feed today's world because population has increased too far and too fast. We must accept and indeed depend upon technology to feed our current population. If people wish to follow extreme faddism in their thoughts and diets, let that be their "bag." However, they shouldn't delude themselves into thinking they're helping anyone.

Certainly, there are legitimate questions we can ask about today's food industry, but we truly believe that such questions are being answered, that controls are becoming more severe, and that voluntary compliance is working. We have come a tremendously long way in the last fifty years. Food production was low in the good old days, and checks and balances were tenuous at best. Now, at least, the consumer is receiving food that is by and large well inspected, of high quality, and available at all times of the year.

Indeed, we are what we eat. This comment from a well-known writer can be interpreted in many ways. Unfortunately, the interpretation of some is that the foods we are eating now do not create a healthy mind or a healthy body. This, in our judgment, is sheer nonsense—and in fact extremely dangerous, particularly to those who do not have the technical background with which to make a proper scientific assessment of writings about food and nutrition.

In the midst of the deluge of materials that scream about our food being poisonous or at least harmful to anyone who partakes of it, we are faced with a serious problem—a problem, moreover, that grows daily: the starvation and malnutrition both in the developing countries and in the United States. Most people are aware of this; what they are not aware of is the magnitude of the problem, or how fast it is approaching crisis proportion. In 1967 the President's Science Advisory Committee Panel on the world food supply estimated that 20 percent of the people in the underdeveloped countries (which contain two thirds of the world population) were undernourished and that 60 percent were malnourished. This means that in 1967 as many as a billion and a half people were either undernourished or malnourished. Other estimates place the number of hungry people at more than 2 billion; of these, an estimated half billion can be described as either chronically hungry or starving. Some of these figures must be increased because it appears that when they were calculated, it was assumed that less calories were required by a person in the tropical countries than in the more temperate zones. However this has since been proved wrong. It is now known that in the tropical countries caloric intake should indeed be increased and not decreased. More recent figures tell us that 2.5 billion of the 3.76 billion people now on earth are critically short of food, water, shelter, and clothing. Some 500 million people in North America, Western Europe, Australia, New Zealand, and some regions of South America live in the lap of luxury compared to this other group. It has become abundantly clear that we are faced with a world-wide crisis situation. People are starving, people are going hungry, people are demanding their rights to adequate food, water, shelter, and clothing. Yes, there is a problem, a very definite problem, one that had better be resolved soon or else violence may shake the flimsy foundation on which many political institutions are based.

Perhaps these figures come as no surprise to the many Americans who know from the popular press that famines do occur, that wars occur, that civil eruptions occur, and that these events create starvation, malnutrition, and undernourishment of large proportions. Unfortunately, we often shrug off these facts and figures because we are living in a society that is reasonably affluent, that provides us by and large with the necessities of life, and that feeds its pets better than most people in the world are fed. It is interesting to note that many Americans feel much worse about a neighbor's dog being run over by a car than they do when they read about hundreds of thousands of people dying from inadequate food and medical attention in some developing country far from American shores.

For this reason, it might be better to discuss some of the nutritional problems in America rather than lingering on the world-wide problems. This does not mean that we are dismissing the world-wide problems, nor does it mean that they are not crucial. It simply means that if we can bring some of these ideas closer to home, they might be more meaningful to the average American. This person seems to worry more about the odd chemical in a certain food—when all foods are only chemicals themselves—than about the many people who are suffering from severe nutritional deficiencies.

At times, a book tells a story in a way that cannot possibly be improved. In order to describe some of the nutritional problems in America, I would like to quote a section of such a book.

> Let me describe what I have seen among fifty or so people who live in four small cabins at the edge of a large plantation. In child after child I have seen evidence of vitamin and mineral deficiencies; serious, untreated skin infections and ulcerations; eye and ear diseases; unattended bone diseases secondary to poor food intake; the prevalence of bacterial and parasitic disease, as well as severe anemia, with resulting loss of energy and ability to live a normally active life; diseases of the heart and the lungs—requiring surgery—which have gone undiagnosed and untreated; epileptic and other neurological disorders; a severe kidney ailment that in other children would warrant immediate hospitalization; and finally, evidence of what can properly and conservatively be called malnutrition, with consequent injury to the body's tissues—its muscles, bone, and skin—accompanied by a psychological state of malaise. Diarrhea, chronic sores, chronic leg and arm (untreated) injuries and deformities— they are everywhere around for a doctor to notice, and in time to overlook and forget.

> I have to remind myself after a while that I am staying in homes that lack screens and running water and even on occasion electricity. I have to remind myself that mosquitoes and flies bear germs, as does stagnant water, that a meal of grits, bread, Kool-Aid or Coke, and occasional slices of "salad meat" or fatback gives the body some calories to burn, but precious little else. I have to remind myself, as a physician, that not all American children are plagued by illnesses with names like trichinosis, enterobiasis, ascariasis, or even a plain-worded one like hookworm disease. I have to keep in mind that dry skin, shrunken

skin, ulcerated skin is rarely seen by the pediatricians who work with my children, with "our" children; nor are rashes, boils, abscesses, furuncles, impetigo, and scars the usual and constant things to be found in child after child.

All that and more goes on. With five other doctors in May of 1967 I went from home to home in several counties of Mississippi. We were shocked, just as I had been horrified and ashamed all these past years. We wrote a report called "Children in Mississippi," and in July of 1967 presented our findings to a group of United States Senators—they were members of a subcommittee on employment, manpower and poverty, and they listened to us and questioned us in a public hearing. To quote myself: Almost every child we saw was in a state of negative nitrogen balance; that is, a marked inadequacy of diet has led the body to consume its own protein tissue. What we saw clinically—the result of this condition of chronic hunger and malnutrition—was as follows: wasting of muscles; enlarged hearts; edematous legs and in some cases the presence of abdominal edema (so-called swollen or bloated belly); spontaneous bleeding of the mouth or nose or evidence of internal hemorrhage; osteoporosis—a weakening of bone structure—and, as a consequence, fractures unrelated to injury or accident; and again and again, fatigue, exhaustion, weakness.

These children would need blood transfusions before any corrective surgery could be done—and we found in child after child (and in adults, too) the need for surgery: hernias; poorly healed fractures; rheumatic and congenital heart disease with attendant murmurs, difficult breathing, and chest pain; evidence of gastrointestinal bleeding or partial obstruction; severe, suppurating ear infections; congenital or developmental eye disease in bad need of correction.

The teeth of practically every child we saw—and of their parents, too—were in awful repair—eaten up by cavities and often poorly developed. Their gums showed how severely anemic these children are; and the gums were also infected and foul-smelling.

Many of these children (and again their parents) were suffering from degenerative joint diseases. Injuries had not been treated when they occurred. Bleeding had taken place, with subsequent infections. Now, at seven or eight, a child's knee joint or elbow joints might show the "range of action" that one finds in a man of seventy who suffers from crippling arthritis.

In child after child we tested for peripheral neuritis—and found it, secondary to untreated injuries, infections, and food deficiencies. These children could not feel normally—feel pressure or heat or cold or applied pain the way the normal person does. What they do feel is the sensory pain that goes with disease;

pricking, burning, flashes of sharp pain, or a "deep pain" as one child put it.

The children were plagued with cold and fevers—in Mississippi, in late May—and with sore throats. They had enlarged glands throughout the body, secondary to the several infections they chronically suffer. Some of them showed jaundice in their eyes, which meant that liver damage was likely, or that hemolysis secondary to bacterial invasion had occurred.

What particularly saddened and appalled us were the developmental anomalies and diseases that we know once were easily correctable, but now are hopelessly consolidated. Bones, eyes, vital organs that should long ago have been evaluated and treated are now all beyond medical assistance, even if it were suddenly—incredibly is the word the people themselves feel rather than use—available. In some cases we saw children clearly stunted, smaller than their age would indicate, drowsy and irritable.

In sum, children living under unsanitary conditions without proper food, and with a limited intake of improper food, without access to doctors or dentists, under crowded conditions in flimsy shacks pay the price in a plethora of symptoms, diseases, aches, and pain. No wonder that in Mississippi (whose Negroes comprise 42 percent of the state's population) the infant mortality rate among Negroes is over twice that of whites; and while the white infant mortality rate is dropping, the rate for Negroes is rising.

Perhaps more valuable and instructive were the comments of five Mississippi doctors who were asked by the state's governor, Paul B. Johnson, to visit the same counties we visited—"in response to certain charges of starvation and conspiracy in the state of Mississippi." Many people in the state, not only doctors and politicians, felt that once again "outsiders" had come upon the Delta and the South to tarnish and malign its "traditions," to single out unfairly this area, that region—when all over the country certain people have trouble finding work, a decent place to live, and even enough food to appease their hunger, their children's hunger. Let our own doctors go see what really exists, Mississippi's governor said—and by prompting such a step he provided the kind of leadership the nation certainly craves and doesn't always find. Here are some observations from the medical report submitted to Governor Johnson, and then to the United States Senate:

> "The situations encountered were indeed primitive. In one locality eight families were found to share one faucet and one privy. The mother of one of these families states that she obtained surplus commodity food and that her welfare check was seventy-one dollars per month. She said she had been unable to get work for some time. Her monthly rent is fifteen dollars. She has no children in either of the

Head Start programs, but her house does have electricity and a new refrigerator. Sanitation in the area was not acceptable by modern standards. Six of her eight children were seen. Several of them had infected lesions and all appeared to have some degree of anemia, but none was on the verge of starvation."

"At one house visited, there was one outdoor privy serving "nine or ten families." Not far away was a single water faucet which constituted the only water supply for the same people. Garbage and refuse were strewn about the premises and the smell of human excrement was unmistakable. . . ."

"Hospital facilities for indigent patients was virtually nonexistent. . . ."[1]

In case some reader feels that this quotation is sensationalism and really not typical of the facts, here are some remarks by Senator Ernest F. Hollings about the problem of hunger in America.

Fifteen million desperately poor Americans are going hungry in America today. Most of them are young children whose brains and bodies will be forever stunted by a lack of food. Many others are women and old people for whom America's promise of plenty has been a lifelong sham. These are Americans who will forever live outside the normal systems of society and free enterprise and whose contribution to the future of America will be virtually nonexistent until something is done to reverse the horrible cycle of poverty. Most of these Americans are either beyond the reach of, or have been overlooked by, our expanding system of social welfare and the feeding programs which have grown so rapidly in the past two years.

The problem of hunger in America has grown worse rather than better in the past decade. And within the last few years, poverty has increased rather than diminished. This depressing fact was acknowledged by the Nixon administration. The Office of Economic Opportunity has recently estimated that 25.7 million persons were below poverty level in 1970, an increase of 1.1 million from the previous year. This reverses a general downtrend in the number of those officially classified as "poor." Nearly all economists and specialists in the poverty field agree that the number of poor families has increased because of tightened economic conditions.[2]

Senator Hollings goes on to say that most Americans do not believe that hunger is a serious national concern. Therein lies a large part of the problem. Hollings says that

---

[1] Robert Coles and Al Clayton, *Still Hungry in America.* Copyright © 1969 by Robert Coles, pp. 83–88. Reprinted by arrangement with The New American Library, Inc., New York, N.Y.

[2] Ernest F. Hollings, "Hunger in America." *Supermarketing Magazine.* June, 1971, 41–60.

it is easy for us to say that our food stamp and commodity food programs are serving more than 10 million persons and, therefore, nobody should be hungry. The truth is more elusive.

Americans are going hungry because the food stamp program does not work for large numbers of them. They are going hungry because they do not have the money to buy food. They are going hungry because the free commodity program is a farce. They are going hungry because the world's largest food delivery system, the food industry, has for the most part ignored the poor who so desperately need our help.

These obstacles can be overcome but first American citizens are going to have to be convinced that there is a major, ongoing problem which only aroused public opinion can solve.[3]

So, you see, there is indeed a problem. In order to arouse public opinion to solve this problem, we must understand not only the poverty around us but also the food we are eating today. The latter understanding is essential because of the dangers that may result from believing the misinformed people who claim that technology is ruining our food supply. We cannot feed our ever growing population either in this country or in the world by going back to nature's ways, whatever that means. We can only feed this population by taking advantage of the available technology and by attempting to slow, if not stop, the rapid expansion in births. This can be done only if all of us become better informed. We do not become better informed by reading sensational books and articles by people who do not know the facts about food and nutrition and who are so self-centered that they worry more about what they themselves eat than about the world-wide food problem.

Food is indeed a basic problem. We speak of equality, we speak of equal rights, and we speak of equal job opportunities. All of these things must come if we are to feed our population and the population of the world.

There are many reasons why we eat, social, cultural, and physical. They must all be considered when we attempt to feed a given population. We cannot expect to feed everyone the same way, nor can we expect the people we supply with food to accept it gracefully as a handout given by some patron of the poor. Therefore, we are making a plea for people to understand more about their own bodies, about nutrition, about food science.

The world today is faced with the triumvirate of food, energy, and population problems. Food prices are soaring, as any consumer can attest, the energy problem is critical and becoming more severe,

[3] *Ibid.*

and still we see some 90 million children born a year. America is no longer the richest country in the world; it now lags behind the oil-producing countries, who bulge with petro-dollars. Some degree of cooperation between energy-producing nations and food-producing nations, as well as a curtailment in world-wide population growth, is necessary if the world is to survive.

BIBLIOGRAPHY

Coles, Robert, and Al Clayton, *Still Hungry in America.* Cleveland: The World Publishing Company, 1969.

Ehrlich, Paul R., *The Population Bomb.* New York: Ballantine Books Inc., 1968.

Ehrlich, Paul R., and Anne H. Ehrlich, *Population, Resources, Environment.* San Francisco: W. H. Freeman and Co., Publishers, 1972.

Paddock, William, and Paul Paddock, *Famine 1975! America's Decision: Who Will Survive?* Boston: Little, Brown and Company, 1967.

White House Conference on Food Nutrition, and Health: Final Report. Washington, D.C.: U.S. Government Printing Office, 1969.

chapter **2**

Some Insights into Nutrition

According to portions of the press, other media, and some consumer groups about which we hear and read, there is a tremendous demand for more knowledge about nutrition. Unfortunately, this statement is not the whole truth. In general, people shy away from knowledge about nutrition and about what food can do to help them maintain health and well-being. However, they do want to know how food can make them stronger, happier, more creative, less prone to illness, and sexually capable to a degree unheard of in most societies. That is, they want something that will prevent disease or work miracles. This unfortunate state of affairs can in part be blamed upon consumers themselves, many of whom do not want to read facts but desire a panacea; upon scientists, who at times write primarily for other scientists and not the people; upon faddists or quacks who write about such panaceas, either because they believe in them or because they want to sell books or a particular product; and upon the media, which at times would much rather communicate sensational cures or ills caused by foods rather than a common-sense, logical approach to the problem of food and nutrition.

The authors hope that this chapter will convey a broad view of nutrition and provide information with which the reader can evaluate some of the sensationalism and pap that is found from time to time in the press and in books. Perhaps a little knowledge is a dangerous thing, but no knowledge or the belief that food has an all-consuming power is much less desirable than some actual knowledge, however small, of what food can do for us. Therefore, we shall treat the known and more accepted nutritional facts rather than presenting a series of theories based on preliminary or virtually nonexistent experimentation.

In Chapters 3 and 6 we will discuss food fads in more detail, but we think it might be of interest at this point to mention one of the more amusing food fads, and perhaps the first one, developed in America.

In 1796 Dr. Elisha Perkins discovered the secret of perpetual good health. Surprisingly enough, it was quite simple. Dr. Perkins fabricated two metal rods each 3″ long and each of specially compounded materials. By placing the tractors—as they came to be known—over the area of the body suffering from pain, heat, or disease of some kind, then drawing them out to one of the extremities, Dr. Perkins could remove the illness.

Within a matter of weeks Dr. Perkins found that his own healing hands were not needed to guide the tractors. Anyone could do it. Quite understandably Americans rushed to buy tractors from their benefactor. No price was too large for such a boon. It is recorded, though not well documented, that one Virginian, in selling his home, accepted tractors enough to total the entire value of his estate.

Elisha Perkins had become the first great American quack.

Of course, action was taken by the authorities at once. President George Washington immediately bought tractors for his entire family. And Supreme Court Chief Justice Oliver Ellsworth, after calm judicial reflection, took an even more foresighted course. Having purchased tractors from Perkins and tried them, he took care to introduce the good doctor, with the highest recommendations, to his successor, Chief Justice John Marshall. Medical historians are convinced that Perkins was sincere. To this conclusion they adduce the evidence of the great yellow fever epidemic which struck New York City in

1799. Dr. Perkins rushed to the very heart of the plague and tended the stricken. Seeing that the fever racked the entire body of its victims, he realized that tractors alone were not enough. Vinegar, quaffed in judicious combination with the magical tractors, he was certain was the answer. Confidently, fearlessly, he applied his cure. Three weeks later Dr. Elisha Perkins was dead of yellow fever. In so dying Perkins at once advanced and refuted the first important food fallacy. He also left the heritage of the tractors to his son, Benjamin, who was a quack of the most vicious sort. Cynically, he plied his tractor trade in both the new world and the old, was honored where-ever he went and in building a fortune never for a moment gave credence to his father's medical faith. This is a pattern which we shall see again and again.

[Is this story merely a] wry vestige of a distant past? Not quite. For recall Dr. Perkins' finest hour, his ultimate discovery—vinegar to cure yellow fever. Recall Dr. Perkins' vinegar and then consider "folk medicine," by Dr. DeForest C. Jarvis. Dr. Jarvis is said to have sold over half a million books so far. Not surprising when one understands that Dr. Jarvis offers relief from headache, arthritis, diabetes, vague physical weakness, and other scourges. And his method is so easy. One need only know the proper combinations and dosages of two monumental nostrums. One of these is honey. And the other—shades of Elisha Perkins—is vinegar.[1]

We did it then, and we are doing it again today. Accepting any possible cure for any possible disease, the pie-in-the-sky ideal, the kind of cure that will easily make us feel better, lose weight, increase our sexual potency, and destroy many of our bodily malfunctions. All nonsense, but all truly believed because there is a glut of misinformation on the market and very little reliable information.

When one considers nutrition, one must also consider where nutrients come from—food. This seems like an innocuous and unnecessary comment. However, when one also considers what else food gives us, it is not difficult to understand why nutrition is perhaps considered one of the last things one should know about when eating. The majority of people eat food not for nutrition but for many other reasons. People will tell us that this is not the case, but it is, and the fact can be documented. Let's consider some of the functions of food. Dr. Madeline Leininger summarized some of these functions in her book, *Dimension of Nutrition.*[2] First, food is used

---

[1] Ronald M. Deutsch, *The Nuts among the Berries* (New York: Ballantine Books, 1967), pp. 11-12.

[2] M. L. Leininger, "Some Cross-Cultural Universal and Nonuniversal

universally to provide body energy to satisfy man's hunger. Second, food is used universally to initiate and maintain interpersonal relationships with friends, kinsmen, and strangers. Third, food is used to determine the nature and extent of interpersonal distance between people. Fourth, a universal function of food is for the expression of socio-religious ideas. A fifth universal function is the use of food for social status, social prestige, and for special individual and group achievements. Sixth, food is used to help man cope with his psychological stresses and needs. Seventh, food is used to reward, punish, or influence the behavior of others. An eighth function is to influence the political and economic status of a group, Finally, food is used to detect, treat, and prevent social, physical, and cultural behavior deviations. Is it any wonder, then, that although we stress our need to know more about nutrition, we are engulfed by many other factors when we consider what foods we will eat other than those that maintain us in good health?

Food choices are the result of many personal attitudes and beliefs. Food is really one of the most personal things that we have, because eating is such a personal thing. Think about this for a minute: what is more personal than perhaps sexual relationships or bodily functions that are nonsexual or non food oriented? When we eat, we do so for our own reasons. When we taste, messages go to our brain, and as a result we feel pleasure or displeasure with what we have tasted. Another way of defacing the argument that the nutritional knowledge of food is truly desired by the consumer at large is to consider the amazing array of foods people put into their mouth in order to alleviate some illness or psychosomatic disorder. By and large, the vast majority of fads are illogical: we put things into our body because we believe something that is written—in many cases by a person without the proper credentials or authority. Would you do this with your car? With your television? With any material possession in your home? We think not. You would not stop putting oil into your car, because you paid 5 or 6 or 10,000 dollars for it, and you wouldn't take a chance on ruining it. You would not put some handmade tube into your color television set because it might blow up, and then you would have to pay up to 1000 dollars to replace the set. But how shocking it is that the human body, your most important possession, may be fed a totally unsound diet almost at a whim.

In order to understand what food can do for us, we must know something about the body, its chemical makeup, and the chemical makeup of food. We must also remember that we eat not only to obtain nutrients but for many other reasons, which by and large are

Functions, Beliefs, and Practices of Food," in *Dimensions of Nutrition*, ed. J. Dupont (Boulder, Co.: Colorado Associated University Press, 1970), pp. 154–63.

far more important to us on a day-to-day basis than the nutritional adequacy of the food we consume.

In order to understand what the body requires for the maintenance of adequate health, we should look first at what the body is made up of. The human body consists primarily of carbon, oxygen, hydrogen, and nitrogen atoms. These atoms make up the vast majority of all forms of life. These elements, along with lesser amounts of other compounds, are combined in our bodies in the form of various chemicals. The fear of chemicals that faddists have been putting into consumers' minds seems unrealistic, since humans and food are both merely chemicals. The chemicals that make up the human body include:

1. water
2. proteins
3. fats
4. carbohydrates
5. minerals
6. vitamins

A hollow tube, so to speak, extends through the body. At one end of this tube is the mouth, where we ingest food; at the other end is the anus, where we excrete waste materials. As food travels down this long tube, we absorb and assimilate the ingredients we require in order to maintain the chemicals in our body; the food ingredients we don't require, we excrete.

Treated in such a way, the human body seems a rather simple creation, and indeed it is. Materially, it costs very little, even in these days of inflated prices: for about thirty dollars we could purchase from the local supermarket, drug stores, and chemical houses all the ingredients that make up the body. However, before we deflate your ego totally, we should note that chemicals of the human body are organized in the form of cells. Cells are tiny, intricate bundles of life that are responsible for vast numbers of chemical reactions. They contain such things as the genes and chromosomes that determine our heredity and the components of the nervous system that allow us to think and act as rational beings. Each of the billions of cells that we are made up of is like a tiny city containing factories that assemble parts, energy plants, blueprints, and engineers who take the blueprints off the drafting table and put them to use in the factories to create the components that we need to live. This chapter, however, is not aimed at even a simple discussion of molecular biology, and we will now leave our discussion of cells in order to evaluate further what our body needs from the simple materials known as food.

WATER

Approximately 75 percent of the body is water, which is distributed among the fluids inside the cells, the fluids between the cells, and the fluids in the blood. The water within the cells provides a medium in which chemical reactions take place. The function of the water outside the cells is to transport substances and chemicals from one part of the body to another. The third function of the water in the body is to maintain body temperature. When we perspire, water is released through our skin. This water evaporates and thereby cools us, due to what is known as the latent heat of evaporation of water. This cooling effect allows us to maintain the very delicate balance of temperature required to sustain life; we all know the feeling that occurs when we are ill and have a high fever.

A fourth function of water is to wash out any toxic by-products or end products of the chemical reactions going on within the body. We should stress again that we are dealing with chemicals and with chemical reactions. These are not scary nor are they unknown. In any chemical reaction, there are quite often by-products or end products that are toxic. Many of these by-products are extracted from the blood by the kidneys and excreted through the urine. The kidneys can handle most toxic substances that are adequately diluted. However, if toxic substances become too concentrated, the kidneys cannot handle them; as a result these substances build up, eventually causing body malfunctioning and perhaps even death. Such common elements as sodium, which occurs in table salt, can build up and become toxic unless diluted with water. This is well known by the organs of the body; and when sodium begins to build up, the organs send a message through the nervous system to the brain, which then informs us that we are thirsty. This is a phenomenon that everyone has undergone after eating a salty meal or otherwise consuming large amounts of salt. Another simple chemical, urea, is formed from the nitrogen in proteinaceous foods. Because of the body's need to dilute urea, we feel thirsty after eating a high-protein meal such as a large steak, a large roast beef dinner, or a large fish dinner. There are other bodily chemicals that need to be diluted, but these two common ones serve to illustrate the fourth function of water in the body.

People can live for very long periods of time as long as they ingest sufficient water. Obviously, there are not many people who would wish to volunteer for an experiment designed to find out how long one can live without water; the longest period on record is seventeen days. The body requires about two quarts of water a day under normal living conditions. However, under stress conditions— when we are very hot, perhaps as a result of being in a desert or working very hard—the requirement could go up to eight to eleven quarts per day. We obtain a great deal of our water requirement from food. Vegetables are 90 to 95 percent water, fruits are 80 to 85 percent water. Meat, fish, and poultry can run as high as 70 to 75 percent. We are told by some of the faddists that we should consume minimum amounts of water. We hope that this discussion has pointed out that this is a very dangerous approach to nutrition, and that a healthy body requires water much more than it requires food.

ENERGY AND CALORIES

Prior to discussing the individual nutrients that the body requires, we should consider how foods give us the energy to run this intricate machine. Food supplies us with energy, which we express in terms of calories. We can define a calorie scientifically as the amount of heat required to raise the temperature of one kilogram of water $1°C$. However, this definition does not really allow us to conceptualize the function of the calorie. To do this, it might be simpler to think of a calorie as a unit of energy going into the body and supplying it with a certain amount of power, just as a gallon of gas powers a car. Different food groups give us different amounts of calories: in general, a gram of protein supplies us with four calories; a gram of fat, nine calories; and a gram of carbohydrates, four calories. We can see that a given weight of fat supplies us with more than twice the energy of the same amount of protein or carbohydrates. This is why fats are considered "fattening." If we take in more energy than we require, this energy is stored in the body as fat and in time leads to overweight and obesity.

The total energy requirement of an individual can be divided into two parts. First, the body needs energy in order to perform the work involved in the process of living—the beating of the heart, breathing, the activity of the glands, and keeping the muscles in a normal state of tension. This involuntary work is necessary to life and continues twenty-four hours a day throughout life. The rate at which calories are burned in the performance of this work remains reasonably constant over long periods of time, and is called the basal metabolic rate (BMR). The second part of the total calorie requirement depends considerably on how active the individual is in his or her work and leisure activities. The person who holds a sedentary job and has no vigorous leisure pursuits will certainly require far less energy in the form of calories than one who has a physically demanding job or who pursues active recreations. We can say, then, that the first demand for calories is in the form of involuntary energy requirements; the second demand is in the form of voluntary energy requirements—that is, requirements besides those that sustain life. The BMR of an individual is normally constant; any large variation is a sign of poor health. One's BMR may be determined by instruments that measure oxygen utilization, respiratory capacity, and so on, or it may be determined by certain simple formulas.

The BMR of juveniles is much higher than that of adults, per unit of weight. This is due to the stimulus of growth in juveniles and to the different body composition of juveniles and adults. The BMR is highest per pound of body weight at about age one, and then drops somewhat with slight variations until the individual stops growing.

Having discussed the two basic requirements for calories, we can begin to understand the problem of weight control. Weight control has become almost an obsession with the American public, and for good reason. Overweight and obesity are often associated with atherosclerosis and subsequent heart conditions which constitute one of the leading causes of illness and death in this country. Every year Americans, to make themselves physically fit, buy and believe in exercise gadgets that promise to melt fat while they relax watching television. They trust that a once-a-week round of golf in a cart, an evening of bowling while sipping a glass of beer, or a short swim and a long sunbath will keep them trim, vigorous, and youthful. They pound and rub and roll their fat in an effort to "break it down" or move it from hips to bust. They look for instant and lasting rewards from sporadic efforts to tone their sagging muscles. And when they discover a jogging session or a set of tennis leaves them sore and strained, they become disenchanted; they feel betrayed by vigorous exercise and head for the steam or sauna bath. They expect the impossible from exercise because they do not understand what the possible is. In addition, they believe in diets that do not provide them with all the essential nutrients, diets that are low in certain nutrients such as carbohydrates and high in others such as fat.

How much energy does a person require? We know that our body requires a certain number of calories to sustain itself—that is, to maintain its basal metabolic rate. This amount is about 1400 for an average woman weighing about 121 pounds, and about 1600 for an average man weighing about 143 pounds. Any excess calories that we consume must be burned up by the work we do or the recreational activities we engage in; otherwise, they turn to fat.

It is a simple and easily remembered fact that 3,500 excess calories will produce one pound of fat. These 3,500 excess calories typically accumulate not in one day or two days but over a period of time. That is, if you consume 500 calories more per day than your body requires (that is, 500 calories more than are required to sustain your BMR plus your voluntary activities), then in one week you will gain a pound. Conversely, if you consume 500 calories a day less than what your body needs, you will lose a pound. This is a simple fact. It does not tell you that you can eat all you want. It does not say that "calories don't count."

Many of the proponents of the high-protein diets to which we are exposed in books, the press, and other media tell us that we can eat all we want as long as we avoid certain foods that contain carbohydrates. At best, this is a dangerous diet; at worst, it can result in very serious illness. On March 14, 1973 the New York County Medical Society denounced Dr. Robert C. Atkins's revolutionary no-carbohydrate diet as "unscientific," "unbalanced," and "potentially dangerous," especially to persons prone to kidney disease, heart disease, and gout. At a news conference called by its committee on public health, the society said that "the side effects of the kind of diet that Dr. Atkins promotes in his best selling book may include weakness, apathy and dehydration, loss of calcium, nausea, lack of stamina and a tendency to fainting."[3] This in itself should persuade people not to partake of such a diet. However, many other medical experts have agreed vehemently with the comments of the society. Dr. Ethan Allan Sims, obesity expert at the University of Vermont medical center, cited one of the most inhibiting aspects of the Atkins diet: "It's a jet set diet. Poor people couldn't afford to live on the proteins and fats. Besides, America is already living off the top of the food chain—its resources couldn't support the consumption of more animal proteins."[4] You can see that such diets are transitory. They are a faddish way to lose pounds quickly, and the major reason they work is boredom. One tires very soon of eating nothing but high-protein foods. People who have tried this diet will tell you that the thought of another steak or another piece of fish is rather revolting, and that they dream at night of spaghetti and bread rather than sugarplums. There are other diets that promote the use of high-protein foods, such as the Stillman diet, but these suffer from the same problems as the Atkins diet.

One of the major causes of obesity in this country is the fact that we have become a sedentary nation. We do not exercise nearly as much as we used to, but we have not cut down on our food intake in proportion to our lesser amount of exercise. In other words, we don't work as hard, but we eat as much.

[3] *New York Times,* March 14, 1973, p. 50.
[4] *Ibid.,* p. 50.

Exercise is often said to be ineffective in reducing weight, because in order to lose a pound of fat you must exercise for seven or eight hours—longer, if you don't exercise very vigorously. For instance, it is said that you must walk thirty-six hours to lose a pound of fat. This is true, but you could instead walk a half-hour per day for ten weeks, a rather pleasant exercise, and lose the same pound of fat.

Many of the fad diets and so-called exercise machines and rubberized girdles that claim to remove inches of fat from the user are based upon the fact that fat cells in the body contain a high proportion of water. When one uses these rubberized girdles or exercise machines while sitting and watching television, there is indeed a dehydration effect and the person's fat cells lose some of the water inside them. Now if you consider that the body contains a great many fat cells, and if each cell is reduced in size due to a loss of water, you can see that an inch or an inch and a half may certainly disappear from a particular part of the anatomy. However, this is simply transitory, and as soon as enough liquid is ingested the so-called loss is replaced immediately.

Some weight-reducing plans advertise a fat loss of as much as fifteen pounds a week. Think back to the 3,500 calories required to lose one pound of fat. Normal, healthy people do not lose fat at that rate. In order to lose fifteen pounds in a week, you would have to consume 7,500 less calories a day. Consequently, you would have *to need* 7,500 calories per day to begin with. This means that for a week you would have to exercise harder than an athlete training for competition and not eat one calorie. Anyone who knows anything about nutrition should disregard such advertisement.

In order to maintain or lose weight, we must understand the balance between caloric intake and energy expenditure. Our body is just like a bank: if we put more calories into it these calories will accumulate; the only way we can take them out is to spend them by exercising. Therefore, the really healthful method of weight reduction is to cut down, to some extent, the caloric intake and to increase energy expenditure through pleasurable exercise. As Jean Mayer has stated, the faddish way to lose weight should be described as the "rhythm method of girth control."

More and more Americans are being pushed by a sedentary way of life into a zone of inactivity where their appetites exceed their need. Such individuals have only three choices in regard to weight maintenance: to be hungry all their lives, to become fat, or to exercise more.

Technically, only those who are obese should lose weight. Obesity is different from overweight, in that it refers only to being "over-fat." In any case, it is unwise to undertake a severe diet without a physician's supervision. If weight loss is kept to a pound or two a week, and if a properly balanced diet is maintained, there is not much danger of harming oneself. However, if one undertakes a severe diet or even a moderate one that is unbalanced, anything from a vitamin deficiency to nervous-system damage could result.

PROTEIN REQUIREMENTS AND SOURCES

Proteins, about which we hear a great deal, are simply large molecules composed of nitrogen and containing amino acids. Proteins are constituents of every living cell in the human body. Half the dry matter of an adult is protein, and of this amount one third is in the form of muscle, one third in bone and cartilage, one tenth in skin, and the rest in other tissues and in body fluids. All enzymes are protein in nature. (Enzymes are biological catalysts that speed up the rate of the chemical reactions that occur in the body, and in this way they are essential to life.) Many hormones are either proteins or protein derivatives. (Hormones are similar to enzymes, but they transport messages in the body.) Materials in the cell that are responsible for the transmission of genetic information and for cell reproduction often occur in combination with proteins as nucleoproteins. Bones, muscles, hair, nails, cell membranes, and just about everything else in the body is composed at least partly of proteins. Because these tissues regularly need additional proteins for maintenance, the body must have a regular supply of protein in the diet.

Once ingested, proteins are broken down into their component amino acids, which are then resynthesized into new proteins that the body can use. Interestingly, a fad that has recently appeared in several books recommends certain foods because of the enzymes they contain. Just above, we described an enzyme and stated that it is a protein. Now all enzymes are broken down once they enter the digestive system and are resynthesized into compounds that the body requires. Therefore, the ingestion of enzymes is rather pointless, since any enzymes you eat will be broken down immediately.

New proteins formed by the body are used for regulating the internal water and acid-base balance, for energy, for building enzymes, antibodies, and some hormones, for growth in children and pregnant women, and also for lactation. Protein is needed also for tissue repair and in case of injury or blood loss. It is recommended that 60 grams (2.1 ounces) of protein be consumed per day by men aged eighteen to twenty-two, and 55 grams by women the same age. It is generally recognized that this figure is a bit generous for our daily needs, but it is nevertheless accepted because a slight surplus of protein is necessary in case of tissue trauma. The body can tolerate as much as 300 grams daily without harm, as long as sufficient water is drunk so that the nitrogenous waste can be disposed of through the kidneys. Remember, when large amounts of protein are ingested, the nitrogen has to be diluted so that the kidneys can handle the urea production and so that toxic end products won't accumulate. The large amount of water in the Stillman diet is partly for this reason. But it makes no sense to ingest so much protein that you have to drink more water than usual in order to rid your body of toxic products. This kind of diet seems rather ridiculous. It should be emphasized that there is no advantage to an excessive intake of protein, even though some athletes maintain that excessive protein builds up muscle tissue.

The word protein has a magic ring to it in our society. We are told to eat this high-protein food and that high-protein food in order to build our bodies large and tall and strong and sexy. Interestingly recent surveys have indicated that most Americans, no matter what ethnic group or economic level, ingest two to three times the amount of protein that their body requires. We believe ourselves deficient in protein and feel that somehow protein doesn't add calories; it only adds "goodness." This is not to deride the importance of protein but simply to attempt to place in proper perspective the amount of protein we ingest. Once tissue demands are satisfied, excess protein is simply used as calories and therefore such protein may be classified as having "empty calories."

There are some twenty-three amino acids in nature that combine chemically in different ways to form protein. Eight are considered "essential" in adults, and ten are considered "essential" in children. These amino acids are termed essential because the human body cannot synthesize them in enough quantity to satisfy its demands. Fifteen amino acids can be synthesized from the chemicals which we receive from food, and are considered nonessential in that sense. The eight essential amino acids in adults must be obtained intact from the foods we eat, and this is one reason why vegetarian diets can be dangerous for those that do not know what they are doing. Vegetables are not normally considered a good source of high-quality protein. The quality of a protein depends on the number of essential amino acids it contains and the amount of such amino acids. Meat, fish, cheese, milk, and eggs all contain high-quality protein in fairly large amounts and therefore the essential amino acids. Individual vegetables, however, do not generally contain all eight essential amino acids. Therefore, people on a vegetarian diet must eat mixtures of vegetables at the same time so that their body may obtain all the essential amino acids. For amino acids to be used properly, all eight must be received in the stomach within approximately four hours of one another. If one or two essential amino acids are not present, the other six or seven will not be utilized as efficiently as if all were present. Therefore, those wishing to follow the vegetarian way should have some knowledge of the amino-acid balance in vegetables prior to beginning such a diet.

There are many terms associated with the quality and quantity of amino acids in protein. With the advent of nutritional labeling and with the increased interest in nutrition, we should at least be familiar with these terms. Biological value (BV) is the ratio of nitrogen retained in the body to nitrogen absorbed by the body, multiplied by 100. This tells us the quality of the protein or the number of essential amino acids present, because if not all the essential amino acids are present, protein synthesis in the body will not be complete. Another widely used term is the protein efficiency ratio (PER). This is the weight gained by a rat divided by the protein consumed by the rat after four weeks of feeding trials with a test protein versus a casein-based protein. The PER of casein (milk protein) is usually considered to be 2.5, and the PER of the test protein is adjusted correspondingly. For example, if a test PER is determined to be 80 percent caseins in a particular test, the test protein's PER is reported as 80 percent of 2.5, or 2.0. Another common term used with proteins is the net protein ratio (NPR). In conducting the NPR assay, one group of rats eats a test protein while a second group eats a diet that contains no protein. The NPR is defined as the weight gained by the test group plus the weight lost by the nonprotein group, divided by the protein consumed. A fourth term often used is net protein utilization (NPU), which is similar to NPR except that body nitrogen rather than body weight is used. NPU = (retained nitrogen ÷ food nitrogen) × 100. The NPU value is considered to be equivalent to the biological value of the food times digestibility. Another commonly used method for assessing protein quality and quantity is the slope-ratio method, but this measure is not used as widely as the others.

Some nutritionists and food scientists feel that none of these methods or terms adequately assess both the quality and the quantity of food protein. They prefer another method of doing this, which they have named "biologically utilized protein" or "utilizable protein." This concept supposedly recognizes the inherent interrrelations between nutritional quality and quantity and applied nutrition. The term "biologically utilizable protein" may be defined as a food's crude protein content measured by chemical analyses and multiplied by the ratio of NPR, NPU, or slope-ratio values of the particular protein to lactalbumin or casein. The resulting value gives some idea of the quality of the protein, the digestibility of the protein, and the amount of the protein present in the food.

We stated previously that protein is involved in a tremendous number of bodily functions and is extraordinarily important. The importance of protein in world nutrition has been emphasized in the last two decades with the identification of the protein-deficiency disease known as kwashiorkor. This disease, which is more prevalent in the developing countries than in the developed countries, normally occurs in children between two and five who are weaned from their mother's milk and begin to consume a diet of starchy foods rather than milk. It is caused by a deficiency in the quality and quantity of dietary protein in the presence of a normal intake of calories. (Marasmus, on the other hand, is a condition resulting from a caloric deficit that is usually accompanied by a protein deficiency.) The many clinical symptoms of kwashiorkor include failure to grow, mental changes, accumulation of fluids in the tissues, skin changes, changes in hair, enlargement of the liver, and anemia. The ability of the afflicted child to combat infection is very low, and death from the disease is usually attributed to an infection such as measles or pneumonia that is not normally fatal.

Recently, many studies have indicated that the severe protein deficiency that exists in diseases such as kwashiorkor may be alleviated to a great extent by an increase in calories. If calories are increased by means of nonprotein sources, then the protein ingested can be used to build and replace tissue rather than for energy. Adequate calories thus have a "protein-sparing" effect. This concept has many ramifications for developing countries because it implies that the world food problem is due not to a protein shortage but to a calorie shortage. Perhaps we should be looking at more efficient methods of utilizing carbohydrate crops as food.

It should be mentioned at this point that there is a danger in the zen macrobiotic diet, which has recently become somewhat popular in this country. (This diet is discussed in more detail in Chapter 6.) Its advocates suggest that all animal proteins be removed from the diet and replaced by selected plant foods, and that water intake be limited. This diet is not too severe if tried by a young adult, say a twenty-year-old, for a period of a year, since such a person will have had adequate nutrition most of her life, but it is extremely severe if applied to a child at a very early age. Such a regimen of only selected plant foods rather than milk and a wide variety of other foods may result in some irreversible retardation of brain development in the child. This, we feel, should be categorized as child abuse and considered a criminal act.

Foods that contain high quantities of high-quality protein are generally expensive. This is why kwashiorkor is seen most often in the developing nations of the world. One need only look at the prices of foods of very high biological value, such as eggs, milk, fish, and beef, to realize that these animal foods are not available to many of the people in the ghetto areas of this country, nor to many of the people in the developing areas of the world.

Certainly, a case can be made for replacing animal protein with vegetable protein if the vegetables are chosen properly. Certain vegetables have a fairly well-balanced content of amino acids and quite a high biological value. Soybeans, the bean family in general, and the nut family are good sources of protein, particularly when one is consuming a mixed diet. Soybeans are slightly deficient in one of the essential amino acids, methionine, but this nutrient can be obtained from other sources if one is eating a mixed diet. In general the grains, such as corn, wheat, and rice, are deficient in one or more amino acids. Wheat in particular is deficient in lysine. This is a very important deficiency because wheat is the staple food for most of the world. The use of vegetables as a sole protein source, then, requires some knowledge of their protein quality. Since protein deficiencies do exist among the various vegetables, it is essential to eat the right combination of vegetables at the same time. The American Indians did this unknowingly when they consumed succotash, a mixture of corn and beans. Another problem with vegetable protein is its digestibility. Vegetables are high in cellulose, a carbohydrate that is not digested by humans. Cellulose is bound intricately with protein in vegetables, and because of its nondigestibility it decreases the digestibility of the protein present—to about 70 or 80 percent at times.

In general, top-quality proteins are found in lean meat, poultry, fish, seafoods, eggs, milk, and cheese. The next best group of foods for proteins are dry beans, peas, and nuts. Cereals, bread, vegetables, and fruits provide some proteins, but of lower quality. In general, plant and animal products that are related to reproduction and care of the young are excellent sources of protein, as you can see in this list, whereas leafy or stalky vegetables are poor sources.

Certainly, an important and increasingly popular development is the use of vegetable protein that is flavored to taste much the same as meat. (This will be discussed in detail in Chapter 10). This is a valuable contribution to nutrition (and one that will become even more valuable in the future), since the human diet should be about

Peanuts
(1 1/2 oz.)

Almonds
(1/3 c.)

Navy Beans
(1/4 c. uncooked)

Ham
(2 thin slices)

Beefsteak
(1/2 serving)

Whole Wheat Bread
(3 1/2 slices)

Cheese
(1 1/2 oz.)

Milk
(1/2 pt.)

Salmon
(1/4 c.)

Liver
(2 oz.)

Rolled Oats, uncooked
(3/4 c.)

Bacon
(1/4 lb.)

Eggs
(1 1/2)

Figure 2-1: Protein Equivalents (Each of the above contains ten grams of protein.)

15 percent protein (0.434 grams per pound of body weight per day) and half of this should be of high quality.

CARBOHYDRATES

Quick energy sources? Fattening foods? The cause of tooth decay? Empty calories? These are only a few of the terms and thoughts that the general public applies to carbohydrates. Although they have come under fire from many different sources, carbohydrates are merely another set of nutrients that the body requires. They should form about 50 to 60 percent of one's diet.

Carbohydrates are chemical compounds of carbon, hydrogen, and oxygen. In their simplest form they consist of such molecules as glucose and fructose, which are known as monosaccharides. These monosaccharides combine chemically to form larger and larger molecules, all of which are carbohydrates and retain the basic chemical make-up of carbon, hydrogen, and oxygen. Two monosaccharides combined are known as disaccharides; for instance, one molecule of glucose combined with one molecule of fructose makes sucrose, or simple table sugar. Other combinations can produce trisaccharides or even larger units known as dextrins, which are the compounds that are missing from "low-calorie" beer. In terms of molecular weight, the largest compounds in the carbohydrate family are starches and cellulose.

The carbohydrates we normally consume are sugars and starches, and in some cases dextrins. We do eat cellulose, but we are unable to digest and assimilate it, and thus we can't use it as an energy source. Animals, in particular grazing animals, contain in their intestinal tract bacteria that can break down cellulose and thereby make it available as an energy source. Cellulose in plants acts in much the same manner as muscle in humans: it gives rigidity to the plant and acts as a stabilizing or binding force in its structure. In our discussion of proteins we mentioned that the proteins from plants are not as high in quality as those from animals. We noted that one of the reasons for this is that plant proteins are interwoven so closely with the cellulose that they cannot be digested to as large an extent as if the cellulose were not present. Cellulose does, however, have one important function: it provides roughage, which aids the rhythmic contractions that move food through the intestinal tract.

In America, slightly less than 50 percent of all foods consumed are carbohydrates. In the last several decades, the consumption of raw carbohydrates, in particular grains and potatoes, has tended to decrease, and the consumption of refined carbohydrates has tended to increase. It is probably because of this that the term "empty calories" was coined. This term is an unfortunate misnomer because it implies that one is obtaining nothing from certain food groups. But one *is* obtaining something, for the calories in these food groups are, like all calories, the essential sources of energy for the body. However, refined carbohydrates lack certain nutrients that are contained in unrefined carbohydrates. That is, pure sugar or honey, which are 99 percent refined carbohydrate, lack certain nutrients that are contained in a raw carbohydrate such as a grain or a potato: some vitamins, a very small amount of protein, certain minerals, and a very small amount of fat. Nevertheless, there is nothing toxic about refined sugar, as some authors would have us believe. Conversely there is nothing magical about honey. Chemically, both are very similar.

There is no conclusive scientific evidence that sugar causes heart disease, hypoglycemia, diabetes, or obesity. In fact, the Food and Nutrition Board of the National Academy of Sciences has not recommended a limit on sugar or carbohydrate intake.

The role of sugar as a calorie source may well become important in the alleviation of world food problems. Table 2-1 shows that sugar is a very efficient crop in the production of calories per acre of land, in comparison with other common crops.

Remembering that calories have a "protein-sparing" effect, it becomes evident that an economical source of calories, particularly one that has a high yield per acre, might well become a staple in the world food supply.

Table 2-1.

Food Source	*Acres of Land to Produce one Million Calories*
Sugar	0.15
Potatoes	0.44
Corn—as corn meal	0.9
Wheat—as whole-wheat flour	0.9
Wheat—as refined wheat flour	1.2
Hogs (pork and lard)	2.0
Whole milk	2.8
Eggs	7.8
Chickens	9.3
Steers	17.0

From Fredrick J. Stare, "Role of Sugar in Modern Nutrition." *World Review of Nutrition and Dietetics*, 22 (1975) 239-47.

For the past fifty years, Americans have been consuming approximately 100 pounds of sugar per person per year, as shown in Figure 2-2. Thus, we have not seen the dramatic rise in sugar consumption in recent years, as some would have us believe.

Convenience foods, natural foods, and fortified foods generally contain sugar. This sugar may be present naturally, or it may be added. In either case, it normally adds to the flavor and acceptability of the food, and no matter how nutritious a food is, it must be acceptable in order for people to eat it.

In order to illustrate how far-fetched some of the charges against sugar can be, one need only look at the allegations made against the sugar content of cereals. A good breakfast should supply approximately one fourth of the daily requirements for energy, protein, and most vitamins and minerals. This requirement may be met for a child as follows:

1 cup presweetened fortified cereal with milk
2 slices of toast with butter or margarine
4 ounces of orange juice
8 ounces of whole milk (fortified with Vitamin D)

In this breakfast the presweetened cereal provides good flavor—a flavor that most children accept, at any rate—about 3 percent of the child's total daily sugar intake, and one fourth of the U.S. Recommended Daily Allowance of vitamins A and C, thiamin, riboflavin, niacin, vitamins B_6 and B_{12}, and iron.

The amount of sugar in the presweetened cereal, which is generally the point of attack, is about equivalent to the sugar in one tablespoon of jelly, one tablespoon of pancake syrup, or two canned peach halves served with two tablespoons of the fruit syrup. Now is this an inordinate amount of sugar in a well-balanced meal? Of course, a good breakfast does not have to contain a cereal, but with the lifestyle in our society cereal seems to fulfill a consumer demand.

About 15 percent of the calories Americans consume comes from sugar. Much of this sugar is contained in other foods, such as ice cream and bakery products, which, of course, provide other nutrients. These comments are not intended to make a super-food out of sugar; it isn't. Sugar is a food no better or no worse than other foods when eaten in moderation in a varied diet.

Are carbohydrates fattening? Certainly they're fattening, in that they contain four calories per gram, the same as proteins. However, carbohydrates and proteins each contain less than half the number of calories per gram that fat contains. Relatively speaking, then,

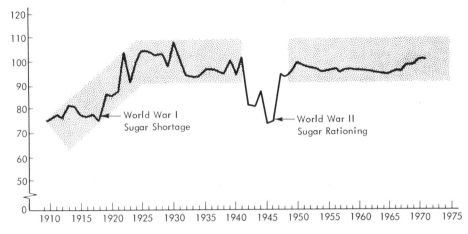

Figure 2-2: Per Capita Consumption of Sugar (both household and industrial),
1909–1971 (official data published by U.S. Dept. of Agriculture)

carbohydrates are not particularly fattening. A medium-size potato contains only about seventy-five calories. Nevertheless, it has come under scrutiny by dieters, who tend to view it as fattening and push it away at the dinner table. The potato is not the problem here, but rather the large amounts of butter or gravy that are placed on it.

The body obtains energy in many ways, and carbohydrates are certainly one very important source of energy. Carbohydrates are also essential to health: in their absence—for instance, when one is on certain high-protein diets—ketosis may occur. As far as the quick-energy claim is concerned, one food material will not provide quicker energy than another food material. It is true that simple carbohydrates such as the monosaccharides are absorbed slightly faster by the body than carbohydrates of larger molecular weight, such as starches, but none of these will really provide energy any faster than other food sources. The normal body has large stores of energy, and when proteins and carbohydrates are ingested and broken down to simple chemicals, the liver converts these chemicals into glycogen, the only starch that the human body makes. Blood sugar makes up about one tenth of one percent of the blood. It is a ready source of fuel for cells, and as it is used the liver breaks down some of the glycogen and converts it into sugars, which are released into the bloodstream. Too much sugar in the blood results in a condition known as diabetes. An abnormal decrease in blood sugar is known as hypoglycemia. The latter term is often used by Dr. Atkins in defense of his diet (see page 22). However, medical authorities are unaware of the apparent large-scale problems believed by Dr. Atkins to result from hypoglycemia.

Do sugars cause tooth decay? It seems that from time immemorial parents have screamed at their children not to eat so much "sweet stuff" because of the tremendous number of dental caries that would result. There is no question that sugar or carbohydrate substances act as food for the bacteria that grow on our teeth and in our mouth. It is rather frightening to most people that their mouths are full of bacteria, but in reality bacteria are everywhere—in the air, in our mouths, and on our skin. The bacteria responsible for dental caries are so-called fermentative bacteria, and carbohydrates are their favorite food. The end products produced by bacteria consuming a carbohydrate are mainly acids, and these eat into the tooth enamel and the structures surrounding the tooth, resulting in dental caries. Therefore, an unduly large amount of carbohydrate could lead to more dental caries. However, normal use of carbohydrates will not lead to dental caries so quickly that one should avoid them. Because bacteria feed on sugar in the mouth, it is a good idea to get rid of this sugar as quickly as possible after eating. If you can't brush your teeth, rinse your mouth out with water. (It should be noted that water is just as good as most of the mouthwashes that claim to prevent tooth decay.)

Although the issue of white flour isn't concerned strictly with carbohydrates, it is pertinent here. Somehow, a feeling has evolved that the food industry purposely removes all the vitamins and minerals in making white flour. This, of course, is entirely untrue. Flour is made from wheat because wheat contains appropriate amounts of the protein gluten, or wheat protein, which allows wheat to be structured into forms such as bread and cakes. Certain other grains (such as barley) do not contain gluten and for this reason cannot be used in making these commodities. (Barley, however, can be fermented, as can all carbohydrates, and is the source of many of our palatable liquors, such as whiskey and beer.) One of the major reasons for milling flour, of course, is that historically, people have been accustomed to eating white flour. The same is true of rice: in the Orient white rice is a status symbol, and many people do not want to eat brown rice since it indicates a lack of status. But there are other reasons for milling flour. If flour were not milled and large amounts of whole-grain flour were produced instead, a storage problem would ensue. For household use, whole-wheat flour may be suitably stored in the refrigerator. However, if we consider the millions of tons of flour used world-wide, the matter of storage indeed becomes a problem. Whole-wheat flour contains reasonably large amounts of fat. In the humid climate that exists in many parts of the world, this fat would become rancid immediately, making the flour inedible as well as less nutritious. Therefore, the removal of fat in the milling process allows us to store the flour for longer periods of time. This, of course, is the reason for processing all foods. Our crops grow only at certain times of the year, and processing allows us to eat all year long. In this country, flour is usually enriched. All bread is enriched, and enriched white bread is certainly as nutritious as whole-wheat bread. In the Philippines, rice has been enriched since the early 1950s, and many of the problems associated with the use of white rice instead of brown rice have been eliminated.

Research has attempted to determine whether there is an association between refined carbohydrates and atherosclerosis. This is a condition in which the flow of blood through the arteries is disrupted because of substances that build up and partially block these vessels. The resulting evidence has suggested that both the kind and amount of carbohydrate may be important in this disease. Sucrose has been suggested as being associated with a higher incidence of atherosclerosis and heart disease, but the consumption of sucrose in this country is too low for us to be concerned about this matter. In addition, genetic factors have to be taken into consideration with this evidence. At this point in time, one can conclude only that there is no hard scientific evidence that sugar is a causative factor in heart disease at the levels currently used.

There is certainly a need for simple carbohydrates for aesthetic reasons, in that many people enjoy a sweet flavor in certain foods. This is easily proved by the widespread use of sugar substitutes by people who want their foods to taste sweet but do not want to gain weight. Carbohydrates are not particularly fattening, as we noted above, but overuse of sugar as a sweetener can lead to an increase in weight. Saccharin and cyclamates have been used in the past as sweeteners. Cyclamates are currently off the market due to some studies that are really not conclusive. These studies concluded that cyclamates were possible cancer-causing materials when consumed at extraordinarily high levels. These levels have been calculated for humans to amount to seven or eight hundred bottles of diet soda per day for a lifetime. (This concept of massive doses of materials will be discussed in more detail in chapter 4.)

Alcoholic beverages constitute another calorie source. Alcohol is produced by the fermentation of a carbohydrate compound by bacteria. It is frightening that alcohol accounts for seventy-six calories per day for the average American. Considering those who don't drink, someone seems to be working overtime on the consumption of alcohol. The metabolizing of alcohol by the body requires a rather large amount of water. One ounce of whiskey requires about four ounces of water in order to be metabolized. Most people who drink have at some point undergone the "thirst syndrome" the morning after. This occurs when people don't consume enough other liquids along with their alcohol. Therefore, when you're extremely hot it's better to have a couple of glasses of water rather than quickly downing several very strong drinks, because your body has already lost water and will lose even more as the alcohol is metabolized.

Foods that originate from fruits, vegetables, and grains contain reasonably large quantities of carbohydrates. In fact, carbohydrates are found almost exclusively in foods of plant origin. In general, vegetables are about 5 to 8 percent carbohydrate and fruits are about 10 to 15 percent carbohydrate.

Milk contains some carbohydrates in the form of lactose (milk sugar), but this is the only important source of animal carbohydrates. Lactose is a problem for certain people who are apparently deficient in the enzyme lactase, which is essential for the proper metabolizing of lactose. Such "lactose-intolerant" people cannot digest milk properly; instead, they suffer from diarrhea and flatulence. This condition may be seen in children as well as in adults. Obviously, milk cannot be considered a major food source for such people.

In sum, carbohydrates are just the same as all other food nutrients: they don't work magic yet they are essential in the diet of a normal human being.

FATS

Fats—or, more correctly, lipids—are chemical compounds of carbon, hydrogen, and oxygen. They differ from carbohydrates in that they contain a much lower ratio of oxygen to carbon and hydrogen. Per gram, fats contain more than twice the calories of either protein or carbohydrate.

Certainly, one cannot dismiss the nutritive importance of certain fats, but by and large Americans eat far too much fat. The consumption of fat by Americans has been increasing dramatically. It is currently estimated that fats constitute about 50 percent of the average American's diet; this figure should read from 25 to 35 percent.

Certain fatty acids, which are components of fat, are necessary for health. These acids are linoleic acid, linolenic acid, and arachadonic acid. We need only linoleic acid from the food sources, since the human body can make the other two acids from it. Excellent sources of these essential fatty acids are corn, cottonseed and soy oils. Peanut oil is also high in essential fatty acids. Animal sources of food have more saturated fatty acids than vegetable sources, many of which are non-essential, but pork and beef do contain some of the essential fatty acids.

Consumers are deluged with the words saturated and unsaturated, in reference to fatty acids. Chemically, the difference is this: if the carbon molecules in a fat are attached to two molecules of hydrogen and two other carbon atoms, a saturated fatty acid is produced; an unsaturated fatty acid is produced when a carbon is attached to only one hydrogen, has a double attachment to one carbon, and has a single attachment to another carbon. A fat is generally thought of as being solid at room temperature, whereas an oil is thought of as being liquid at room temperature. A saturated fatty acid normally tends to make a fat more solid; more unsaturation tends to make a fat more liquid.

In his book, *U.S. Nutrition Policies in the Seventies*, published in 1973, Jean Mayer comments on the relationship between diet and heart disease. One of the major reasons for heart disease is atherosclerosis—hardening of the arteries. This condition is due to an accumulation of fatty materials (lipids)—in particular, cholesterol—in the walls of large or medium-size arteries. As the arterial walls harden and decrease in diameter below a critical size, circulatory impairments become evident. This means that by the time the condition is detected, it is already in an advanced stage. Occlusion of the coronary vessel, which interrupts the blood supply to part of the heart and causes myocardial infarction, and occlusion of an artery irrigating part of the brain, which interrupts the blood supply and causes stroke, are the most dramatic consequences of atherosclerosis. One million Americans are killed or permanently disabled every year by coronary atherosclerosis, the number one health problem in the United States. Mayer lists several changes that we must make if we are to decrease the evidence of this disease:

1. Modify our national diet; to cut drastically our intake of saturated fat and cholesterol, particularly among middle-aged men.
2. Cut down the excess calories in our diet.
3. Launch a much more vigorous antismoking campaign.
4. Conduct a nationwide campaign of detection and correction of hypertension.
5. Provide universally accessible facilities for adult physical exercise, and reform and extend our physical education programs in schools; plan urban renewal with health problems in mind.
6. Create a network of facilities for immediate, appropriate cardiological treatment of victims of myocardial infarction.
7. Develop systems of information for the public concerning nutrition (in-

cluding labeling), smoking, hypertension, exercise, and signs of mild myocardial infarction requiring treatment at appropriate facilities.[5]

From this list you can see that saturated fats and excess calories are factors in atherosclerosis, but they are just two of several factors. We are not trying to lessen the importance of a proper diet in preventing atherosclerosis, but people should certainly not panic all of a sudden and attempt to cut all forms of fat from their diet in order to prevent this disease.

It is extraordinarily difficult for the consumer to make rational judgments about what they should eat if they want to keep down the number of calories and decrease the number of fats they consume. We read in nutrition textbooks or we hear from nutritionists that the good sources of protein, several vitamins, and minerals are organ meats (such as liver), eggs, milk, and cheese. Then we read that we're not supposed to eat these same foods, because of their high saturated-fat content and cholesterol. What is the consumer to do? In order to make the difficult choice of eating or not eating certain foods, we must know the composition of these foods as well as being aware of the potential loss of nutrients that might occur if these foods are cut completely from our diet.

Obviously, we cannot stop eating all fat-containing foods, but we can certainly mix these foods with others to make a balanced diet. And instead of listening to misguided people who tell us what to eat and what not to eat, we should look at the composition of the foods we are considering eating. For instance, we hear raves that the amount of fat in a hot dog is inordinately high. But as we shall see shortly, this is not the case. In addition, weiners are 85 percent meat, which is much more than the meat content of the average meat loaf. If the meat loaf recipe calls for an egg, half a cup of bread crumbs, and half a cup of milk to a pound of meat, and if you add a bit of salt, pepper, and onion, then your meat loaf is only two-thirds meat, just over 65 percent. It contains sixteen ounces of meat and nearly eight ounces of other ingredients, but you could not make the meat loaf in any other way because every ingredient does an important job. Federally inspected frankfurters should not average more than 30 percent fat. That may sound like a lot of fat, but it is less fat than is naturally present in some cheeses, and many cuts of fresh meat. In comparison, a porterhouse steak, trimmed the way you would buy it in the market and then broiled, is 43 percent fat; a beef rump roast (considered lean) is 24 percent fat after cooking; pork chops, broiled, are 30 percent fat. This is not a defense of the hot dog or a plea for people to start eating nothing but hot dogs; it is merely an observation that many of the meats that we consider

[5] Mayer, *U.S. Nutrition Policies in the Seventies* (San Francisco: W. H. Freeman & Co., 1973), pp. 44-45.

nonfatty are in fact very fat and contain saturated fats, the prime offenders in heart disease. The visible fats, such as butter, margarine, vegetable fat, and the layer of fat on meat, account for only 40 percent of the fat in the American diet. The remaining 60 percent is present as invisible fat—that is, the fat that is marbled throughout meat fibers and that is present in egg yolks, homogenized milk and milk products, and nuts and whole-grain cereals. Therefore, it is not enough to cut only the visible fats from our diet; we should also look at the nonvisible fats in the products we buy. Nutritional labeling will take care of a great deal of this problem if the consumer is willing to learn it and use it wisely.

VITAMINS

In any discussion of essential nutrients, vitamins and minerals receive the most attention from food faddists and health-food promoters. These nutrients might be termed "micronutrients," for they are looked upon mysteriously by the public as tiny substances that are not always present in the food we eat. Vitamins have become equated with health in our society, and they are indeed essential for a healthy person. In general Americans do not suffer from vitamin deficiencies, though these conditions certainly exist in other countries, particularly developing countries. For this reason, the scare tactics used by purveyors of health food to promote the consumption of vast amounts of vitamins are at the best ill advised and at worst dangerous.

At times, parents come under pressure from advertising—either through legitimate means or through gossip—to feed their children more and more vitamins so that they can "make the team," "be popular with their peer group," "have a healthy complexion," or "have beautiful shiny hair." It is unfortunate to have to recognize that the reason for this is due in part to nutrition education, in part to the food industry, and in large part to health-food faddists. Many times, instead of being told to eat a balanced diet of the foods available to us, we are told that the ingestion of large amounts of certain substances will give us more strength, more sexual potency, and many other attributes because of the many micronutrients that they contain. Moreover, in nutrition education we are scared by the thought of scurvy and our teeth falling out, or by the thought that if we don't ingest enough B vitamins we might experience nervous tension, as suggested by the late J. I. Rodale, the editor of *Organic Gardening* magazine.

Certainly, severe vitamin deficiency is not an unusual problem in some parts of the world. But even though the ten-state nutrition survey that was undertaken in 1967 as a result of congressional hearings has shown that there are some minor vitamin deficiencies in this country, these are not numerous enough to cause panic. We should realize what vitamins exist, and we should know that they are essential and that severe vitamin deficiency can result in disease. On the other hand, we should also realize that the ingestion of vast quantities of vitamins is worthless and, as we will point out later, may lead to illness and death.

The history of vitamins is exceedingly interesting. Prior to the twentieth century it was thought that illness was always caused by eating something, and not by the absence of something that belonged in the diet. This absence of certain nutrients from the diet leads to what we now know are "deficiency" diseases.

History has shown us, however, that long before the deficiency diseases were recognized, they were occasionally cured by luck. In 1535, the French explorer Jacques Cartier and his men explored the coast of Newfoundland. This party was decimated by what we now know was a lack of vitamin C. The expedition was saved by the Indians of the region, who recommended that Cartier and his men drink an extract of spruce needles, which fortunately, were rich in vitamin C. The eighteenth-century Scots discovered that their children could be protected against rickets, a bone-deforming disease, by having them ingest cod liver oil. In eighteenth-century Italy, children suffering from pellagra, caused by a lack of niacin, were treated successfully as soon as they entered special hospitals that ministered to this disease. The cure was probably due to the fact that the children obtained more meat in these hospitals than they did at home.

The definitive study on vitamin C deficiency was done in the British navy. For years this ailment plagued the navy, and it was felt that the great tradition of British naval power would be lost, not because of the enemy but because of the sickness that constantly attacked the British sailors on long voyages. In 1747 James Lind, a physician to the Royal Navy, carried out what was and still is a marvelously well controlled clinical investigation. He isolated twelve scurvy victims whose cases were very similar and who had all received an identical diet: water-gruel sweetened with sugar in the morning; fresh mutton broth, puddings, or boiled biscuits with sugar for dinner; and barley and raisins, rice and currants, or sago and wine for supper. Lind divided his twelve patients into six pairs and fed them six different remedies. Some of these remedies seem terrible, but some of our health-food faddists would have us eat things as ridiculous as the supposed cures that these men were fed. Four of the pairs received liquid additives such as cider, vinegar, a dilute sulphuric acid mixture, and ordinary sea water. The fifth pair received a remedy "recommended by a hospital surgeon," which consisted of a paste that contained among other things garlic, mustard seed, balsam of Peru, and myrrh. The men in the last team were treated much better: they were each given two oranges and a lemon every day. After six days, one of the men in this last pair was ready to go back to work on board ship; the other was nursing the remaining patients. This showed that citrus fruits contained something that, when absent from the diet, created a deficiency disease. This something, of course, was vitamin C. In order to prevent scurvy from recurring, the British admiralty in 1795 ordered that every British seaman be provided with a daily dose of fresh citrus juice. As a consequence, the Royal Navy's fighting force had doubled by the start of the Napoleonic wars. Interestingly, at that time the British called lemons "limes," and as a result the warehouse area along the docks in London's East End became known as "Limehouse" and British sailors acquired the nickname "Limeys."

The man who really led the way in vitamin research, Elmer V. McCollum, almost died in infancy from a vitamin-deficiency disease— again, scurvy. By the time McCollum was a year old, his family had almost given up on his life. But one day, his mother was peeling apples and she fed him some of the peelings to quiet his whimpering. He seemed to like them, and the feeding continued day after day. In a few days, the mother noted an improvement in the child's health and suspected that the apple peelings were helping him. She thought that the improvement was due to raw vegetables, so she began feeding him these, along with the juice of wild strawberries. This diet was an intuitive one, but of course it became a cure for this particular deficiency disease. McCollum eventually obtained his doctorate and began a career in nutrition that culminated in the discovery of vitamin A and vitamin D.

There is no need to go into the metabolic role of vitamins in the body, but it is interesting to note that most vitamins function as a co-enzyme. Remember that an enzyme is a biological catalyst: it helps along the chemical reactions in the body. A vitamin, then, is an "enzyme helper": it aids in the work of the enzyme. Interestingly, under this generalized definition vitamins C and vitamin E would not be considered vitamins if they were discovered today. A certain number of "helpers" or vitamins are required for efficient and healthy body metabolism; any more than this amount can clutter up the metabolism. An intake of more vitamins than are required can therefore do more harm than good.

In general, vitamins may be subdivided into two large groups: the fat-soluble vitamins and the water-soluble vitamins. Prior to considering the horrendous things that vitamin deficiencies can do, it might be useful to make two generalizations. The first concerns the sources of two categories of vitamins. Fat-soluble vitamins, as their name implies, are soluble in fat. This means that they are not found in water-containing substances as much as in fat-containing substances. Therefore, a good source of fat-soluble vitamins would be fatty materials, such as oils and meats. On the other hand, water-soluble vitamins are not as likely to be found in fatty substances. Therefore, the best sources of these vitamins are foods that contain more water, such as vegetables and fruits, which, you will remember, contain about 90 to 95 percent water and 80 to 85 percent water, respectively.

The other generalization concerns stability. During processing and also during cooking we can lose some vitamins. When cooking vegetables, one should remember that the vitamins we are looking for in these vegetables are quite often water-soluble. Therefore, it makes sense to cook the vegetables in a minimum of water and to utilize the water in which they're cooked as much as possible. If a vegetable is cooked in a large quantity of water and the water is then thrown out, as is often the case, many of the water-soluble vitamins will have been leached out of the vegetable into this water that is thrown out. Not too long ago, in the South, a social stigma was attached to drinking this water or using it as soup stock: low-subsistence whites who did this lost status because the black population also used this water. The blacks called it "pot-likker" and were generally healthier than the whites at the same subsistence level.

The Chinese cook most of their vegetables by stir frying. That is, they place the vegetable in a small amount of oil and cook it very rapidly. The water-soluble vitamins are not leached out because no water is used in cooking, a minimum of heat is applied over a very short time so that fewer vitamins are destroyed by heat, and the oil used for cooking the vegetable may add some fat-soluble vitamins.

The fat-soluble vitamins in a food, on the other hand, are not lost when the food is cooked in water. One thing to remember, though, is that these vitamins can accumulate and be stored in the body's fatty tissues over a long period of time. This has some safety implications: whereas water-soluble vitamins, when taken in excess, are normally removed immediately from the body through the urine, fat-soluble vitamins may be stored and accumulate to a toxic level. The overingestion of vitamins A and D is particularly dangerous.

Water-Soluble Vitamins

Vitamin C: The first point to be made about this vitamin is that it is a chemical, as are all other vitamins and all other nutrients.

Vitamin C is also known as ascorbic acid. There is no difference between vitamin C and ascorbic acid and no truth to the frequently heard statement that vitamin C obtained from a vitamin pill is better than or different from "naturally occurring" vitamin C. This claim will probably be legislated against by the FDA.

As we noted above, a severe deficiency of vitamin C can result in scurvy. A very common disease a hundred and fifty years ago, scurvy results in swollen gums, painful joints, and spots under the skin. These spots are tiny hemorrhages caused by the breaking of the blood-vessel walls. These symptoms are accompanied by a loss of weight and muscular weakness, and the disease eventually leads to death unless treated. However, scurvy has virtually disappeared by now. The ten-state survey conducted after 1967 in this country found that vitamin C was not a major problem among any of the groups studied, although males generally had a higher prevalence of low vitamin-C levels than females, and poor vitamin-C status increased with age. Therefore, we should not immediately begin to consume 5,000 milligrams of vitamin C a day, as Linus Pauling suggests. (The recommended daily level is 45 milligrams per day.) On the basis of current evidence, vitamin C does not cure the common cold. In some definitive work done in Russia, however, overdoses of vitamin C to pregnant rats resulted in the premature birth and subsequent death of some of the litter. This does not indicate any real danger to a human; it does indicate that large overdosages of vitamins not only do not aid health but may possibly be dangerous. The recommended daily allowances we now have tell us what the best science we have currently knows. These allowances are the result of many controlled experiments done over a very long period of time. Therefore, there is no point in adhering to the regimen of another person simply because it works for that person. We are sure that Linus Pauling has not had a cold since he began his regimen, but we are also sure that he has not been run over by a herd of elephants either.

Ascorbic acid is the most unstable of all the vitamins. It is easily destroyed by oxidation, which is speeded up by heat and alkali. In other words, when vitamin C is exposed to oxygen under conditions of heat, as in cooking, and an alkaline atmosphere, the vitamin is easily destroyed. Fortunately, an acid medium in contradistinction to an alkaline medium aids the stability of vitamin C. Fruit juices, which are acid products, lose little if any of their vitamin C value, even after processing.

The best sources of ascorbic acid are fresh, raw fruits and vegetables. Probably the best-liked and most widely used sources are citrus fruits such as oranges and grapefruit, or their juices. But these are by no means the only sources. Strawberries and cantalope are rich in vitamin C, and so are cabbage, green peppers, turnips, tomatoes, and potatoes. Unless it is fortified, apple juice, a common breakfast drink, is very low in vitamin C. The following all produce about one-half the recommended daily allowance of vitamin C:

one serving of cabbage
a quarter of a large grapefruit
half of a large orange
three quarters of a cup of tomato juice
a third of a cup of orange juice
one ounce of green pepper
one serving of potatoes
one serving of turnip

Remember that vitamin C is a water-soluble vitamin and that care should therefore be taken in preparing some of the foods that contain it. For instance, boiling potatoes with their skins on retains more of their vitamin-C value, since the water cannot reach the interior of the potato as easily. For the same reason, all vegetables should be cooked in as large pieces as possible, in as little water as possible, and for as short a time as possible. It also should be noted that when such foods as tomatoes, tomato juice, and citrus-fruit juices are canned, they retain most of their ascorbic acid because of their high acidity. For best retention, the canning is usually done in a vacuum since ascorbic acid is destroyed by oxidation. This is the normal procedure in commercial methods of canning, which for this reason are superior to ordinary home-canning methods, which can't employ vacuum canning. This is not a condemnation of home canning, but merely an illustration of just one of the many cases where industrially processed foods are superior to the foods we process at home.

The B Vitamins: At the beginning of the twentieth century, the many vitamins in what is now called the vitamin B family was thought of as a single vitamin. Today, nine different B vitamins have been named:

1. thiamine
2. riboflavin
3. niacin
4. pyridoxine (vitamin B_6)
5. pantothenic acid
6. cobalamine (vitamin B_{12})
7. folic acid
8. biotin
9. choline

Inositol has been and still is occasionally named as a B vitamin by some health-food people. However, there is little evidence that it is a vitamin. Even if it were essential, we get plenty of it in the foods we eat; a deficiency of inositol has never been shown.

Thiamine, riboflavin, and niacin are the most important B vitamins because the human body requires more of them than it does the others. Let's consider each of these three vitamins in turn.

Thiamine: This vitamin is known also as vitamin B_1. A severe deficiency of thiamine produces the disease known as beriberi (polyneuritis). This disease is still common in certain areas of the Far East among people who subsist mainly on polished white rice. It affects the nerves, and paralyzes the legs in such a way that an afflicted person exhibits a peculiar gait. In some cases the victim's heart enlarges, his heartbeat slows down, his appetite and consequently his weight decreases. In the past, beriberi was cured quite often by feeding the victim whole rice, including the bran, instead of white rice. These days, white flour and rice are usually enriched. In the Philippines, many people used to die from beriberi, but in 1952 enriched rice was introduced commercially in two provinces of that country. At the request of the Food and Agricultural Organization (FAO) and the World Health Organization (WHO), a team of experts evaluated this program. The results were published in 1954 in a bulletin called "Rice Enrichment in the Philippines." It was found initially that enriched rice did not completely prevent the deficiency, but since then, technological advances, along with acceptance of the enriched rice, have virtually eliminated the disease. In North America beriberi is virtually unknown, and this is due to the enrichment programs that have been introduced by legislation and the food industry.

Thiamine, a water-soluble vitamin, may be lost in the cooking process if water is used. Thiamine may also be destroyed more readily in alkaline water.

Often, a vitamin requirement can be satisfied by a single food source that is rich in the vitamin. For instance, a normal serving of orange juice supplies the vitamin C that prevents scurvy, a teaspoon of cod liver oil supplies the vitamin D that prevents rickets, and a large serving of green or yellow vegetables satisfies the need for vitamin A. This is not the case with thiamine. Although there is some thiamine in many foods, there is no single source that can provide all the thiamine needed daily for health. So thiamine must be obtained from many foods or from a diet supplement. This is not intended as a scare tactic. The many foods that one normally eats daily will provide one's daily requirement of thiamine, even though the amount of thiamine in the individual foods is small. Enriched bread, potatoes, green peas, dried peas, beans, and milk all contribute to the satisfaction of the thiamine requirement. Meat is a good source of thiamine, and pork products are the best source. Half a slice of ham or one and a half sausages contains the same amount of thiamine as four slices of enriched or whole-wheat bread. A large pork chop contains the thiamine equivalent of one pound of enriched or whole-wheat bread. In addition, organ meats such as kidney and heart, are reasonably rich in thiamine.

Riboflavin: This vitamin is a very stable part of the B complex, but it is still subject to the problems associated with water solubility and alkaline solutions. It is destroyed by light when in a liquid form. Therefore, an excellent source of riboflavin such as milk should not be left in the sunlight for any length of time if its riboflavin content is to be preserved.

The other vitamins mentioned thus far have been used to cure a particular deficiency disease. Although riboflavin does not cure a particular disease, it helps in the cure of pellagra and other diseases. Moreover, it has a beneficial effect on certain sores that appear around the mouth and nose, and it is necessary for growth.

Variety meats and organ meats are excellent sources of riboflavin. Milk and cheese are also very good sources. One-half cup of milk contains 0.2 milligrams of riboflavin; the equivalent amount may be found in the following servings of food:

one-quarter cup of evaporated milk
one and a half servings of salmon
two tablespoons of dried milk
one-fifth ounce of beef liver
two servings of broccoli
one-quarter ounce of kidney
one and a half eggs
two ounces of cheddar cheese

In general, riboflavin is fairly stable when processed. It is not destroyed by heat, but it may be leached into the cooking water and then lost if the water is thrown away. Little, if any, riboflavin is lost in baking or broiling.

Niacin: Niacin is a specific remedy for pellagra, a deficiency disease marked by dermatitis, diarrhea, and dementia. Pellagra was prevalent in many countries of the world in the early part of this century, and has always been associated with poor diets. At first, it was thought to result from a deficiency of protein, since one of the essential amino acids, tryptophan, is the precursor of niacin. Niacin was originally called the pellagra-preventing (p-p) factor.

Thiamine, riboflavin, and niacin have been called "the big 3" of the B vitamins. We can obtain enough of them if we eat a varied diet, but it is still worthwhile to watch for the word "enriched" on the labels of all flour products. This same care should be taken when buying corn meal, grits, rice, and baking mixes of all kinds, because if these aren't enriched, problems might occur. Most scientific studies of the rest of the B vitamins have shown that they are not deficient in the American diet. However, certain conditions of stress can deplete some of them, and we should therefore include them in our diet. They are obtainable through a varied diet, so most people in North America do not have to worry about them. There may be one exception, however, since a great many people are currently subsisting on a vegetarian diet. Cobalamine (vitamin B_{12}) is not found in vegetables, and although a minimal amount of it is required by the body, it could be depleted if meat or meat products were not consumed.

One other vitamin that is mentioned from time to time is vitamin P. In a very large course that we teach at the University of Massachusetts (Amherst), we have been asked on several occasions about the importance of vitamin P and its necessity in the proper utilization of vitamin C. In the past, and particularly in the 1930s, claims were made on behalf of vitamin P, but by 1950 it was well known that this substance is not in fact a vitamin. There is still some confusion as to what people mean when they speak of "vitamin P." We are told that it is a bioflavonoid that is naturally present in citrus fruits and that is esssential for the proper metabolizing of vitamin C. Bioflavonoids certainly exist in nature, but they have never been shown to have any therapeutic action as vitamins.

Fat-Soluble Vitamins

There are four fat-soluble vitamins:

1. vitamin A
2. vitamin D
3. vitamin E
4. vitamin K

These vitamins have certain properties in common. They are not soluble in water, and they are not destroyed by heat. They can be stored in large amounts in the liver, where they form a valuable reserve to be used in time of need. They are absorbed from the intestinal tract with the help of bile salts. Any interference with the production of bile salts will cause a lessening in the absorption of fat-soluble vitamins. The use of mineral oil either in salad dressing or as a laxative prevents some absorption of fat-soluble vitamins, and this substance should therefore be used only if a physician orders it.

Vitamin A: Vitamin A has two sources, plant and animal, and can exist in two forms. In humans, vitamin A exists as the human requires it; in plants, it occurs as a provitamin (a compound which can break down to form a vitamin) called beta carotene, which forms two molecules of vitamin A after ingestion by a human. In another sense, all vitamin A may be considered to have a plant source, since animals eat plants and make their own vitamin A from this provitamin. There are actually four nutritionally useful carotenes in plants, but the most effective is beta carotene. Not all the carotene in a plant is converted to vitamin A; in fact as little as 25 percent may be converted. For this reason, amounts of vitamin A are expressed in international units (IU), which take into account the actual amount of vitamin A available. Vitamin A is stable to heat and is thus not lost during cooking and processing, but it may be destroyed by exposure to oxygen or to sources of ultraviolet light, such as sunlight. Fats tend to go rancid under the same conditions, so when a fatty material such as meat smells rancid, chances are good that most of its vitamin-A value has been lost.

How often have you heard the expression, "Eat your carrots—they'll make you see in the dark"? Unfortunately, neither carrots nor vitamins will allow anyone to see in the dark. However, a deficiency of vitamin A certainly impairs dark adaptation in humans; that is, it prevents one from adapting from light to dark light as quickly as one should. This is one of the first signs of vitamin-A deficiency in humans. Other symptoms are dry skin and tiny lumps forming in the corner of the eye known as Bitot's spots. If the deficiency is very great over a long period of time, the eyelids may become swollen and sore and the eye disease xerophthalmia develops.

The richer sources of vitamin A are fish liver oils and the livers of all animals. The older the animal, the greater the amount of vitamin A in its liver and, therefore, the richer the source. Beef liver is a better source than calf liver. Milk fat contains both vitamin A and its provitamin carotene, and so does egg yolk. The proportions vary, partly due to the food eaten by the animal and partly due to the breed of the animal.

The richer sources of carotene, or provitamin A, are green and yellow vegetables. However, the available amount of carotene varies. Experimental evidence has shown that in some vegetables only 24 percent is available, whereas in others 74 percent is available. This availability is due to the type of provitamin present. The recommended daily allowance of vitamin A is 5,000 IU per day. If the proper foods are eaten, it is not very difficult to obtain this amount.

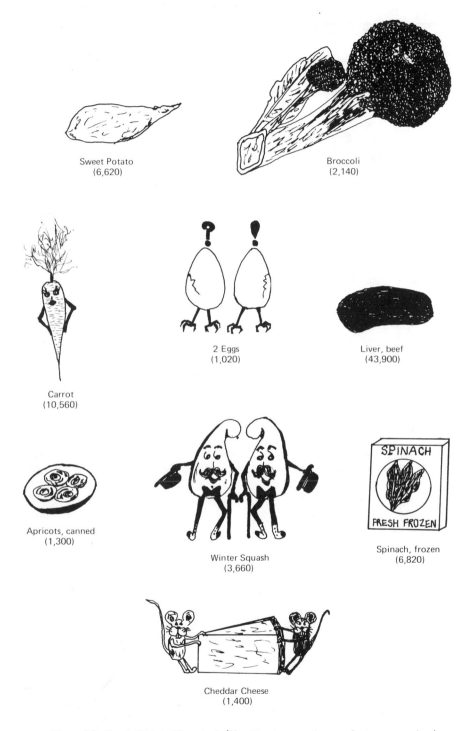

Sweet Potato
(6,620)

Broccoli
(2,140)

2 Eggs
(1,020)

Liver, beef
(43,900)

Carrot
(10,560)

Apricots, canned
(1,300)

Winter Squash
(3,660)

Spinach, frozen
(6,820)

Cheddar Cheese
(1,400)

Figure 2-3: Foods Rich in Vitamin A (Numbers in parentheses refer to one serving.)

However, the ten-state survey showed that the Spanish-Americans in the low-income states, mainly Mexican-Americans, were deficient in vitamin A. In addition, a majority of young people in all subgroups showed low vitamin-A levels. This might be due to the fact that organ meats and vegetables, which are excellent sources of vitamin A, are bypassed by the young and cannot be afforded by the subsistence-level group studied.

Some writers, the late Adelle Davis for one, have recommended that 25,000 international units of vitamin A be ingested per day. This recommendation is most unfortunate, for too much vitamin A is extremely dangerous. Some Arctic explorers have died from vitamin-A toxicity after eating the liver of a polar bear. As two authorities have noted,

> vitamin A given in excessive amounts causes toxic reactions. Adults who ingested 300 to 500 grams of polar bear liver became severely ill. Headache, vomiting, diarrhea and giddiness appear promptly. About a week later, desquamation of the skin and some loss of hair occurred. The intake may have been about seven million international units since the vitamin A content of polar bear liver may be as high as 18,000 international units per gram. Numerous instances of poisoning have been described in infants and children given excessive dosages of vitamin A in the form of fish liver oil concentrates. Scaly dermititis, patchy loss of hair, fissured lips, skeletal pain, irritability and anorexia were common to all these patients. The insidious onset of the symptoms and prompt response to cessation of overdosage are characteristic. Permanent sequelae are unusual. More cases of vitamin A overdosage than of deficiency have been reported in medical journals in recent years. The condition has been studied in a human volunteer. Nothing is known of the biological properties of vitamin A that will account for these reactions.[6]

You can see that a recommendation of five times the amount of vitamin A required by humans is at best shortsighted. Excess vitamin A cannot be excreted by the body because vitamin A is fat-soluble. Therefore, it can accumulate until it reaches a toxic level.

Vitamin D: A deficiency of vitamin D results in a disease known as rickets, which has been recognized for centuries but has been cured only as recently as the early part of this century. We know today that vitamin D cures and prevents this disease, which is easily recognized by the victim's bowlegs, pigeon chest, and enlarged forehead bones. Vitamin D has many different forms, of which two

[6] Charles H. Best and Norman B. Taylor, *The Physiological Basis of Medical Practice*, 8th ed. (Baltimore: The Williams and Wilkins Co., 1966), 1435–36.

are especially important. One is a provitamin called ergosterol, which has a plant source, and the other is the provitamin 7-dehydrocholesterol, which has an animal source. Both these substances are converted to active vitamin D as a result of exposure to sunlight.

For years it was known that children in the tropics hardly ever developed a vitamin-D deficiency, and initially this was not understood. However, it was found that the animal provitamin, 7-dehydrocholesterol, is found in the skin of humans, and that when sunlight reaches the skin it changes this 7-dehydrocholesterol to active vitamin D. The blood then carries the vitamin D to the liver, where it is stored for future use. Fog, rain, and cloudy weather, of course, prevent sunlight from reaching the skin. Also, people who don't live in a tropical climate must wear sufficient clothing to defend themselves from the rigors of the weather, and, thus, they are not exposed to the sunlight necessary to convert the provitamin into vitamin D. Therefore, vitamin D must come from foods or food supplements.

The cause of rickets seems to be the inability of the body to absorb calcium and phosphorus in the right proportions from the intestinal tract. In other words, there can be plenty of calcium and phosphorus in the food ingested, but without vitamin D much of these two minerals are lost in the body. Therefore, to prevent rickets, food that contains calcium and phosphorus should also contain vitamin D. One can now see the great rationality in fortifying milk with vitamin D. Milk contains an abundance of calcium and phosphorus naturally, but it does not contain vitamin D. Since all three nutrients are required for the prevention of rickets, it is logical to fortify milk with vitamin D so that the body may obtain all three nutrients at the same time. In a talk that she presented at the University of Massachusetts (Amherst) in 1972, Adelle Davis stated that she [did] not know of any fortification program [that had] ever worked." It seems to me that this is idiocy. We have already noted that the use of enriched rice in the Philippines helped prevent beriberi, and now we see that rickets is virtually unknown because of the fortification of milk with vitamin D and the use of vitamin D supplements.

Very few foods contain vitamin D naturally. Certain fish, such as herring, mackerel, salmon, and sardines, contain a fair amount, and egg yolks contain some, but other foods contain either none or a negligible amount. Because of this, it has been necessary in the past to consume fish-liver oil concentrates in order to obtain the required supply of vitamin D. The fortification of milk with vitamin D has, of course, eliminated to a great extent the need for fish-liver oils.

Excessive vitamin D may also be toxic:

Excessive intake of vitamin D in experimental animals or in man is deleterious. The first signs of toxicity are digestive disorders (vomiting and diarrhea) with loss of appetite and considerable loss of weight. Kidney damage finally results in death. Excessive doses of vitamin D cause hypercalcemia and calcification of the joints and soft tissues, especially the kidneys, large and medium sized arteries, heart, lungs, bronchi, pancreas and parathyroid glands.[7]

Vitamin E: This vitamin has been described as a cure looking for a disease. Four forms of vitamin E are known to occur naturally, and of these one is always present in natural fats as an antioxidant. Vitamin E is used by the food industry to prevent oxidation and consequent spoilage of some food products. In this case, one of those very bad food additives is in fact a vitamin. Chemically, vitamin E is known as tocopherol.

Vitamin E is necessary for reproduction in rats. It was found that on an E-deficient diet, female rats were unable to bear young, and males became sterile. This research led to the belief that E was a high-potency vitamin that enhanced sexual capability, and people therefore began to consume larger and larger amounts of it. In recent years this has become a fad again: in 1972, sales of vitamin E were up to sixteen million dollars a year. Adelle Davis tells us that vitamin E prevents blood clots, but there is no scientific evidence for this in humans.

There is a recommended daily allowance for vitamin E, but a deficiency has never been found, so we apparently obtain enough from the foods we eat. Vitamin E is found in whole-wheat bread, wheat germ, and leafy green vegetables. The richest sources are plant oils. Margarine is a very/good source, and milk contains vitamin E in direct proportion to its vitamin-A content.

Vitamin K: Vitamin K is known as a coagulation vitamin because it cured a hemorrhagic disease in chicks that was characterized by delayed blood clotting. This delay was caused by a lack of sufficient prothrombin in the blood. When the chicks were given vitamin K, however, the amount of prothrombin returned to normal and the blood clotted in the normal amount of time. Prothrombin is formed in the liver and does not contain vitamin K, but its manufacture is activated by vitamin K.

Plants are the best source of vitamin K. Leafy green vegetables such as spinach and chard contain a lot, whereas cereals and fruits contain very little. Animal foods are almost void of vitamin K. Fortunately, however, it is synthesized in the digestive tract of many animals, including humans, so we are not dependent on food as the sole source of this vitamin. Bile is required for the absorption of vita-

[7] *Ibid.*, p. 1439.

min K, and thus, if the bile ducts are blocked, absorption of vitamin K will be low. Under normal circumstances, there is sufficient K in foods eaten or synthesized in the intestinal tract. However, in surgery, where the clotting time of the blood is most important, extra vitamin K may be given the patient to prevent possible hemorrhage. This is particularly true when the bile ducts are stopped. Newborn infants have little vitamin K, so to prevent them from hemorrhaging, vitamin K may be given to the mother before delivery or to the infant at birth.

MINERALS

Much of what has been said about micronutrients and vitamins applies also to minerals. We are told constantly that we need the trace amounts of minerals that apparently do not exist in plants grown in chemically fertilized soils. The facts have never proved this to be so. Certain minerals are needed for the maintenance of body health, but by and large we apparently receive enough of these in our diet. About fourteen minerals and traces of some others are found in the body, but only about six are required in enough quantity to warrant study here. These are calcium, phosphorus, iron, copper, iodine, and fluorine. The others are potassium, sulphur, sodium, magnesium, manganese, cobalt, and zinc. The latter group are found both in many foods and in water, and, thus, they seem to constitute few problems for the average American.

Calcium and Phosphorus

These minerals are found together as calcium and phosphate mostly in the bones. Small amounts are also found in the blood and the soft tissues. The main function of calcium and phosphorus is to build bones and teeth, but small amounts are important in other ways. Calcium is important to the normal clotting of the blood and in maintaining normal osmotic pressure, and phosphorus forms a part of such compounds as phospho-lipids and phospho-proteins as well as helping with normal osmotic pressure.

Humans need a large amount of calcium per day (800 milligrams; 1200 for children and pregnant women). Remember, however, that no nutrient is useful unless it is absorbed properly by the body. Certain substances can tie up calcium so that it can't be absorbed properly. For instance, spinach contains a great deal of oxalic acid, which combines with calcium and prevents it from being absorbed and utilized properly. Rhubarb leaves are toxic because of the tre-

Broccoli
(1/3 lb.)

Turnip
(3/4 lb.)

Cheddar Cheese
(2/3 oz.)

Navy Beans, raw
(2 servings)

Chard
(1 1/2 servings)

Cottage Cheese
(1/2 c.)

Salmon, canned
(1/3 c.)

Milk, fluid
(1/2 c.)

Milk, dried
(2 tbsp.)

Milk, evaporated
(1/4 c.)

Figs
(4 large)

Figure 2-4: ½ Cup Milk Equivalents in Calcium (0.14 grams calcium)

54

mendously high percentage of oxalic acid they contain, and because of the combination of this oxalic acid with calcium in the body.

One of the best sources of calcium is, of course, milk, and Ronald Deutsch has called this the "gentle tyranny of milk." One of the major problems in our society today is obesity and overweight. Certainly, a large amount of milk may contribute to this. In addition, whole milk contains a great many saturated fatty acids, which may become a factor in heart disease. As a means of avoiding such dangers, Deutsch recommends skim or low-fat milk. However, one may obtain enough calcium from a moderate amount of whole milk without incurring the problems pointed out above. Too much milk, like too much of any other food, does not fit into the healthy pattern of a widely varied diet.

Other excellent food sources of calcium are cheeses and canned salmon (because of the bones it contains). Broccoli and chard are fair sources of calcium. Interestingly, in days gone by we obtained enough calcium because we tended to eat or at least gnaw on the bones of meat and fish. However, with the affluence that our society has offered us we rarely grind our teeth on bones these days. Thus, we have lost this high-calcium source due to the wonders of civilization.

Iron

The amount of iron in the body is small: estimates range from three to five grams, depending on one's size and age. A little over half is found in the hemoglobin of the red cells, about a third is stored in the liver, spleen, red bone marrow, and kidneys, and the rest is found in small amounts in muscles, serum, and iron-containing enzymes. Iron is of great importance to the body since it is responsible for the oxygen-carrying properties of the hemoglobin in the red blood cells, and for the oxygen-using power of the enzymes that contain iron. Therefore, without iron it is impossible for the cells of the body to obtain enough oxygen, which, of course, is required for the combustion and energy-producing reactions that occur in the body. Just as in a car engine, without this combustion we don't have enough energy to fuel us and we eventually die.

It is alarming that an estimated 70 percent of American females are iron-deficient. Males require about ten milligrams of iron per day; females require some eighteen milligrams. These amounts are not actually needed by the body. However, the body absorbs only about 10 percent of the iron ingested, and this is why the larger amounts are required.

It is extremely difficult to obtain enough iron through foods alone unless one eats a great deal of variety meats, such as liver,

White Bread, not enriched
(5 slices)

Milk
(1 qt.)

Rolled Oats, uncooked
(1 serving)

Whole Wheat Bread
(2 slices)

Navy Beans, raw
(1/2 serving)

Broccoli
(2 servings)

Prunes
(5)

Beef Liver
(1/5 serving)

Egg
(1)

Potato
(2 servings)

Beefsteak
(1/2 serving)

Malaga Grapes
(2 medium bunches)

Figs
(2 large)

Figure 2-5: Egg Equivalents in Iron (1.2 MG)

56

heart, and tongue, leafy dark green vegetables (not lettuce), dried fruit, and nuts. There are, however, other food sources of iron. Interestingly, some of these are the commercial cereals that many of the consumer advocates have condemned as being sugar-coated vitamin tablets. Whether this is the case or not (we don't believe it is), at least 85 percent of the dried cereals on the market contain about a third of the recommended daily allowance of iron in one serving. This would seem to be an easy and adequate amount of iron to obtain at one sitting. If adequate iron is not obtained through one's regular diet, an iron supplement should be taken.

Copper

Copper, when ingested in large amounts, can be toxic, but the body requires it in very small amounts for the proper utilization of iron. The ordinary diet contains enough copper for this purpose.

Iodine

Iodine is found in minute amounts in the body—approximately twenty-five milligrams in the adult. Of this amount, fifteen milligrams are concentrated in the thyroid gland and the rest is found in the blood and in other tissues of the body. The thyroid makes thyroxine with some of the body's iodine and stores iodine that is not needed elsewhere. Thyroxine is released into the blood in amounts necessary to regulate the oxygen-consuming function of the body.

When the thyroid gland does not receive an adequate amount of iodine, it does not function properly. Insufficient iodine during adolescence results in a simple colloid goiter, a condition characterized by swelling around the neck directly under the chin. This enlargement is due to an effort by the thyroid gland to make more adequate amounts of thyroxine. This kind of goiter is not accompanied by any toxic symptoms, although it may indicate underfunctioning of the thyroid gland. Medically, it is important in that it may develop later into a serious condition.

Unfortunately, other thyroid-related conditions may be much more severe. Insufficient thyroxine during fetal life may result in cretinism, which is characterized by physical and mental dwarfing. If thyroxine is given to cretins early enough, they may recover completely. If not, they do not develop normally and have a low basal metabolic rate. Cretinism can be prevented by giving mothers sufficient iodine during pregnancy.

The amount of iodine in food is extremely variable. Sea foods such as oysters, salmon, and seaweeds contain fairly large amounts.

Drinking water contains variable amounts. Whether or not any iodine is in a plant depends on whether or not iodine is in the soil. Therefore, people who do not live near the ocean may be deficient in iodine. Fortunately, the food-processing industry produces iodized salt, which supplies more than enough iodine for the human body. It might be a good idea if all salt were iodized by law. There are still some areas in the country where people buy uniodized salt, due to ignorance or perhaps to save a penny or two. This, of course, can result in an iodine deficiency and subsequent health problems.

Fluorine

Fluorine exists naturally in the water supply in some communities. It appears unnaturally in the water supply in others, where the community leaders have been farsighted enough to fluoridate the water. Fluoridated water is very helpful in preventing dental caries, and no adverse conditions have been shown to result from the normal consumption of it.

The minerals other than the six discussed above are normally obtained in enough quantity, so in general we don't have to worry about them. An interesting study was conducted recently, though, to show that the overconsumption of any food material can be harmful. It was found that when whole-wheat flour and bread constituted a major portion of one's diet, the phytate present in the bread and flour combined with the zinc in the body to such an extent that a zinc deficiency resulted. This deficiency in nutritional dwarfism, affects the sexual glands, and has other far-reaching consequences, both physical and psychological. This is just another instance of faddism creating health problems and ignorance breeding danger.

Thus far, we have not mentioned the interdependence of various nutrients. This interdependence is very important. Certain nutrients require the presence of other nutrients in order to fulfill their function properly. However, these relationships are beyond the scope of this book. If a widely varied diet is eaten, adequate amounts of all the nutrients will be obtained and the various dependencies among them will be more than satisfied.

FIBER

A discussion of nutrients in this day and age cannot omit some mention of fiber. Fiber will be the new food fad of the 1970s. In recent years there has been a reawakening to the role of dietary fiber in nutrition. With this renaissance comes evidence that fiber, which has often been the most overlooked dietary component, may have a direct effect on some widespread biochemical-physiological human abnormalities.

Dietary fibers loosely define a group of substances found in practically all foodstuffs of plant origin and absent from foodstuffs of animal origin. Unfortunately, the term "dietary fiber" seems to imply a single chemical substance, or at least a group of very similar entities. This is not quite true. Dietary fibers include cellulose, hemicellulose, lignins, pectins, and other polymers that have traditionally and simplistically been referred to as "undigestible matter." It is perhaps this very concept of undigestibility that for many years had such an inhibiting effect on the research and subsequent enlightenment of this subject.

In the past, we have eaten fiber mainly as an aid to elimination. Perhaps we could consider ourselves a country of laxative eaters, since in some health-food stores as many as thirty-two different laxatives are advertised. One, in fact, is advertised with the statement, "Have you cultivated your inner organic garden recently?" The diet that we are becoming accustomed to in this country contains a lesser amount of fiber than was the case in the past, and concern has arisen over this. One of the areas of concern is colon cancer, which we might add emphatically has not been proved to be directly related to fiber intake. However, some evidence indicates relationships between a high incidence of colon cancer and a low intake of dietary fiber. The thing that frightens us is that dietary fiber might become the next advertising gimmick of the 1970s as a result of this concern. (We can see it now: "Buy this product because it contains 90 percent hay.") We would hope that readers would not build the issue of fiber to these proportions. Nevertheless, it seems that an increase in our dietary fiber—in the form of rougher or less refined food materials— may in some cases be helpful.

In this chapter, we have considered the nutrients we need and the foods in which they exist. Eating should not be a mathematical exercise, and we hope that readers may be able to make some generalizations of their own after reading this chapter. For instance, flour comes from seeds (which are concerned with reproduction) and is therefore a better source of protein than spinach (a leafy vegetable). Such thinking might help one choose the right foods without a list of figures. In addition, such generalizations are necessary because we don't eat all fresh food anymore and there is thus no point in memorizing what every fresh food contains in the way of nutrients. However we do eat pizza, which is a fair source of protein considering the flour and cheese it contains.

Remember, a wise diet is a widely varied diet, one that includes fresh, processed, and "fun" foods.

NAS-NRC 1974 REVISED RDA

The Food and Nutrition Board of the National Academy of Science—National Research Council has completed work on the revised RDA. The new chart appears below. Work on the test is still in progress, and the tentative publication date for the complete report is early summer.

The newly revised table changes classifications in sex and age groupings. The RDA for protein is down except for pregnant women. (Other changes for this category reflect current thought on the nutritional needs of the pregnant woman.) For the first time, there is an RDA for zinc: 15 mg for adults and 20 to 25 mg for pregnant and lactating women. Iron recommendations remain the same, despite current feeling of an increased iron need in pregnant women.

BIBLIOGRAPHY

Deutsch, R. A., *The Family Guide to Better Food and Better Health.* Des Moines: Creative Home Library, Meredith Corp., 1971.

Labuza, T. P., *Food for Thought.* Westport, Conn.: Avi Publishing Co., Inc., 1974.

White, P. L., and W. Selvey, *Let's Talk about Food.* Acton, Mass.: Publishing Sciences Group, Inc., 1974.

Table 2-2. Food and Nutrition Board, National Academy of Sciences National Research Council Recommended Daily Dietary Allowances[1] Revised 1974

Designed for the maintenance of good nutrition of practically all healthy people in the U.S.A.

	(Years) From up to	Weight (kc)	Weight (lbs)	Height (cm)	Height (in)	Energy (kcal)[2]	Protein (g)	Fat-Soluble Vitamins Vitamin A Activity (RE)[3]	Vitamin A Activity (IU)	Vitamin D (IU)	Vitamin E Activity[5] (IU)
Infants	0.0–0.5	6	14	60	24	kg × 117	kg × 2.2	420[4]	1,400	400	4
	0.5–1.0	9	20	71	28	kg × 108	kg × 2.0	400	2,000	400	5
Children	1–3	13	28	86	34	1300	23	400	2,000	400	7
	4–6	20	44	110	44	1800	30	500	2,500	400	9
	7–10	30	66	135	54	2400	36	700	3,300	400	10
Males	11–14	44	97	158	63	2800	44	1,000	5,000	400	12
	15–18	61	134	172	69	3000	54	1,000	5,000	400	15
	19–22	67	147	172	69	3000	52	1,000	5,000	400	15
	23–50	70	154	172	69	2700	56	1,000	5,000		15
	51+	70	154	172	69	2400	56	1,000	5,000		15
Females	11–14	44	97	155	62	2400	44	800	4,000	400	10
	15–18	54	119	162	65	2100	48	800	4,000	400	11
	19–22	58	128	162	65	2100	46	800	4,000	400	12
	23–50	58	128	162	65	2000	46	800	4,000		12
	51+	58	128	162	65	1800	46	800	4,000		12
Pregnant						+300	+30	1,000	5,000	400	15
Lactating						+500	+20	1,200	6,000	400	15

(continued)

Food and Nutrition Board, National Academy of Sciences National Research Council Recommended Daily Dietary Allowances[1] Revised 1974 (continued)

	Water-Soluble Vitamins							Minerals					
	Ascorbic Acid (mg)	Folacin[6] (µg)	Niacin[7] (mg)	Riboflavin (mg)	Thiamin (mg)	Vitamin B_6 (mg)	Vitamin B_{12} (µg)	Calcium (mg)	Phosphorus (mg)	Iodine (µg)	Iron (mg)	Magnesium (mg)	Zinc (mg)
Infants	35	50	5	0.4	0.3	0.3	0.3	360	240	35	10	60	3
	35	50	8	0.6	0.5	0.4	0.3	540	400	45	15	70	5
Children	40	100	9	0.8	0.7	0.6	1.0	800	800	60	15	150	10
	40	200	12	1.1	0.9	0.9	1.5	800	800	80	10	200	10
	40	300	16	1.2	1.2	1.2	2.0	800	800	110	10	250	10
Males	45	400	18	1.5	1.4	1.6	3.0	1200	1200	130	18	250	15
	45	400	20	1.8	1.5	1.8	3.0	1200	1200	150	18	400	15
	45	400	20	1.8	1.5	2.0	3.0	800	800	140	10	350	15
	45	400	19	1.6	1.4	2.0	1.0	800	800	130	10	350	15
	45	400	16	1.5	1.2	2.0	3.0	800	800	110	10	350	15
Females	45	400	16	1.3	1.2	1.6	3.0	1200	1200	115	18	300	15
	45	400	14	1.4	1.1	2.0	3.0	1200	1200	115	18	300	15
	45	400	14	1.4	1.1	2.0	3.0	800	800	100	18	300	15
	45	400	13	1.2	1.0	2.0	3.0	800	800	100	18	300	15
	45	400	12	1.1	1.0	2.0	3.0	800	800	80	10	300	15
Pregnant	60	800	+2	+0.3	+0.3	2.5	4.0	1200	1200	125	18+[8]	450	20
Lactating	60	600	+4	+0.5	+0.3	2.5	4.0	1200	1200	150	18	450	25

(Courtesy of National Research Council, Food and Nutrition Board, Washington, D.C., Recommended Daily Allowances, 8th edition, 1974 Publication 0-309-02216-9.)

[1] The allowances are intended to provide for individual variation among most normal persons as they live in the United States under usual environmental stresses. Diets should be based on a variety of common foods in order to provide other nutrients for which human requirements have been less well defined. See text for more-detailed discussion of allowances and of nutrients not tabulated.

[2] Kilojoules (KJ) = 4.2 × kcal.

[3] Retinol equivalents.

[4] Assumed to be all as retinol in milk during the first six months of life. All subsequent intakes are assumed to be one-half as retinol and one-half as β-carotene when calculated from international units. As retinol equivalents, three-fourths are as retinol and one-fourth as β-carotene.

[5] Total vitamin E activity, estimated to be 80 percent as α-tocopherol and 20 percent other tocopherols. See text for variation in allowances.

[6] The folacin allowances refer to dietary sources as determined by *Lactobacillus casei* assay. Pure forms of folacin may be effective in doses less than one-fourth of the RDA.

[7] Although allowances are expressed as niacin, it is recognized that on the average 1 mg of niacin is derived from each 60 mg of dietary tryptophan.

[8] This increased requirement cannot be met by ordinary diets; therefore, the use of supplemental iron is recommended.

chapter **3**

Organic Gardening:
A Consideration

Interest in organic gardening and the related health food phenomenon are certainly connected with the ecological concern that is overtaking the country for many valid reasons. There is no question that the back-to-nature movement is strong and vigorous, and this is due perhaps to errors that we have made in the last fifty years. However, there is another explanation. It used to be that calories were counted, people were either fat or nonfat, diet meant dieting, and this was about all there was to worry about when one ate. But in recent times, several things have happened to change all that. The Kennedy years ushered in an era in which thinness, vigor, youth, and stylish health were significant. Underfed laboratory rats were living longer and better than their overfed brothers. Rachel Carson and other conservationists were thinking about, writing about, and worrying about the price we all pay for urbanization: the effects of chemicals, poisons, and processing on our food and possibly our genes. Many of the screen heroes of the 40s and 50s—who taught us all how to hold a cigarette and drink—were dying young and in the worst ways possible. Nutrition, health, and extended youth were starting to become a major concern to that group of decorative doers that writer Marilyn Bender has called the beautiful people. Heathful eating had to become a major concern to them, as it should be to you, because they found themselves faced with a serious problem: Paris and Seventh Avenue were becoming increasingly merciless about styles. You couldn't hide anything, anywhere, anymore after 1965. At the same time, the demands of beautiful living stepped up: a beautiful person had to be more places, do more things, do them more quickly. A woman had to get the most out of every bite of food she put in her bodily engine. She needed high-octane foods and she needed them fast. The standard weight charts also had to go, despite the inevitable protestations from the medical profession. Who now wanted to weigh 146 pounds at five feet eight inches? Better, under 130 pounds! Better yet, 125! And with the standard weight chart went many of the conventional ways of thinking about food. And, so, people began to think seriously about such things as vitamins, blood sugar, proteins, minerals, and supplements. We now want to know where and how food is grown and what it does once it's in our body. All this is very admirable, as long as we are not carried away by faddism or cultism.

This new awareness, whether it be well founded or not, is showing itself at every level, including that of the university. Not too long ago in March 1972, John Birchfield, president-elect of the National Association of College and University Food Services, told the executive board of that association that "students have strong feelings that something has to be done to stop the trend of destroying their surroundings. They want to live without the garbage and pollution that is choking our communities."[1] In addition to the concern for environmental pollution is a concern for personal physical pollution. Organic foods conform to the dictum that no chemical fertilizers, conditioners, pesticides, or insecticides may be used in growing foods, and no preservatives, artificial coloring, or artificial flavorings may be added to the products. Equal in importance to the organic purity of natural foods is, of course, their nutritional value. The same journal that contained Birchfield's remarks also contained

[1] "Health Foods Enter Student Diets," *College and University Business* (March 1972), p. 51.

an article about the University of Massachusetts.[2] This article pointed out that of the 10,000 students who had contracted to board at
the university, slightly more than 1,000 were using this service,
according to meal counts.

DEFINITIONS

In a discussion of the organic food movement, it is first necessary to define the term organic foods. One of the first definitions of
organic gardening was presented in *The Organic Directory* (1971), a
catalog of organic food stores throughout the country compiled
by the editors of the magazines, *Organic Gardening and Farming* and
Prevention. According to this directory, "organically grown" describes foods and crops that have been raised in soil fertilized by
organic methods only. In particular, it indicates that no chemical
fertilizers, conditioners, pesticides, or preservatives have been used at
any time in the growing or preparation of these products. The following standards were established by a group of West Coast shops that
joined together in an assorted-trade association in 1971; no organic
merchant will sell any food containing artificial flavor, artificial
color, monosodium glutamate, synthetic sugar substitutes, synthetic
salt substitutes, synthetic preservatives, emulsifiers, or other synthetic food chemicals, corn syrup, white sugar, bleached white flour,
cottonseed products, or hydrogenated fats. Thus, organic foods are
foods grown without the use of any agricultural chemicals and
processed without the use of food chemicals or additives (White,
1972). A wider definition has been supplied by Food and Earth Services, Inc. (1970). This same group sponsored a forum on food and
nutrition on May 7, 1971 at the Massachusetts Institute of Technology, Cambridge, Mass. This forum brought together concerned
specialists ranging from small bio-dynamic gardeners to huge commercial producers and marketers—with the addition of scientists,
researchers, and educators. The unifying concern among the partici-
pants was for nutritional quality. The purpose of the forum was to
approach three questions: (1) Is there a way to guarantee the nutritional content of the food that consumers buy? (2) If so, then how?
(3) Is there a role for an objective, nonprofit, public-service organization dedicated to this proposition? During the course of this
forum, it came to light that the Food and Earth Services group felt
that censorship of literature on nutrition was widespread. One of
the organic representatives reported the existence of a list that rated

[2] Ibid., p. 86.

books on nutrition. This list compiled by the Chicago Nutritional Association, employed three classifications: "Recommended," "Recommended for Special Purposes," and "Not Recommended." It was pointed out that most of the books considered worthwhile by the organic people were classified "Not Recommended." The commercial people were unaware of this list and requested to see it, but apparently the list was unavailable. Libraries generally followed the list's recommendations, it was reported, and therefore withheld from the general public all books that did not follow the party line.[3]

POPULARITY AND SALES

No matter what truth or fiction is embodied in the organic movement, the fact remains that organic foods are commanding more attention and more of the market. Health food stores sell organic foods, which were defined earlier as foods that have not been chemically treated and that contain no additives of any kind. The prices of the foods in these stores are, in general, about twice those of commercial products distributed through conventional channels.

The appeal of health-food stores is growing rapidly, to the point where they may be considered a threat to the commercial producers of all types of foods. According to *Barron's* (1972), the National Nutritional Foods Association states that there are about 275 major health-food manufacturers and distributors, plus another 300 or so who supply one or two items. At least 2,800 stores retailed natural foods, compared with a maximum of close to 2,000 in 1972. One of the few firms to conduct market research is the William T. Thompson Co., which figured that in 1970 health-food stores sold $100 million at wholesale ($140 million at retail), and in 1971, $140 to $150 million at wholesale ($200 million at retail). If mail-order firms, door-to-door concerns, supermarkets, discounters, and drug stores are added, the total may have run to $400 million.

Therefore, a large viable industry is emerging and is currently attracting the attention of major food companies. Whether the latter trend is good or bad is a matter of personal opinion, but it would seem that the food industry may be lending respectability to rather fraudulent claims and thus indirectly admitting that the "natural" movement is in some ways correct. Television advertising implies that "natural" or "no-additives" is somehow better. This takes ad-

---

[3] Food and Earth Services Inc., 1970. Forum on Food and Nutrition. Massachusetts Institute of Technology, Cambridge, Mass., May 7, 1971.

vantage of the consumer's confusion and implies that other foods are somehow not as good.

The frightening result of people deserting modern methods of agriculture is implied in the following remarks.

> Any proof that some small grower has succeeded in growing crops with organic methods is meaningless. Today, of about 3 million farms in the U.S. (half as many as in 1940) about 1% or 30,000 farms account for over 60% of our vegetables, 45% of the fruit and nuts, and 35% of all poultry products, according to the U.S. Department of Agriculture. What counts in food production is what these giant farmers do. If these relatively few farms were put out of operation, as for example by any catastrophic occurrences, the country would have a severe food shortage. All of these big farms use scientific methods, including full use of chemical fertilizers and pesticides. Furthermore, the trend is still fewer and bigger farms, requiring increased mechanization and the application of the highest skills of the agronomist. On the other hand, in areas of Asia, the Near East and Africa where farming methods could be called organic, famines are recurrent and hunger and malnutrition are common.
>
> In the real world of farming today, there is no room for the cult that regards natural methods as good, and all improvements on nature, bad. Many of the organic food cultists who go arm in arm with the health food faddists appear to have a semi-religious conviction that what is natural is a manifestation of God's purpose while what is scientific is a denial of God's plan.[4]

In an article in the *Boston Globe*, Christina Robb in 1971 pointed out that although overall retail sales dropped 5 percent in metropolitan Boston retail sales of organic foods doubled. The number of retail outlets for organic foods doubled also. An article in the *Boston Sunday Globe* pointed out that a gentleman in Boston named Doroska makes his living selling compost and fertilizer that he makes organically. It boggles the mind to think what would happen if his methods were used on a world-wide level. This gentleman mixes one bushel of manure, two bushels of sawdust, and one bushel of leather dust. He puts this mess into a big barrel and adds water. The manure provides bacteria that heat up the mess and cause the sawdust and leather dust to rot. This perks for fourteen days. Then he draws off the water at regular intervals, and the stuff is ready for use. Another composting method is to put down layers of organic matter

[4] R. A. Selig, "The 'Organic Food' Kick," Supply letter of the United Fresh Fruit and Vegetable Association, June 9, 1971, pp. 1-3.

mixed with cow manure and keep it wet. This is left on the ground and takes up to one year to cure. Other organic materials that can be used are grass clippings, mulch leaves, old plants, and anything else that rots. The water that Doroska uses in his perking method he also sells, by the gallon. This is mixed one cup to a gallon of water and is used as a liquid fertilizer. One must wonder at how such preparation of fertilizer if used nationwide would affect the production of America's crops.

ADVANTAGES AND DISADVANTAGES
OF THE ORGANIC WAY

Thus far, the organic movement has been defined and has been shown to be a viable, growing portion of our national economy. It now becomes essential to examine exactly what the organic way is supposed to accomplish.

To its youthful enthusiasts, organic farming represents the wave of the future and abounds in political and ecological overtones. These include cooperation in place of competition, and humans working with nature instead of conquering and exploiting it ("Organic—Pro and Con," 1972).

To its opponents, organic farming represents a perverse spurning of the miracles of modern agricultural production. They see organic farmers as irrational dilettantes who simply refuse to come to grips with the very substantial problem of feeding a growing world. As Dr. Earl Butz has pointed out in the New Jersey Farm Bureau's "This Week" report of July 10, 1971, "We can go back to organic agriculture in this country if we must. We know how to do it. However, before we move in that direction, someone must decide which 50 million of our people will starve."

Most of the claims for the wonders of organic gardening border on the ridiculous. These claims not only are made on behalf of organic foods but also spread into other areas. A report in the *Wall Street Journal* described one such area.

> The woman who feeds her family organically grown foods, recycles her soft drink bottles and keeps phosphate out of her washing machine has a few questions about a related matter: How, in good conscience, can she walk out of the house in the morning knowing that she has just bathed her body in cosmetics that are saturated with chemicals? Well, here's what she can do: she can wash her face in raw eggs and beer. Or condition her skin with strawberries. Or rub it with avocado or cantaloupe or pat it with cucumber or celery juice. Or take a bath in herb tea. Indeed, there are any number of things she can do for skin

with fruits and vegetables and other natural ingredients, and when she's finished, she can take the container back to the store for a refill.[5]

The ecology movement has touched the cosmetic business only lightly. It isn't much more than a touch, because most of the six-billion-dollar-a-year beauty industry goes on as before. Within two months of its introduction, the Bonne Bell line of cosmetics was being sold in 4,000 stores in all fifty states. Mr. Bell predicted that sales would hit $2 million the first year, and he stated that the line was already profitable after its first few months. Amelia Bassin, who owns Apothecare, Inc., wouldn't talk about her sales and earnings figures, but she stated that business was going well. Her products were being sold in ten stores, and often the customers brought in their own bottles to be filled. Meanwhile, other cosmetics makers maintained that business was just fine and that they didn't have to resort to new gimmicks. One reason for this, they said, was that in this environmental age girls and women want a "natural" look, and according to Lester Rand, president of Rand Youth Poll, the natural look is causing teenage girls to use more cosmetics than ever before.

A discussion of the marvels of organic gardening would not be complete without mention of the late J. I. Rodale. Wade Green (1971) has discussed some of this gentleman's ideas in an article in the *New York Times Magazine.* "[The increase of interest in organic methods has] made me so much happier," said the late Rodale. "In the old days, I used to get such clobberings and insults, you know, and if I wasn't so well nourished, it would have affected me, but I stood up under it, because I had plenty of Vitamin B, which is the nerve Vitamin." Well, J. I., as he was known to friends and followers, would have good cause to rejoice these days. An idea whose time has come—following in the footsteps of hotpants, waterbeds, and even revenue sharing—organic foods, to use the term that he himself gave to the language, came to J. I. Rodale thirty years ago, and he above all nourished it to its current popularity. Superstitious, faddist, unscientific, nostalgic, the organic movement's critics say. Still, signs of the revival are everywhere—in smart conversation and in the sprouting of little stores with barrels and bins and quaint names such as "Ounce of Prevention," "The Good Seed," and "Mother Earth and Sons." Among other things, these stores dispense soybeans, brown rice, herbal tea, alfalfa sprouts, and a philosophy: organic or natural food is better, or at least favored, for earth dwellers. The Mecca of the organic movement is the small Lehigh Valley town of Emmaus, Pennsylvania, a biblical name bequeathed by Moravian settlers in the area. The movement's foremost prophet, since the death of J. I.

---

[5] S. H. Slom, "Lovely to Look at, Delightful to Hold—Her Secret: Celery," *Wall Street Journal*, June 14, 1972, p. 1.

Rodale, is a son, Robert. Associates in Emmaus disseminate a monthly magazine with the prosaic name, *Prevention*, which with a mixture of evangelical tones and scientific terms espouses health and nutrition. Concerned more specifically with organic food and how to grow it is *Organic Gardening and Farming*, periodic bible of the organic movement. According to the *Whole Earth Catalog, Organic Gardening* is "the most subversive" publication in the country. *Organic Gardening* readership nudged 700,000 copies and climbed 40 percent in the last year alone. Rodale did not conform to many organic food orthodoxes. Many organic dieters are vegetarian. Perhaps this is due partly to expense. Two dollars will get you a pound of organic hamburger, or only half as much as the unorganic stuff. However, Rodale frequently denounced vegetarianism; he thought people needed the zest of a good peice of meat. And unlike the late Adelle Davis, the organic-minded popular nutritionist, he thought milk was bad for people, except babies. When asked why he thought there was a basic superiority in using organic fertilizers, Rodale used what seems to be the ultimate argument of many organic believers, one that is based on an intuitive—almost mystical—conviction, or at least suspicion:

> We feel that with inorganically grown food you have things you don't even know exist. I'll give you an idea of an experiment to show you how little man does know. In an aquarium in London, they brought in some seagoing fish, but they didn't have seawater, so one of the curators said, "we could make seawater; we have the formula." He gets out his book and they make it, and they put in some fish, and in a few days the fish are dead. They did this any number of times. One of the curators then said, "let's put in a little pinch of seawater." The next thing, the fish could live. In other words, in their formula for seawater there's a little gleam of something that is missing.[6]

Rodale blessed the youth for their popularization of the organic movement, but he felt that there should be no organically grown marijuana! (In fact, the organic philosophy appears to be making its mark on the drug scene; marijuana is okay to some people because it's organic—from a plant—whereas LSD is spurned because it's a synthetic substance.)

Organic Gardening and Farming issues a seal that certifies that a farmer is "organic " and that he is using recognized organic growing practices to raise his crops. The seal and certification had been awarded to some forty-five farms in California by 1974. What is organically grown food? According to Rodale, it is food that has been grown without pesticides or artificial fertilizers; that has been grown in

[6] Wade Greene, "Guru of the Organic Food Cult," *New York Times Magazine*, June 6, 1971, p. 30.

soil whose humus content is increased by the addition of organic matter and whose mineral content is increased by natural mineral fertilizers; and that has not been treated with preservatives, hormones, antibiotics, and so on.

Thus far, it may seem that the organic movement is either a panacea or a total fraud. Neither seems to be the complete truth, as one writer has pointed out :

> I farmed for a number of years before going to college. For various reasons I farmed "organically" and read quite broadly on the subject. Two experiences during that time motivated my later course of studies. One summer a Soils Extension Agent at Kansas State University published in a national magazine a scathing condemnation of organic gardening and farming. He listed seven rules for good soil husbandry. That very month "Organic Gardening and Farming" published a scathing condemnation of the Agriculture Universities and the Chemical Industry. They listed seven rules of good soil husbandry. Both sets of rules were identical, almost to the word. Needless to say, there developed in my mind a bit of a credibility gap toward both.[7]

Because of this degree of uncertainty, which still exists both in the lay community and the scientific community, it is essential to consider scientific fact. T. H. Jukes (1970) states that there is no such thing as organic nutrition, that plants utilize only inorganic forms of plant food:

> Compost and manure are broken down by bacteria to components such as nitrate, potassium, iron and phosphates before they are assimilated. Hydroponics, in which plants are grown inorganically without soil, lead to the production of vegetables and fruits with the same proteins, carbohydrates, vitamin and mineral content as when the same strains of plants are grown in the ground with lots of manure.[8]

There are no magical properties in organic matter, as far as the plant itself is concerned. However, a good supply of organic matter in the soil (if soil is used) is of great value in farming, for it improves soil structure, reduces water runoff, and aids soil aeration and the development of soil organisms. Both chemical fertilizers and plant and animal manures may be used as needed. Isn't soil improvement important? Yes it is, but it is not true that soil improvement increases the nutrients in a fruit or vegetable, except in an extremely limited

---

[7] R. Adams, Jr., *Organic Gardening*, 1971. Personal Communication to J. M. Clydesdale.

[8] T. H. Jukes, "Facts and Fancy in Nutrition and Food Science," *Journal of the American Dietary Association*, 59, no. 3 (1971), 203.

way. Endemic goiter is the only established example of a direct relationship between a soil deficiency and a human disease, and manure wouldn't necessarily supply iodine. The answer to the iodine-deficiency problem has been iodization of salt, not application of fertilizer. Soil improvement can increase the size of crops, but not in nutritional characteristics. You cannot increase the supply of ascorbic acid in an apple to equal that in an orange by any amount of fertilization. This is because the composition of an apple and the composition of an orange are determined primarily by the genes of the fruits.

Some interesting facts have been brought to light in an extension publication called "Facts about Organic Gardening" prepared by L. H. MacDaniels, Professor Emeritus, Cornell University, Ithaca, New York. According to MacDaniels, the concepts of organic gardening are not new. Some appreciation of the value of organic matter in maintaining the structure and fertility of soils is as old as agriculture. About thirty or forty years ago, organic gardening appeared as a cult with a somewhat mystical background. This movement made extravagant claims as to the superior value of crops grown with composts and organically derived fertilizers, compared with crops fertilized with inorganic materials. Much of what was written about crop production thirty years ago is still relevant today, but the world in which that writing took place has changed drastically. The greatly increased population has necessitated increased food supplies. And there is an increasing awareness these days that the resources of this planet are finite, and that increased agricultural and industrial wastes and the unwise use of pesticides have contaminated the environment to the point where human survival on this planet is seriously questioned. Organic gardening is proposed as an answer to many of the problems related to these issues. MacDaniels concludes that some of the concepts and recommendations of organic gardening are basically sound and important, some are half-truths, perhaps plausible but limited in their application, and some are contrary to the best scientific evidence available.

The truth in organic gardening is basic and important. Agronomists agree that organic matter is an indispensable or at least a very valuable ingredient in most soils. It improves soil tilth through granulation of the soil particles, increases the soil's water-holding capacity, slows erosion, and through its decay releases nitrogen and other nutrients to growing crops. Carbon dioxide from decaying materials helps bring minerals into solution and thus makes them available to plants. Many soils the world over that once were productive are now barren wastes, due largely to the depletion of organic matter that followed too much cultivation. With the loss of organic matter, water penetration and the water-holding capacity of the soil are greatly reduced, resulting in runoff and erosion. A major problem in restoring such soils is to build up their organic-matter content by any means feasible. However, it is a half-truth either to state or imply that the use of composted materials and the absence of chemical fertilizers is adequate to build up the organic-matter content of soils over large areas, or to solve the problems of crop nutrition under present conditions. Over the wide area of the earth's surface where foods are produced in large quantity, it is impossible to accumulate enough plant refuse to increase the organic matter in the soil adequately. The organic gardening literature has stated that composting is adequate because the compost applied to the soil may last for twenty years. It is true that some of the more stable forms of humus remain in the soil for a long time, but the residue from leaves and other composted material is lost in a few years, at best. If this were not so, leaf mold in forests would build up very rapidly, which it does not. It is well known, too, that in the composting process much of the nutrient roughage value of the material is lost. Not only is the material greatly reduced in bulk but nitrogen is lost in the form of ammonia and some other elements are leached out.

Organic gardening emphasizes the use of mulches. In general, mulching is good practice, particularly if cheap mulching materials are available. These may consist of old hay, straw, sawdust, woodchips, shredded bark, or any other such material. Such a mulch conserves moisture, helps control weeds, and, if renewed yearly, releases nutrients from the decay of the material next to the soil. Mulching with newspapers, fertilizer sacks, and similar materials can also be beneficial. Black plastic is useful for controlling weeds and conserving moisture. In the organic gardening literature even rocks are recommended as a mulch. It is true that flat rocks around a tree will help control weeds, but the use of rocks as a mulch obviously has very limited application. Mulches, however, also have their drawbacks. There are always the hazards of fire burning the mulch and mice living in the mulch and destroying the plants. Also, it has been shown that in the spring, frost damage is greater over a mulch than in the open ground.

A feature of organic gardening that appeals to many, particularly young people, is the recycling of waste products. Considered broadly, everything that is produced on this planet—whether by nature, agriculture, or industry—eventually becomes a waste, either solid, liquid, or gas, or is dissipated as energy. Composting recycles biodegradable substances and puts them to good use. Reusing all waste materials appeals to organic gardeners as a conservation measure. However, there is a fallacy in this thinking. In order to recycle waste as in the form of mulch or compost, one must have a large yield on a given plot of land in order to plow it under. If chemical fertilizers are not used, the yield is normally lower and there is far less material to plow under. One may recycle all one wishes, but if the nutrients are not available, the recycling process merely implants less nutritive biological systems back into the soil until these are totally degraded. It is only common sense that when a tomato plant grows and a human eats the tomatoes, some nutrients are taken away from the plant. If this plant minus its tomatoes is plowed back under, it is bound to supply less nutrients than it would have, had the tomatoes been left on the plant. Therefore, a cycle exists: as long as we eat the fruit-bearing portion of the plant, we take away more and more nutrients from the soil and return fewer and fewer of them.

A claim found in organic gardening literature that is contrary to any known evidence is that a nutrient that comes from an inorganic fertilizer and is supplied to a plant and absorbed by or combined within it will produce a crop that is less nutritious than if the same element came indirectly from some organic source. In fact, in a recent book, *Fertilizer Technology in Use*, W. H. Allaway (1971) states "that at the present time there is no basis in the results of well-conducted experiments for statements that crops grown with organic fertilizer are nutritionally superior to those fertilized with inorganic forms of nutrients."

Another half-truth in the organic gardening literature is that organic material will control plant disease and insect pests and still result in healthy crops. It is true that under some conditions, crops that are growing rapidly as a result of adequate fertilization, either organic or inorganic, appear to be freer from insect and disease damage. In most cases this is apparent rather than real, in that with the larger amount of foliage that appears on the healthier plants, the insect damage seems to be less noticeable. On the other hand, the opposite can be true; a plant growing rapidly with an adequate nitrogen supply is likely to be much more susceptible to any of several diseases than if it is growing slowly as a result of a lack of nitrates. Some crops, particularly bulbs, tubers, and roots, are more likely to be damaged in soils high in organic matter than in soils low in organic matter (MacDaniels).

The position of organic gardening on pesticide use is valid up to a point, in that it calls attention to the limits and dangers of pesticide use and demands that materials and methods be changed to minimize damage to the environment. To say that no pesticide should be used under any conditions, however, is wholly unrealistic in light of the tremendous volume of food that must be produced to feed the world's population. Where hundreds of acres of crops are concerned, it should be obvious that picking potato bugs or using the ladybug approach is not practical. This is an important consideration, for it is in these larger operations that foods for the millions are produced.

The control of insects and plant diseases is a very complex problem. With the pressure of a greatly increased population, there is growing concern on the part of scientists not only to control plant diseases and insects but to breed new, resistant plants and use better soil management to increase food production. The answers to these problems involve far more than the presence or absence of organic matter in the soil.

Another misleading claim by the organic gardening movement is that inorganic fertilizers are in some way responsible for many of the ills of mankind, and that in order to lessen or prevent this condition it is necessary only to shift to the "organic way." This fallacy may be exposed by a simple comment. The soil in parts of Florida lack certain chemical elements necessary for the normal growth of livestock. These deficiencies are being corrected effectively by the addition to the soil of inorganic salts containing the necessary elements. No amount of compost or organic material grown on these deficient soils would supply the needed nutrients.

On a worldwide basis, there is a high correlation between the increased longevity of the population and the increased use of fertilizers. It is, of course, difficult to separate the effects of fertilizer on nutrition as such, from other changes that occur along with their use. In the developing countries, for instance, the use of fertilizers greatly increases the yields of food crops. This frees land for the growth of a greater diversity and abundance of food, which contributes to better nutrition and to increased longevity. After a comprehensive world survey, W. H. Allaway (1971) made the following statement:

> Thus the use of fertilizers accompanied by other changes, including the development of commerce to distribute food, usually leads to a more abundant and varied food supply. People living in a developed country generally have the opportunity to select a more nutritious diet. There is no evidence that the nutritional quality of this diet has been jeopardized because fertilizers were used to produce the food crop.[9]

One area in which the organic gardening philosophy is relevant is the recycling of organic wastes. Because of the high labor costs of raising food and mechanizing agriculture, organic refuse from farms and feedlots are not being recycled as they once were and as in the long run they should be. The cost of handling animal wastes prohibits the effective use of these materials, and as a result they accu-

---

[9] W. H. Allaway, "Feed and Food Quality in Relation to Fertilizer Use," in *Fertilizer Technology and Use*, ed. R. A. Olson et al. (Madison, Wisc.: Soil Science Society of America, 1971).

mulate or are disposed of in a way that increases the pollution of our environment. These waste materials, which were once regarded as an agricultural asset, are now a liability in many instances because their use is not profitable. The emphasis of organic gardening on recycling these wastes is basically sound and should be the concern of everybody.

According to MacDaniels, some apparent fallacies in the organic gardening position are as follows:

1. Composting organic waste in piles is an adequate way to build up or maintain organic matter in the soil over a wide area.
2. Food produced with organic fertilizers is superior in nutritive value to food grown with inorganic material and, hence, should command a higher price.
3. Inorganic fertilizers, as such, are in some way ruining our health and shortening our lives.
4. Under present conditions it is possible to produce the food necessary to feed the world's millions without any chemical pest control.[10]

Due to a lack of understanding, certain difficulties are experienced by the organic gardening advocates. L. A. Hodgkinson (1971) has pointed out that it is common practice in modern commercial farming to plow in sod crops, known as "green manure" corps, in rotation planting. This supplies the soil with the organic matter necessary to maintain its good quality, and at the same time it recycles some of the chemical elements not taken from the soil by the previous crops, thereby helping to secure them from being leached out and wasted. So in gardening, whether it be commercial or hobby, incorporating organic matter into the soil is very important. We really can't do without it, as any good farmer will attest. However, when individuals who have little or no training in biology, particularly in the chemistry of soils and plants, decide to garden organically, their lack of understanding sometimes results in difficulties (low yields, need for spending much time and labor, infestation, disease, infection of plants). The decision to garden organically may lead quite logically to medical and food faddism. Or if a person is first a medical or nature-food faddist, he or she is then apt to become an organic gardener.

Plants take up fertilizer and other elements from the soil that are dissolved in water. These substances enter the plants through the roots and to some extent their foliage. Whether they come from dead plant or animal material or from a bag of chemical fertilizer, these elements dissolved in water can enter plants only in the inorganic chemical state. The plants then combine these elements into various combinations with the carbon atoms that are part of the simple

[10] L. H. MacDaniels, "Facts about Organic Gardening." Published by Hampshire County Extension Service, Northampton, Mass., 1971, pp. 1-6. Originally by Cornell University, Ithaca, N.Y.

sugars that the plants manufacture during the process of photosynthesis. These sugars are created from the inorganic chemicals, carbon, hydrogen, and oxygen in the presence of sunlight. The plants obtain the carbon from carbon dioxide in the atmosphere, the hydrogen from water and the oxygen from both water and carbon dioxide. After this process takes place, oxygen is left over. This is given off into the atmosphere and is the oxygen that man and other oxygen-breathing organisms need to remain alive.

There isn't a food grown under natural organic methods that is better than the same food grown with chemicals. Here in part is what a group of experts had to say on the effect of organic versus inorganic fertilizers on the nutritional quality of plants.

Soils that have a high content of organic matter usually have many desirable physical properties. For example, they are easy to till, absorb rain readily, and tend to be drought resistant. Because soils high in organic matter have these desirable properties, some people have speculated that they might also produce plants of superior nutritional quality and that the use of organic composts or manures would result in plants of superior quality to those produced with inorganic fertilizers. A number of experiments have been conducted to check on this speculation. The nutritional quality of plants grown in soils that have received large amounts of organic manures has been compared with that of plants grown in soils that have received only inorganic fertilizers or, in some cases, with plants grown on culture solutions containing only inorganic salts of the essential elements. Any differences in their content of the essential elements or vitamins that have been noted have been too small to be of any nutritional significance, and have been in favor of the inorganic fertilized plants as often as in favor of those grown with organic materials.

This result is to be expected when one considers the relationship between the plant and the soil. For the most part, the elements essential to plant growth enter the plant in the inorganic form. If an element is originally present in the soil in some organic combination, this organic combination is broken down to an inorganic form by the microorganisms in the soil before the element enters the plant. Once converted to inorganic forms, the atoms of this element are indistinguishable from other atoms of the same inorganic forms that have never been a part of an organic combination.[11]

[11] Lewis A. Hodgkinson, "The Effect of Soils and Fertilizers on the Nutritional Quality of Plants." Publication 299 (September 1971), Agricultural Research Service, U.S. Department of Agriculture, in cooperation with Cornell University Agricultural Experiment Station and Soil Conservation Service, pp. 3–4.

It is pertinent to point out that the present-day countries of the world that, for various reasons, have not used agricultural chemicals, among them, "chemical" fertilizers, are the countries where famine exists and where millions have died from starvation. These countries grow by the natural method, the "organic" method. (The Bible has ample references to famines, and these occurred, of course, when people had no chemicals and all were organic gardeners.) On the other hand, the countries that grow great surpluses and feed most of the world's population are those that use "chemicals," understand the chemical and physical properties of soil and organic matter, and know the role that organic matter plays in modern agriculture. "Nature's way" means competition—competition between humans and the things that prevent them from growing food: insects, diseases, drought, and flood. And competition implies elimination: millions of people have been eliminated having to live "nature's way."

R. A. Seelig (1971) has pointed out that sixteen elements are necessary for the growth of plants. These are carbon, hydrogen, oxygen, nitrogen, phosphorus, potassium, calcium, magnesium, sulphur, zinc, iron, manganese, boron, copper, molybdenum, and chlorine. In addition, plants absorb many other elements. At least twenty-seven elements have been identified in certain samples of white pine wood. More than half of the elements in the periodic table have been found in plants, and it seems probable that every element occurring in the root environment is absorbed, including toxic elements. Furthermore, assuming "organic" compounds are in the soil, it should be noted that plants do not absorb food; rather, they absorb elements or compounds, which they then convert to food. The organic substances in the soil decompose, and the inorganic elements, nitrogen, phosphorus, and potassium are released in their inorganic forms. *However, potassium is not known in any organic compound, and it is one of the big three in fertilizers; nitrogen and phosphorus are the others.*

From such studies as the above, it becomes increasingly apparent that the organic way has something to offer, but only a minor fraction of what its proponents claim.

Having established the general uses of organic material, it now becomes necessary to look at the hard facts of the effect of the organic way upon food production.

Dr. Kenneth C. Beeson (1972), former director of the U.S. Plant, Soil and Nutrition Laboratory and Professor of Soil Science, Cornell University, points out that few scientifically controlled experiments have been devised to compare the quality of crops grown exclusively with organic fertilizers and those grown with inorganic chemicals. However, one such experiment was reported several years ago at the University of California, Berkeley. Essentially, this was a comparison of fruit grown with compost with fruit grown in a water culture in which inorganic water-soluble chemicals served as a source of plant nutrients. The mature crops were fed to guinea pigs for a period of twelve weeks. The animals in both groups showed equal growth, excellent skeletal and muscular development, healthy fur, and clear eyes. The conclusion drawn was that the organic matter in soil—the humus—had no different effect than the artificial water-culture media on the grass-fed guinea pigs. However, because of certain technical difficulties in eliminating completely either organic matter or inorganic chemical compounds from the nutrient media, unequivocal conclusions based on the results of this experiment may not be justified.

In 1938, several scientists in southern agricultural experiment stations began a unified effort to study the factors affecting the nutrient composition of foods of vegetable origin. This study, which became known as the soil-weather project, included experiments that tested the effects of soil, climate, and management practices on the amount of measurable nutrients in food crops. Emphasis was put on the turnip leaf which was used extensively in the South as a vegetable. The published results may be summarized with the following correlations:

1. High radiation—high Vitamin C concentration and lower than average iron concentration.
2. High relative humidity—high carotene concentrations.
3. High soil temperatures—high concentrations of the B vitamins and minerals.
4. High in the soil levels of organic matter—high concentrations of carotene, thiamine, and iron in the plant but low levels of riboflavin, magnesium, and sodium. No effect on vitamin C was noticed.
5. High rainfall—high concentrations of vitamin C, riboflavin, thiamine, magnesium, and sodium.
6. Weather factors, including soil, moisture, and temperature, and the age of the plant were dominant over soil properties in determining the concentrations of most of the vitamins in the plant.

Despite these two studies, experiments to resolve the controversy of organic versus inorganic fertilizers have been extremely difficult, if not impossible, to design. In an attempt to investigate the problem further, an experiment using both pot cultures and field tests was conducted at the Cornell Laboratory. Carrots, snap beans, and potatoes were grown in the pot. Half of the pots received compost only, and the remainder received inorganic chemicals only.

Exactly the same quantity of nitrogen, phosphorus, and potassium were present in each of the fertilizers applied. The crops were planted so as to mature at about the same time. No differences were found in the concentrations of either vitamin C or carotene in the harvested crops. The Long Island branch experiment station of Cornell University maintained some experimental plots that had received nothing but compost or animal manures for over twenty-five years. Two crops, rye and potatoes, were grown on these plots and on comparable plots that received only inorganic fertilizers. No differences were found in the concentrations of vitamin C, carotene, iron, or copper in the crops from the two soils.

In order to understand the difficulty of interpreting the experimental work cited above, we must first clarify the term "nutritive value." First, it should not be confused with the taste or flavor of the food. Mother's bread or the apple grown in the family garden may invoke a flavor that seems quite different from that of the bread from the local bakery or an apple picked immature to be shipped thousands of miles. But are they different nutritionally? A tomato picked when still slightly immature may have a higher vitamin C concentration than one that is fully ripe but better tasting. The term nutritive value or nutritive quality applied to a given food refers to all of that food's nutritive components, known or unknown. It is impossible at present to describe these components in terms of a single unique value that is abstracted from the conditions of the method of production of the food. Furthermore, as we noted above, there is no valid evidence that crops grown solely with compost, manures, or other organic sources of plant nutrients are superior to those grown with inorganic chemical compounds. There is ample evidence that many factors influence the concentration of nutrients in our foods, but that the nature of the fertilizers added to our soil does not rank high among them.

R. L. Carolus (1971) agrees with some of the physical advantages of the organic way, but he cautions that most refuse available to gardeners is so low in nitrogen that microorganisms will utilize most of the available soil nitrogen as they multiply in decomposing the added organic material, which results in a temporary deficiency of nitrogen for the growing crop unless additional nitrogen is supplied when these materials are used. In composting, the high carbon-to-nitrogen ratio in the organic material is slowly reduced by oxidation of the carbon, and although the material becomes suitable for use, it supplies only about three or four pounds of nitrogen per ton of dry sawdust or straw, or twelve pounds per ton of fresh cow manure. In many overpopulated areas of the world where soils are low in nitrogen and nitrogen fertilizers have not been available, crops grown the organic way are poor, pale, and unproductive, and both the people and their livestock are emaciated. Many local varieties of rice, wheat, and other crops in these areas have adjusted through centuries of natural selection to a low level of nutrition and show little response to fertilizers. However, the international maize and wheat improvement center—where Dr. Norman E. Borlaug, who was awarded the Nobel Peace Prize in 1970, is in charge of the wheat research and production project—the International Rice Research Institute, and other agencies have recently developed varieties that respond to fertilizer with four to five times the yield of the local types. In Asia, facilities have been developed to produce ammonium nitrate and urea, excellent sources of nitrogen, from the air. In Japan—where more agricultural fertilizers and pesticide chemicals are applied per hectare than anywhere else in the world—rice yields are the highest in the world, food self-sufficiency has been reached, and the young people, because of more and better foods, are several inches taller than their parents.

Organic material such as legumes, hay, animal by-products and seed meals, which contain sufficient nitrogen to promote their satisfactory decomposition, are generally too valuable as livestock feeds, and animal manures are seldom available in quantity or in the right place to be used economically by most large commercial food producers. Hower, organic materials containing high levels of nitrogen are available in the United States in limited quantities to organic gardeners, at prices that commercial growers could not afford.

Followers of the organic way are inconsistent and arbitrary in recommending materials to supplement the low content of plant nutrients found in most organic matter. Some, for example, have advised the use of ground granite and green sand, both very low in available potassium, when other natural materials with complete availability of potassium are much cheaper and many times more effective. For some unknown reason they ban the use of nitrate soda, nature's own product, which is derived from the weathered residues of bird droppings, obtained along the west coast of South America. Perhaps their reluctance to use highly available fertilizers is due to the potency of these materials. Many commonly used fertilizers contain over 50 percent available nutrients that will injure plants when applied in excess.

Chet Huntley once observed that some environmentalists would commit genocide to accommodate nature. Agriculturalists are now being confronted as never before in this century, by many groups with antiquated ideas who would, unwittingly, curtail efficiency in food production drastically. Recently computed data by Dr. F. G. Viets of the Agricultural Research Service of the United States

Department of Agriculture indicate that without fertilizer, corn yields in Illinois would fall 37 percent; vegetable yields in Alabama, 55 percent; and grapefruit yields in Florida, 94 percent. If pesticides were banned, the nation's food supply would fall far short of its present needs. Fertilizers do not impair soils or reduce crop productivity, as indicated by records from the oldest agricultural experiment station in the world, located at Rothamsted, England. According to these records, which cover ninety-eight years, wheat yields resulting from annual applications of high-nitrogen fertilizer averaged 6 percent higher than yields from fourteen tons of barnyard manure per acre.

More progress has been made in food production in the past thirty years than in all previous years of human history. In the United States since 1940, for example, wheat productivity has increased 156 percent, corn 142 percent, potatoes 190 percent, and tomatoes 260 percent. We now require only half as much feed to grow a chicken and two-thirds as much feed to grow beef as we did in 1940. Now an agriculturalist can produce enough food for forty persons, as opposed to ten in 1940.

Gene Logsdon (1971) has discussed this controversial area. Most soil scientists and commercial farmers disagree sharply with exponents of the organic way over the latter's often quoted criticism that long use of inorganic fertilizers removes organic matter from the soil, eventually leading to sterile land and plants without nutritional value. As early as 1947, Dr. Firman Bear observed, "Of particular significance is the discovery that fertilizers, even though they may contain no organic matter, are the most fruitful means of adding organic matter to the soils, by reason of the more abundant residues and roots of crops that have been liberally treated with them."

Nor do commercial fertilizers inhibit microbial content in the soil, says L. R. Frederick, an Iowa State University agronomist. Frederick applied inorganic fertilizers at the excessive rate of 100,000 pounds per acre. Even under these conditions, the number and activity of soil microbes were seldom reduced, and the total weight of the microbes actually increased. Organic farmers disagreed with these results, of course. John McMahon, a full-time small farmer in Indiana, with a degree in chemistry, explained his position:

> It is pretty easy to pick out flaws and what you call "myths" in organics. I could do the same with establishment agriculture. It's fully upon which bag of convictions a man wants to carry around with him through life. If some people are willing to work hard to produce organic food and some people are willing

to pay for it, why get up tight? If organic can convince people that food quality is more important than the color of their television sets, that's what agricultural marketing is all about. There is a dangerous trend in this country: ownership of the land going into the hands of fewer and fewer people. Organics might keep more of us on farms, and isn't that what farm organizations have always proposed to do?[12]

Other hard facts have been presented by Ken Skarien (1971) who wrote on the research conducted by Dr. Robert C. Lambe, Virginia Polytechnic Institute, which showed that insects and soil-borne disease organisms wiped out certain organically grown vegetable crops and caused low yield in others. Five rows of tomatoes, for example, yielded 446 pounds in the chemically protected plot and 141½ pounds in the organic plot. Five rows of cucumbers yielded 205 pounds in the chemically protected plot and 28¾ pounds in the organic one. Results for other vegetables were equally dramatic. One row of white squash, grown under chemical protection, yielded 157 pounds, compared to 3 pounds for a row grown under organic methods. No eggplant was produced from the organic plot, due to flea beetles that attacked the plants while they were quite small; 154 pounds of eggplant were yielded by the chemically protected plot. A total of 1,954 pounds of vegetables were weighed from the chemically protected garden, whereas 237 pounds came from the organic garden. Vegetables and fruits grown included black-eyed peas, tomatoes, peppers, okra, lima beans, cabbage, eggplant, yellow squash, white squash, cucumbers, cantaloupe, watermelon, and corn. The trial gardens were planted in May for the purpose of determining the need for fungicides and insecticides in preventing diseases and controlling insects in home vegetable production. Two adjoining plots of the same soil type, measuring one tenth of an acre each, were used. A soil sample of the area, which had been cropped to corn previously, showed it to be low in nutrients. The organic garden was fertilized with 1,000 pounds of dehydrated cow manure, at a cost of $50.00. The chemically protected plot received 100 pounds of 10-10-10 fertilizer, at a cost of $3.15. Both gardens received the same amount of nitrogen, phosphorus, and potassium, according to Lambe. In both cases, fertilizer was broadcast over the field and incorporated in the soil. Before planting, the chemically protected garden was treated with methyl bromide, a fumigant applied to eradicate weeds, soil insects, nematodes, and soil diseases—total cost, $37.08. Weeds in the organic garden were removed by hoeing, at a cost of $18.00, based on labor costs of $2.00 per hour. Both fields were irrigated twice during the summer, receiving equal amounts of water. "When costs for labor, fertilizer, seed, fungicides and insecticides are added up, the chemically protected garden turns out to be a little more expensive," Lambe said. "The figures are

[12] Gene Logsdon, "Organic—Magic Words at the Counter, Many Doubts on the Farm," *Farm Journal* (December 1971).

$158.18 for the chemically protected plot and $141.95 for the organic plot, but this difference is compensated for by the larger yields and the attractive, healthier fruits and vegetables."[13]

Another area of concern to the organic gardener is the influence of growing factors and the type of fertilizers on the chemical composition of the plant. However, there is small cause for worry. As E. J. Russell (1943) has pointed out, the amount of crop growth can be varied greatly by such factors, but the composition of a plant does not vary nearly as much.

Appledorf et al. (1972) compared health and traditional foods for proximate composition, cost, microbial content, pesticide levels, and polychlorinated biphenyl (PCB) contamination. They found only minor differences for proximate composition and microbial content. No pesticides were detected but two samples of health foods contained PCBs. The greatest difference between the samples was cost, the health foods being considerably more expensive.

More extreme denials of the organic way have appeared in writing, and it is pertinent to mention them since their authors are recognized experts. G. M. Knox (1972) has quoted several of these individuals.

Dr. Robert E. Olson, head of the Department of Biochemistry at St. Louis University, states that "food faddism persists despite incontrovertible scientific evidence denying its validity. . . Food has an emotional rather than an intellectual value to the average person, and the food faddists have capitalized upon this fact."[14] Dr. Ruth Leverton of the USDA states, "We want to capitalize to the fullest extent possible on the public awareness that food is important to health. However, we find it hard to understand how so many people could so rapidly have become experts in the field of nutrition without benefit of training and with their only experience having been that of eating."[15]

The Food and Drug Administation (FDA) states flatly that "there are no significant differences in nutritional values of food grown under either the organic or conventional condition." The USDA is also convinced of this. Dr. Frederick J. Stare, chairman of the Department of Nutrition at Harvard University, states, "Fertilization regardless of the type does not influence the nutrient composition of the plant in regard to its content of protein, fat, carbohydrate or the various vitamins. These nutrients are influenced primarily by the genetic composition of the seed and the maturity of the plant at harvest."[16]

[13] K. Skarien, "Organic Growing Is Only Dreamer's Hobby," *Seedman's Digest*, December 1971, p. 6.

[14] G. M. Knox, "How Healthy Are Health Foods?" *Better Homes and Gardens*, June 1972, p. 12

[15] *Ibid.*

[16] Personal Communication to F. M. Clydesdale.

In fairness, it should also be pointed out that more neutral points of view have been raised by equally qualified persons. For example, Dr. Milton Salomon, chairman of the Department of Food and Resource Chemistry, University of Rhode Island, has stated,

> It has only been about a century since the introduction of commercial chemical fertilizers. Since that time, they have become the major source of plant food. Previously, the maintenance of soil fertility depended on the use of animal manures, composts and crop rotation. This does not mean that chemical fertilizers are better than applications of manures, but rather they have become a recognized and tested means of filling new and special demands on the land. This need was associated with expanding population and industrial revolution and an amazing growth of cities.[17]

However, Dr. Salomon goes on to say that most of the organic cult's claims for the superiority of organically grown foods are unfounded.

STANDARDS FOR ORGANICALLY GROWN FOODS

A real problem in the merchandising of organically grown foods is the problem of standards or certification. H. Buchard points out that all but one of three dozen local organic merchants interviewed by the *Washington Post* said they could not be certain all their merchandise was truly organic, and most said they favored adoption of federal standards and regulations governing production and sale. Shoppers in organic stores will find labels that range from a simple, unsupported statement that the product is organic to exhaustively detailed accounts of where, when, how, and by whom the product was produced, along with an invitation to drop in for a tour of the farm.

According to Dr. Virgil O. Wodicka, former director of the Bureau of Foods of the FDA, there doesn't seem to be any way to inspect the end product. He has also indicated that there are no laboratory tests showing which kind of fertilizer has gone into something. In fact, the authors cannot find any proof of real differences between organic and nonorganic foods.

At December hearings held by the New York City Department of Consumer Affairs, producers, sellers, and consumers generally agreed that strict regulations should be imposed. Some states, notably California and Florida, have adopted labeling standards for some organically produced foods, but most local retailers say they don't feel any agency but the federal government has the money and manpower to handle the necessary inspection, testing, and en-

---

[17] Milton Salomon, "Natural Foods—Myth or Magic." Association of Food and Drug Officials of the United States Quarterly Bulletin, 36, no. 3 (1972), 131-37.

forcement of standards for the industry.

There are two main (and separate) questions involved in the organic food phenomenon. The first is whether the host of sprays, dyes, preservatives, extenders, and other food additives permitted by the government are bad for people. At the very least, it cannot be argued that the absence of such additives is going to help anybody. (Chapter 4 is devoted to a consideration of additives.) The second question is whether organic food is more nutritious than food produced by factory farms. As far as fruits and vegetables are concerned, believers in organic farming give an unqualified yes, and the United States Department of Agriculture and such universities as Harvard and Rutgers give a somewhat qualified no. "Here at Rutgers we've grown plants on solely organic sources and others on solely inorganic ones," Dr. Russell B. Alderfer said. "We analyzed them for nutrients, vitamins, etc.; we could measure no difference. But as to whether the human body can—I'd be the first to admit my ignorance. There may be a trace of something or a chemical complex formed in a slightly different way. All I can say is, if there are nutritional differences, we haven't found them."[18]

TYPICAL USES OF ORGANICALLY GROWN FOODS

Knox (1972) points out that breakfast for a true believer in organic eating might consist of a big bowl of toasted brown rice, mixed with ground-up flax seed, sesame seed oil, and raisins. Lunch is a colorful spread at a modest restaurant where the health seeker might choose an alfalfa-sprout and beet salad, a sandwich containing raw-milk cheese, or maybe the special of the day: hot nut-rice loaf. The drink would be milk, but not the ordinary kind.

Not only are such meals eaten in restaurants and communes, but they are becoming more popular in the house. James Trager (1972) has some interesting comments on why the use of natural foods is increasing in middle-class homes. In this world of foul air and water, of ugly technology, in this time of yearning for an idyllic, simple, unspoiled past, the virtues of nature do seem a kind of salvation. There may be nothing much a woman can do about some things, except to write letters and join protest groups, but there is something she can do about what she feeds her family. She can feed them "pure," natural foods and see them glow with health. What a fine, satisfying thought that is! Trager then points out some of the dangers inherent in such an approach and presents a convincing argument against the organic way. However, his comments on the reasons for the use of organic foods are worth consideration.

Vegetarianism is one of the more visible organic concepts. An

---

[18] H. Burchard, "Organic Foods Safer? More Nutritious?" *Springfield* (Mass.) *Union*, March 23, 1972, p. 52.

interesting comment on vegetarianism was made by S. K. Majumder (1972):

> [If] vegetarianism is [to be] completely above the alleged status of a fad or blind faith, it must satisfy three major criteria: (1) from the nutritional point of view, vegetable diets must be complete with the standard daily requirements of the human body; (2) they must alleviate, if not eliminate, the food crisis in certain parts of the world; and (3) they must make positive contributions to the enhancement of "bioethics" among the members of the next generation with regard to wildlife, agriculture and conservation of natural resources.[19]

These dicta might well be applied to the place of organic gardening in the world today.

ECONOMICS

Probably the first area in which economics should be considered is in the price of fertilizer, or more important, the price per pound of nitrogen, since nitrogen causes problems in 80 percent of the cases where there is a deficiency. Dried cow manure supplies us with nitrogen at a cost of $4.00 per pound. Compost of garbage supplies us with nitrogen at $12.00 per pound. Commercial chemical fertilizer, on the other hand, supplies us with nitrogen at 15 to 30 cents a pound.

Seelig (1971) states that in spite of the existing evidence, organic-food faddists buy low grade foods that they believe are "organically" grown, for up to 100 percent more than what they would pay for first-rate merchandise in a supermarket. They are being fooled. The fruits and vegetables offered as "organic" are in almost all cases grown commercially with chemical fertilizers and pesticides. The same author claims to have purchased commercially grown California strawberries at a health food store that proclaimed on a big sign that all the produce was grown "organically." At the same store, Seelig bought commercially grown oranges with a label from an area where regulations require that all groves must be sprayed to keep them free from contamination by pests. Honey was advertised as being organically produced. How would a bee know what flowers were fertilized with manures only? Consider the final irony: the same health food stores that tout "organic" substances sell vitamins that are produced largely by chemical synthesis, such as vitamins A, C, and B_1. No matter what the evidence, however, adherents are buying and growers are producing. Logsdon cites one grower who wrote his own contract for the sale of his organic produce.

[19] S. K. Majumder, "Vegetarianism Fads, Faith or Fact?" *American Scientist*, 60, no. 2 (1972), 175-79.

CONCLUSIONS

On the basis of the evidence, it is safe to say that organic gardening alone is not the answer to a better environment and a more abundant life in the twenty-first century if we wish to feed even the present world population. We have passed the point of no return to nature's way, except in the instances where it serves as a hobby or recreation. Organic gardening does have some beneficial results, of course; it is of some benefit in efforts to alleviate the pollution problem, for instance. Growing crops the organic way involves considerable additional work and expense, but it is a healthful outdoor exercise and may serve as a therapy to reduce boredom, frustration, or tension for those few who wish to believe and have time to spare. However, rational people should directly evaluate the facts and challenge false concepts of the organic way that, if widely adopted, would jeopardize the potential world food production.

Perhaps the best conclusion to a consideration of organic gardening is this one by Boysie E. Day (1971): "In a sense the advocates of the organic way have been right all along, but for the wrong reasons. There are sufficient good reasons for organic farming, without giving credit or credence to the phony claims made by cultists. For my part, to be right for the wrong reasons is very close to being wrong entirely."[20]

BIBLIOGRAPHY

Adams, R., Jr., *Organic Gardening*, 1971.

Allaway, W. H., "Feed and Food Quality in Relation to Fertilizer Use," in *Fertilizer Technology and Use*, ed. R. A. Olson, T. J. Army, J. J. Anway, and V. J. Kilmer. Madison, Wisc.: Soil Science Society of America, 1971.

Appledorf, H., J. A. Koburger, and W. B. Wheeler, "Health Foods vs. Traditional Foods: A Comparison." Personal communication of a report of research.

Barron's, "The Business Front. Not All Milk and Honey." September 11, 1972, p. 11.

Beeson, K. C., "What About the Organic Way?" *New York Times*, April 16, 1972, p. 33.

Burchard, H., "Organic Foods Safer? More Nutritious?" *Springfield* (Mass.) *Union*, March 23, 1972, p. 52.

Carolus, R. L., "Organic Gardening Isn't the Answer?" *Horticultural Science*, 6, no. 3 (1970), 192-93.

Day, Boysie E., "Organic Gardening—Right for Wrong Reasons," *California Agriculture*, August 1971, p. 2.

[20] Boysie E. Day, "Organic Gardening—Right for Wrong Reasons," *California Agriculture*, August 1972, p. 2.

Food and Earth Services, Inc., Forum on Food and Nutrition at the Massachusetts Institute of Technology, Cambridge, Mass., May 7, 1971. Suite 909, 1346 Connecticut Avenue, N.W., Washington, D.C. 20036.

Greene, Wade, "Guru of the Organic Food Cult," *New York Times Magazine*, June 6, 1971, p. 30.

Hodgkinson, L. A., "So You're Going to Be an Organic Gardener," *Middlesex County Bulletin* (Worcester, Mass.), September 1971, pp. 1-6.

Hotton, P., *Boston Sunday Globe*, May 16, 1971.

Jukes, T. H., "Facts and Fancy in Nutrition and Food Science," *Journal of the American Dietary Association*, 59, no. 3 (1971) 203.

Knox, G. M., "How Healthy Are Health Foods?" *Better Homes and Gardens*, June 1972, p. 12.

Logsdon, G., "Organic—Magic Word at the Food Counter, Many Doubts on the Farm," *Farm Journal*, December 1971, p. 16.

MacDaniels, L. H., "Facts about Organic Gardening." Ithaca, N.Y.: Cornell University, 1971. Published by Hampshire County Extension Service. Northampton, Mass., pp. 1-6.

Majumder, S. K., "Vegetarianism Fads, Faith or Fact?" *American Scientist*, 60, no. 2 (1972), 175-79.

The Organic Directory. Emmaus, Pa.: Rodale Press, 1971.

"Organic—Pro and Con," *Research*, Fall-Winter, 1972.

Robb, Christina, *Boston Sunday Globe*, May 16, 1971.

Russell, E. J., "Trends in Agriculture and Relation to Nutrition," *Chemistry and Industry*, 62 (1943), 210-14.

Seelig, R. A., "The 'Organic Food' Kick." Supply letters of the United Fresh Fruit and Vegetable Association, June 9, 1971, pp. 1-3.

Skarien, K., "Organic Growing Is Only Dreamer's Hobby," *Seedman's Digest*, December 1971, p. 6.

Slom, S. H., "Lovely to Look at, Delightful to Hold—Her Secret: Celery," *Wall Street Journal*, June 14, 1972, p. 1.

Trager, James, "Exploding the Health Food Myth," *Family Circle*, July 1971, p. 58.

White, Hilda S., "The Organic Foods Movement," *Journal of Food Technology*, 26 (1972), 29-33.

chapter 4

Food Additives

Food additives! This is probably one of the most emotional subjects relating to our food supply and probably one of the issues least understood by the consumer. The 1974 book *Eating May Be Hazardous to Your Health*, by Dr. Jacqueline Verrett and Ms. Jean Carper, contains this statement on its flyleaf: "In this consumer-oriented exposé of corruption and inefficiency within the FDA, one of the FDA's leading scientific researchers claims that instead of keeping food free of dangerous chemicals and additives, the FDA at times actually endorses and promotes their use."[1] Further, on page 36 of this book appears the statement, "Almost any food imaginable can now be fashioned by the dexterous mixing of artificial chemi-

[1] New York: Simon and Schuster.

cals." One of the present authors had the opportunity of reviewing *Eating May Be Hazardous to Your Health* for the *Journal of Food Technology*. He found that this book was full of the misinterpretations, misapprehensions and false information that creates consumer scares and misunderstanding. Quoting from that review,

> Initially appalled, I was then saddened by the wealth of misinformation and the many, many misleading statements which I found between the covers of this book. The sadness arose from a questioning as to why a scientist would write such a book. . . . Certainly they did not write this book to promote the health and well-being of Americans. If this were the case, then we would have to virtually stop eating every food on the marketplace whether processed, unprocessed, natural or organic. . . . [The book] does not bring truth into the subject, in fact, it avoids the truth in many instances [and] uses sensationalism as its top priority item. The consumer, the governmental agencies, the industry cannot be helped by this book. It can only bring misinformation and damage to the already confused consumer who is attempting to find the truth, find some education, in this vast maze of concern about the safety of our food supply.[2]

Confusion and disagreement about the role of food additives exists in the scientific field. Some scientists decry the use of food additives; others feel that they are entirely safe. The authors of this book are in the latter category and feel that they share the majority opinion among reputable scientists.

There is currently a tendency among consumers to link the words "natural" and "safe," and "synthetic" and "harmful," and to forget that the human body safely handles naturally occurring food substances that are far more toxic than any currently permitted food additives. For some reason, consumers are beginning to believe that synthetic chemicals are different from natural ones. We wish to assure you that there is absolutely no difference: a chemical is a chemical. Verrett and Carper seem to be classifying a new breed of chemicals—"artificial chemicals"—in their book. We really don't know what an artificial chemical is; again, a chemical is a chemical.

The only rational way for the two of us to allay the fears of the consumer about the food that is in the marketplace today is to present the facts as we see them and as most scientists see them. This involves a consideration of what food additives are, why they are

[2] F. M. Clydesdale, ". . . Is It, Really?" *Journal of Food Technology*, February 1975, pp. 18-26.

used, how they are regulated, and how dangerous are they within the context of our total diet.

A food additive, according to the Federal Food, Drug and Cosmetic Act (U.S. Code, Section 321) is a substance "the intended use of which results or may reasonably be expected to result, directly or indirectly, in its becoming a component or otherwise affecting the characteristics of any food . . . ," with certain exceptions. Excluded from the requirements of this act is any substance that is "generally recognized among experts qualified by scientific training and experience to evaluate its safety, as having been adequately shown through scientific procedures. . .to be safe under the conditions of its intended use. . . ." Such substances are commonly referred to as GRAS substances. With respect to GRAS substances in use prior to 1958, the basis of the judgment of safety may be either "scientific procedures" or "experience based on common use in food," but after 1958 the basis must be "scientific procedures."

There are intentional additives, which are added on purpose to perform specific functions, and incidental additives, which have no function in the finished food but become a part of the food product during some phase of production, processing, storage, or packaging. The term "food additives" does not include substances that find their way into a food accidentally. The term also does not include pesticides, color additives, new animal drugs, or any substance used in accordance with a sanction or approval granted prior to the effective date of the food additives amendment to the existing laws in 1958.

That's how things look today. Are they worse now, or better, or about the same as they were back in the good old days? Well, in 1902 Dr. Harvey W. Wiley established what became known popularly as "Dr. Wiley's poison squad." This squad was set up by the Federal Food, Drug and Cosmetic Act "to enable the secretary of agriculture to investigate. the character of food preservatives, coloring matters and other substances added to foods, to determine their relation to digestion and health and to establish the principles which should guide their use." At that time—back in "the good old days"— there were no checks at all, people could add almost whatever they wanted to their foods, and as long as they didn't kill someone these additives did not have to be tested or screened by any governmental agency. Volunteers for this "poison squad" were recruited from among the employees of the Department of Agriculture. Dr. Wiley said, "I wanted young, robust fellows with maximum resistance to deleterious effects of adulterated foods. . . .If they should show signs of injury after they were fed such substances for a period of time, the deduction would naturally follow that children and older persons more susceptible than they would be greater sufferers from similar causes."[3] Twelve men volunteered. This squad was responsible for taking many dangerous food additives off the market, but during the nearly seven decades that have passed since Wiley's time, analytical procedures have increased tremendously. The testing that is done in the food industry today makes our food supply abundantly safe compared to what it was in the "good old days."

The Pure Food and Drug Act of 1906 requires that our food supply be safe. The law states that substances (chemicals) may be added to food only under the following two conditions: that the substances be safe for human consumption and that they serve a useful purpose. A 1938 amendment to this act provided the government with the leverage for enforcing the regulations but it contained an inherent weakness. The Food and Drug Administration had to prove the presence of a deleterious substance before it could act against it. However, the color additive amendment of 1960 closed this loophole by stating that no chemical can legally be used in any food until the manufacturer has proved to the FDA that it is safe. This means that the manufacturer has to do the research, has to pay the bills, and has to prove beyond the shadow of a doubt to the FDA that a food additive is safe prior to its use. This means that you, the consumer, do not have to shoulder this burden of payment in the form of taxation.

As you can see, we have come a long way: we now have regulations that are enforced and that keep our food supply safe. How do food additives rank among what are thought to be possible dangers to our food supply? Dr. Virgil Wodicka, former director of the Bureau of Foods of the Food and Drug Administration, has listed the following major food hazards in their order of importance:

1. *Microbiological contamination:* includes conventional food poisoning and botulism.
2. *Malnutrition:* affects a large segment of our population, especially the poor.
3. *Environmental contaminants,* such as mercury in fish.
4. *Hazards from toxicants that occur naturally in foods.*
5. *Pesticides:* residues of such substances as DDT.
6. *Conscious food additives:* in spite of all the publicity they have received, they are considered the least important hazard from a food-safety point of view.[4]

[3] M. A. Bernarde, *The Chemicals We Eat* (New York: McGraw-Hill Book Co., 1975), p. 108.

[4] R. L. Hall, "Food Additives," *Nutrition Today,* July/August, 1973, pp. 20-28.

According to Dr. Wodicka, "In spite of the fact that there is considerable public concern and suspicion of the minor constituents used in formulated foods, there is no credible evidence that the permitted ones are, in fact, harmful."[5]

HOW FOOD ADDITIVES ARE APPROVED

Prior to discussing the process of approval, a discussion of the Delaney Clause might prove informative to those of you who worry about the possible carcinogenic (cancer-causing) effects of food additives.

The Delaney Clause was added to the Pure Food and Drug Act as a result of an amendment offered by Congressman Delaney in 1958. It established a food additive regulation prohibiting the addition of any cancer-producing substance to human food. Upon initial reading, this appears to be a very admirable proposal. Indeed it is, except that it does not specify the amounts required for substance to become carcinogenic. Almost any substance added to the body in large enough quantities will cause cancer. For instance, it has been estimated that one barbecued steak contains the same amount of benzopyrene (a potent carcinogen) as 600 cigarettes. Yet, we eat steak and don't see an increase in stomach cancer. In fact, we have seen a decrease, as we will point out later in this chapter.

Much of the scare concerning cyclamates, DES (diethylstilbestrol), Red No. 2 (a food color), and other additives has resulted from experiments in which massive dosages of these compounds were given to animals. At these tremendous levels, cancer has at times occurred. However, the dosages are so much higher than we could ingest that it seems incredible to ban them on this basis. The scare has also developed from experiments in which these compounds were injected by syringe into the brain, implanted in the uterus, or injected into chick embryos—hardly the way we consume food additives.

Rest assured that we don't want cancer any more than you do. However, we are convinced that the food additive testing incorporates such a large safety factor that additives are safe. For instance, based on the experiments that have been conducted, a human would have to consume some 500 twelve-ounce bottles of diet soda per day for a lifetime in order to possibly incur cancer from cyclamates. And one would have to consume 250 tons of liver per day for fifty years in order to equal the amount of DES contained in one dose of an approved day-after oral contraceptive.

Based on such facts, we feel that the Delaney Clause should be amended or modified.

[5] *Ibid.*

A substance newly proposed for addition to food must undergo strict testing designed to establish the safety of the intended use. A petition must be presented to the FDA that includes the following information:

1. The identity of the additive, its chemical composition, how it is manufactured, specifications necessary to assure its reproducibleness, and any other means necessary to establish what the composition of the additive is.
2. Information on the intended use of the additive, including copies of the proposed labels.
3. Data establishing that the additive will accomplish the intended effect in the food and that the level sought for approval is no higher than that reasonably necessary to accomplish the intended effect.
4. An analytical method capable of measuring the amount of the additive present at the tolerance levels.
5. Data establishing that the intended use of the additive is safe. This requires experimental evidence, which is derived ordinarily from feeding studies using the proposed additive at various levels in the diets of two or more appropriate species of animals.

ARE FOOD ADDITIVES
AND GRAS SUBSTANCES SAFE?

There is no way in which absolute safety can be guaranteed, as is the case in any area of life. Every time you step into a car you are accepting the risk it entails. Premarketing clearance requirements under the Food Additives Amendment to the Pure Food and Drug Act do assure that the risk of the occurrence of unanticipated adverse effects is at an acceptably small level, at least for food additives. Such assurances may not be available in the case of those GRAS substances that were exempted from the need for laboratory testing by the definition in the law. Recognizing this problem, President Nixon in his Consumer Message of October, 1969 directed the FDA to review the safety of each item on the GRAS list, which is currently being done.

The establishment of premarketing clearances for a particular substance should be understood to be based on the scientific knowledge available at that point in time. Since our scientific knowledge is dynamic and expanding, we must periodically review our earlier decisions at later times to assure that our assessment of the safety of the substances added to our foods remains up to date. Thus, when changes are made in previous clearances these should be recognized as an assurance that the latest and best scientific knowledge is being applied to enhance the safety of the food supply.

WHAT IS THE FDA DOING
ABOUT THE GRAS LIST?

As a result of President Nixon's directive to review the safety of the GRAS substances, the FDA has launched a threefold information-gathering effort. First, a fifty-year retrospective search for the toxicology-related literature on each substance is being conducted. Second, the FDA has contracted with the National Academy of Sciences to send a questionnaire to all manufacturers, processors, and users of GRAS substances. The questionnaire is designed to develop accurate figures on the total production of each of the substances. The academy will utilize this information along with consumption figures to develop the measure of consumer exposure expected with each GRAS substance, and will then provide the FDA with these measures. Third, various laboratories will test the individual compounds in chick embryos for teratology, and in four species of animals (mouse, rat, hamster, and rabbit) for mammalian teratology and mutagenic effects.

This information will be collated, compiled, and finally reviewed by a group of distinguished scientists, who will thereupon recommend to the commissioner of the FDA a status for each substance. The status will be selected from the following categories:

1. Continued GRAS status.
2. Food-additive regulations.
3. Discontinue use until further studies are done.
4. Insufficient information for final decision without chronic toxicity studies.

When this review has been completed, we should have as adequate a scientific basis for the use of GRAS compounds as we do for food additives.

WHY DO WE USE ADDITIVES
IN OUR FOODS?

The use of additives is not new in the twentieth century. When humans first learned that fire would cook and preserve their meat and that salt (sodium chloride) would preserve it without cooking, they began to use additives. Food colors were used in ancient Egypt. In China, kerosene was burned to ripen bananas; the reason this method succeeded, although the Chinese did not know it, was that the combustion produced the ripening agent ethylene. Flavoring and seasoning were arts in many ancient civilizations, and as a result, spices and condiments were important items of commerce. Columbus sailed for the Indies in search of food additives—that is, spices. As our knowledge of food preservation and technology has increased, our use of additives has also increased.

More than forty functions now served by food additives can be listed. In this discussion, however, it is simpler to group additives into five broad categories: flavors, colors, preservatives, texture agents, miscellaneous substances. Let's look at each of these groups.

Flavors   Spices and natural and synthetic flavors are used to complement, improve, and enhance the flavor of the foods we eat.

Colors   These are used mainly to give food an appetizing appearance, on the tested assumption that the way food looks has an effect on its palatability.

Preservatives   Spoilage can be prevented or retarded not only by additives but also by physical and biological processes such as heating, refrigeration, drying, freezing, fermenting, and curing. Some of these processes, however, achieve only partial preservation. Additives, therefore, have a role in prolonging a food's keeping qualities—a major need if we are to feed our modern, urban society effectively.

The seriousness of the problem of spoilage is shown by the World Health Organization's estimate that about 20 percent of the world's food supply is lost in this way. Indeed, shortages of food in many parts of the world could be alleviated by the wider use of preservatives.

Texture Agents   These are used to stabilize and thicken. Many of the newer convenience foods have become practicable only as a result of the development of new and improved emulsifiers and stabilizers.

Miscellaneous   This group is so numerous that we can indicate only a few of the functions they serve. Among other things, they help retain moisture and they add nutrients such as vitamins and minerals. Moreover, the acids, alkalies, buffers, and neutralizing agents included in this category are required for the quality production of baked goods, soft drinks, and confectioneries.

Do we want to continue to use additives? Only the consumer can answer this. Consumer acceptance, after all, keeps the manufacturer in business. If consumers will accept bread that stales and molds in a few days, oil and fat products that rapidly grow rancid, wine that discolors, frozen products that separate and become watery, and overall spoilage and waste of food to the extent that we would have difficulty feeding our population—then we can eliminate additives.

ARE FOODS SAFER THAN FOOD ADDITIVES?

There is no real difference under the law between those substances we call "foods" and those we call "food additives." Meat and potatoes, for example, would clearly be considered "additives" instead of "food" when served as stew, except that they are more appropriately considered as GRAS substances. Preservatives such as sodium and calcium propionate are produced naturally in Swiss cheese. Citric acid, a widely used food additive, is present in all citrus fruits. On the other hand, many so-called natural foods contain toxic substances. Safrole, a carcinogen, is found in sassafras roots. The *Whole Earth Almanac* recommends the use of sassafras roots as a beverage and to flavor foods. Sassafras is known as the root beer tree, but in 1960 the FDA banned the use of safrole as a flavor in root beer. Oxalic acid is found in spinach and rhubarb, and certain goiter-inducing substances are found in some vegetables. Solanine, a toxic alkaloid, is present in potatoes. Patulin, a natural carcinogen, is found in flour and orange juice. Other natural carcinogens in foods are thiourea and several related chemicals in cabbage and turnips, and tannin in tea and wine. The list is much longer, but the point has been made: alarm about additives may have diverted us from some more serious concerns about food. Most additives (except those on the GRAS list, which are now being studied, as we have discussed) have been tested for safety far more often than most naturally or traditionally processed foodstuffs. Dozens of familiar foods about which there is not the slightest concern would surely be banned if all foods were tested as much as additives are, and if Delaney Clause standards were applied to them. With per-capita consumption of additives in the United States being only 139 pounds or so a year, versus about three quarters of a ton for all other foods, the additive threat might by itself be viewed as relatively minor.

In any evaluation of the threat of food additives, it is also worth noting that the American diet as a whole is apparently becoming safer all the time. Data compiled by the American Cancer Society and the National Cancer Institute suggest that our eating habits are less likely to cause cancer than they once were.[6] To be sure, the death rate from the disease has increased markedly since 1930, but most of the increase seems to be attributable to lung cancer and presumably, therefore, to cigarette smoking and air pollution. In contrast, deaths from stomach cancer have declined—from a rate of 30 per 100,000 in 1930 to about 10 per 100,000 now. Some of this decline can be attributed to improvements in medical care, but stomach

[6] Official U.S. Government Statistics.

cancer is still fatal in about 90 cases out of 100, and so the decline almost certainly has to do with diet. And since the liver is the primary organ responsible for detoxifying the substances we eat, the substantial decline in liver cancer may also be due to a healthier diet. Whether additives have had anything to do with these declines or not, we must be doing something right. One possible explanation was suggested recently by Dr. R. J. Shamberger of the Department of Biochemistry at the Cleveland Clinic Foundation. According to Dr. Shamberger, the startling decline of gastric cancer in the United States in recent years is due to the high level of consumption of processed cereal.[7] The explanation: cereals are rich in selenium, an antioxidant that occurs in the soil and that apparently prevents cancer in mice. Further, cereal manufacturers have added certain antioxidants (BHA and BHT) to their products, and these substances have the same anticancer effect in mice. However, the authors would like to emphasize that this is merely a postulation and up to this time has not been proven scientifically.

Previously, the per-capita consumption of food additives per year was given as 139 pounds. The reader might be interested in the kinds of additives that make up this 139 pounds. The most widely used food additive is a natural product, a single chemical of high purity that is produced in abundance. This additive is sucrose—that is, ordinary cane or beet sugar—and each person in North America consumes an average of 102 pounds of it per year. The second most widely used additive is sodium chloride (ordinary table salt), of which we use about 15 pounds per year. After salt comes corn syrup, about 8 pounds, and then dextrose (a simple sugar), 4 pounds. Note that the 139 pounds has dwindled to 10 pounds if we exclude sugar, salt, corn syrup, and dextrose from our list. Following these are about 33 different additives, which account for 9 pounds a year. Of these 33, 18 are used either as leavening agents or to adjust the acidity of food. Yeast, sodium bicarbonate, citric acid, black pepper, mustard, and the much abused but innocent monosodium glutamate (MSG) are among the most often used of these 18.

We hope that you are beginning to realize why we are not concerned about food additives. Our list is now down to one pound, which is spread over the some 1800 other additives we use. The median level of use of these is about one-half a milligram per additive per year—the weight of one grain of salt per year! These are the facts. Are you still concerned? We hope not, since additives not only have legitimate functions in food, they also save us a lot of money. In terms of money saving, consider these data.[8] If additives were re-

---

[7] E. M. Whelan and F. J. Stare, *Panic in the Pantry* (New York: Antheneum Press, 1975), pp. 124–25.

[8] J. F. Angeline and G. P. Leonardos, "Food Additives: Some Economic Considerations," *Journal of Food Technology*, April 1973, pp. 40–50.

moved from white bread, we would have to change our whole bread distribution system. This would not only waste much needed food, it would also cost the American consumer $1.1 billion per year. Yes, *$1.1 billion.* The removal of additives from margarine would cost consumers $600 million. The removal of nitrates and nitrites from processed meats would cost another $600 million, and the removal of potassium sorbate from processed cheese would cost you $32 million. These four products, without additives, would thus cost you, the consumer, $2,332,000,000 per year—a sizable figure.

How many times have we heard consumer activists attacking the food industry as a big business supposedly uninterested in the consumer? Much is made of natural foods. But some companies have found a good thing in the additive scare. The "natural," "organic," and "health food" businesses are growing at a tremendous rate. In 1972, sales in health food stores and other retail outlets for natural foods reached about $550 million, up from $400 million in 1971.[9] This too is big business, and the same criteria applied to the food additive business (which grosses $500 million) must be applied to the health food business.

At this point, we would like to reproduce a paper entitled "Toxic Substances Naturally Present in Food," which puts the matter of food additive safety in its proper perspective.

It should be no news to anyone that there is a basic dichotomy in our Food, Drug and Cosmetic Act respecting its treatment of imitation or synthetic foods as against "natural" ones.

This statutory posture is not peculiar to the United States; many European countries, Germany for example, go even further in according favored treatment to "natural" foods and food ingredients. Even in its extremes, such a policy must still permit the manufacture and supply of food in an industrialized economy, and this often requires a definition of "natural" as remarkable for its ingenuity as for its comprehensiveness. We play this game too; the law says in Section 402:

A food shall be deemed to be adulterated—(a) (1) If it bears or contains any poisonous or deleterious substance which may render it injurious to health; but in case the substance is not an added substance (i.e., a "natural" one) such food shall not be considered adulterated under this clause if the quantity of such substance in such food does not ordinarily render it injurious to health; . . .

An "added poisonous or deleterious substance," however, renders the food adulterated unless the additive is used within the other provisions of the Act, such as the Pesticide, the Food Additive, and the Color Additive Amendments. The regulations issued under these amendments extend, though they do not clarify this distinction between "added" and "not added" or

[9] "The Business Front. Not All Milk and Honey," *Barron's,* Spet. 11, 1972, p. 11.

as it is more often said, between "natural" and "synthetic." An example is the listing of synthetic and natural flavorings in CFR 121.1163 and 121.1164. Successive hairsplittings have finally brought us to the point where purification by distillation results in a "natural" product, while crystallization generally produces a "synthetic" one. We might as well say of these distinctions themselves, that some are natural, and some are synthetic.

Now, ridiculous as this becomes, by the time we have expended our legal and administrative ingenuity on it, there is a substantial underlying reason. We are attempting, in a fumbling way, to express a higher degree of confidence in the safety of "natural" foods and ingredients than in wholly synthetic ones. This confidence often has an emotional and irrational basis, as in the case of the organic gardener. But there is a more scientifically respectable basis for much of it. It is an attempt to apply the results of human experience in the evaluation of safety. If it lacks precision and consistency, and occasionally even common sense, we should consider the alternatives and what can be done by refinement before we abandon the concept.

There is an alternative, or rather a complex and expensive set of alternatives with which we have become increasingly, but often only superficially, familiar. This is the approach of toxicological investigation, employing primarily animal feeding studies. These are an extremely useful tool, providing valuable insights into the degree and nature of hazards which may be associated with a particular substance. But now we are seeing the development of a new breed of fanatic, comparable in his messianic enthusiasm to the organic gardener, who insists that every ingredient must be "thoroughly tested" until it is "proved safe."

I should like to comment briefly on the strengths and limitations of both testing and experience. Then, in a somewhat whimsical example, I'd like to explore the impact and contradictions involved in their application to safety evaluation.

The advantages of human experience in assessing safety are:

1. The experience is gained with the species with which we are concerned—avoiding the problem of interspecific differences.
2. The experience is with the diet composition and within the range of dietary levels normally consumed—avoiding the problems of the consequences of untypical methods of administration and of metabolism by pathways not involved in normal feeding levels.

The limitations of human experience are:

1. Controlled experiments cannot ordinarily be run, although comparative epidemiological studies can sometimes be made.
2. It is not possible to determine the limits of safety by test. Such informa-

tion ordinarily comes from the study of accidental overconsumption or industrial exposure, or from results in some other application, such as drug use.

The advantages of animal studies are that:

1. Controlled experiments can be run—meaning that you can isolate the use or non-use of a particular substance as the single test variable and determine how the response varies with the dose. In observations on humans, this is usually impossible because of the complexity of both our human genetic makeup and our environment.

2. One can determine the nature and extent of the hazard—and damage— to the test animal with a precision limited only by the skill and equipment of the experimenter, since risk to the animal is of no consequence and the pre- and post-mortem observation may be as extensive as necessary and desired.

3. One can do lifetime, and even multigeneration, studies in animals with a short life span.

These are large advantages, but they are balanced by serious disadvantages:

1. The test animal is not the same as the human animal—not even the same as a miniature human would be. The metabolic pathways may, and often do differ; the susceptibility to damage of the individual organs, or of more generalized bodily functions, will almost certainly differ from those of the human. The susceptibility may be greater or less, and usually in a manner and extent impossible to predict beforehand.

   In part, because of these differences, it is customary to apply a safety factor, often 1/100, to "no-effect" levels observed in animals when using these experimental results to estimate safe levels in humans. The result of this is to require in animals doses at least 100 times higher than the functionally effective level intended for human food. In avoiding one trap, we fall into another.

   Any substance any animal consumes is either excreted unchanged, or in a few cases, is stored (accumulated) or is modified by the body in some way prior to excretion or storage. This modification, or metabolism, generally takes place by one or a few processes (metabolic pathways) which the organism favors over other paths, presumably because in evolving, these have worked out to the least disadvantage to the organism. As the level of intake of a substance increases, these normal pathways become loaded to capacity, and the organism calls upon other pathways or the substance temporarily accumulates. These other paths will often involve intermediate stages which are more toxic, or mechanisms which place a greater strain on the animal. In any case, they are not necessarily related to the paths, and effects, encountered at lower levels. Thus, the second disadvantage of animal testing is that:

2. To obtain an adverse effect, and to provide an arbitrary but large safety factor, feeding levels must be so high, compared with intended human consumption, that valid analogies very often cannot be made.

   The demand that everything be thoroughly tested until safety is proved actually comes from a naive, desperate, and quite unsupportable faith in the extent and certainty of the conclusions which may be drawn from animal tests.

One may well point out that where doubt exists about the applicability of animal data to humans, the decisions should always be made conservatively; and if this is the case, why all the fuss? There are at least two rejoinders to this, one of which is obvious from recent events.

"No effect" in animal studies has every limitation of negative evidence. It simply means that under conditions of that experiment, that experimenter did not find anything. It provides no reason to assume that under some different set of experimental conditions, or with better analytical tools, or a more skilled observer, an effect could not have been found.

We should not ignore another aspect. Not to use a particular substance because a more or less thorough investigation showed some significant potential of hazard is not to avoid a danger. It merely exchanges one risk, recently estimated, for another risk which is often unknown. Nowhere is this more apparent than in the attitudes, congealed into regulation, with which we regard "natural" and "synthetic" food ingredients. For like an old tin-type, our food laws, regulations, and company policies present these attitudes as they once were, their rigidity exaggerated, as in a tin-type, by the laborious process of recording them.

Let's consider a reasonably elaborate and attractive, but not at all exotic dinner menu [Figure 4-1]. And let us approach it, not with the infectious, rules-be-damned enthusiasm of Graham Kerr, the Galloping Gourmet, but with the flinty-eyed inflexibility of Dr. Constance Care, the Galloping Toxicologist. Connie, of course, reads the literature and has heard of the concept of toxicological insignificance, so she concedes that a trace—or possibly the shadow of a trace—may indeed be negligible. But she thinks about carcinogens, teratogens, and mutagens; and she vows never to depart from the 100-fold safety factor which stands between us and disaster. Natural or synthetic, it will kill us all the same. Now let's evaluate our menu from Connie's point of view, as if we must regard each food not as it is treated under the law as natural food, but as it would be treated if manufactured from added ingredients. We will become alarmed only by foods containing substances which, following the assumptions inherent in present toxicological protocols, could not survive these assumptions and safety factors. The Delaney Clause will be applied with the reverent concern properly due revealed truth.

Among the toxic substances naturally present in certain foods are some cholinesterase inhibitors of unknown structure. Cholinesterase inhibitors interfere with the transmission of nerve impulses; many potent modern pesticides are based on such activity. These are present in measurable quantity in radishes, carrots, celery, and most particularly in potatoes. In the case of potatoes, the alkaloid solanine [Figure 4-2] is responsible, and is often present with less than a ten-

Figure 4-1: An Attractive Dinner Ahead

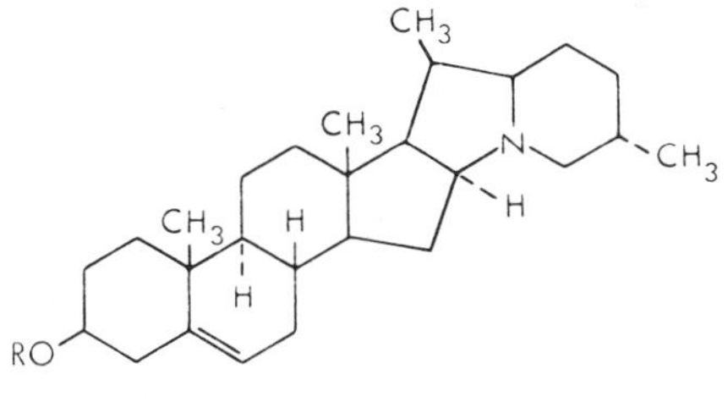

Solanine — R = *l*-rhamnosyl- *d*-galactosyl- *d*-glucasyl-

Solanidine — R = H

Figure 4-2: Cholinesterase Inhibitors

fold safety factor between the normal level and levels that have caused human poisoning. Thus fall the first items from our menu [Figure 4-3].

105

Figure 4-3: Some Items Must Fall

A number of food contain glycosides which break down dur-ing cooking or digestion to yield hydrogen cyanide. Among those with this disconcerting property are almonds and lima beans. This is no idle concern; lima beans, high in HCN, have been the cause of several serious poisoning outbreaks. Tch Tch.

Oxalates and free oxalic acid occur in a number of foods—spinach, cashews, almonds, cocoa, and tea. Our menu is beginning to suffer [Figure 4-4].

Stimulants occur widely in foods. Nutmeg contains myristicin; tea, coffee, cola, and cocoa contain caffeine. Tea contains theophil-lyne and cocoa, theobromine. Even more ominously, myristicin is a hallucinogen, and occasionally abused for that purpose. But nutmeg also contains small quantities of safrole, a carcinogen. Unfortunately, we used nutmeg on our spinach, and, of course, the depressant alco-hol is not tolerable with a reasonable safety factor, and its hazards are well known.

That alone would rule out the liqueurs, but high intakes of menthol have caused cardiac arrythmia and the glycerine in Coin-treau is toxic at only small multiples of normal use.

Figure 4-4: A Few More Items of Concern

Goitrogens, substances which promote goiter, are present in many foods. The white turnip contains 1-5-vinyl-2-thiooxazolidone, and cauliflower contains a thiocyanate. It would only take about 22 pounds per day of cauliflower to cause thyroid enlargement, and as careful readers of recent adverse toxicological reports know, this is a wholly inadequate margin of safety. The peach, pear, strawberry, Brussels sprouts, spinach, and carrot have all been shown to demonstrate goitrogenic activity in man. A shame, since more items must be dropped [Figure 4-5].

Pressor amines, which raise the blood pressure, are common [Figure 4-6], and present a real hazard to susceptible persons, and especially to those who are taking drugs such as the tranquilizer, Parnate. Since, by this time, we are sufficiently worried to be gobbling tranquilizers, we should eliminate bananas, pineapples, cheese, especially Camembert cheese, and wine.

Now, we probably need pressor amines, though their essentiality has not been conclusively demonstrated. But this dilemma is presented even more sharply by several of the Vitamins—A, D, and K—and several of the essential minerals, which we could not begin

Figure 4-5: Our Menu sans Goitrogens

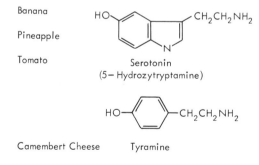

Figure 4-6: Pressor amines

to tolerate at 100 times normal consumption levels. But our rule is sacred, and the Vitamin D and A in egg yolk and butter, Vitamin D in milk, and the zinc and arsenic in seafood rule them out [Figure 4-7]. In addition, egg yolk is reportedly carcinogenic in the diet of mice.

Figure 4-7: "Safe," But What's Left to Eat?

Most of you have heard of the recent concern over the nitrite or nitrate content of foods, and the proved capability of these substances not only to cause methemoglobinemia in man, but also to be transformed in the stomach to the potent carcinogens, the nitrosamines.

These involve not only the cured meats such as ham and bacon, but certain vegetables if they have been fertilized—spinach particularly. Finally, smoked foods almost inevitably contain small amounts of the polynuclear aromatic hydrocarbons, and the role of these as dietary carcinogens in man is confirmed by epidemiological surveys of the northern European countries where smoked foods are much consumed, and cancer of the stomach is unusually common. Let's remove the smoked salmon.

We can, perhaps, retain the rolls if we can ignore the ricket-promoting factor in yeast and the hazards of amino-acid imbalance. Butter has been eliminated, although, if it were devitaminized, we could retain it, labeling it, of course, for added color.

If space permitted, it would be interesting to speculate on how foods would be labeled, especially if complete declarations of naturally occurring ingredients were required, as in the case of added substances. Some interesting warning statements would be needed—ones that would make the cigarette warning seem hesitant by comparison. Since some of the toxins we have discussed are a characteristic and even essential component of the foods in which they occur, we would have to take steps to eliminate these, with appropriate labeling; degoitrogenized, imitation cauliflower, for example.

"Hazardous, but essential substances, like the fat-soluble vitamins, could be available on a prescription basis. Those of less clearly justified merit, for example the pressor amines and alcohol, would be available on a non-refillable prescription only. We can't have people taking these things indiscriminately!

"In all this nonsense, however, there is a serious point. For safety is a serious matter. The whole thrust of this article is that all sources of relevant information should be used. Indeed, this is the underlying concept of general recognition of safety (GRAS), in which both experience based on common use in food, and scientific procedures may be used. Combined, they are still insufficient, and always open to new evidence. Animal testing may be of crucial value—but it may also be irrelevant to human safety. Human experience, for all its directness, may remain an enigma. The utility of both should be improved. In part, this may be achieved by using in animal tests those species previously shown for each instance to be suitable metabolic models for man, instead of those that are handy, cheap, or customary. We need more, and more detailed, national dietary studies coupled with better reporting and analysis of individual health.

Let there be no misunderstanding on one point. We must use the mass of human experience, not mass human experiments. By this, I mean that prior to the broad intentional use of a material in human food, we should have information from animal and human studies which allows expert judgment to conclude with confidence that use of the material will not significantly increase overall risk. But, we must recognize that experience is the final determinant, no matter how encouraging the results from animal tests. We need not only to recognize this, but to improve our utilization of feedback from human experience, in improving our quality of life.[10]

Having stated the case for the benefits and safety of food addi-

[10] Reprinted by permission of the author, Dr. Richard L. Hall, Vice-President for Research and Development, McCormick and Co., Inc., and the Food and Drug Law Institute, the original publisher, 1973.

tives, let us leave you with this thought. The benefits of additives are often ignored, and the risks are often overstated. At this point in time, quite a few additives have been banned because of questions about their safety. Yet, there is no known case of any illness other than the kind of allergenic reactions that many foods can cause. Even mishaps from improperly used additives—huge overdoses taken by mistake—are so rare as to be medical curiosities.

BIBLIOGRAPHY

Bernarde, M. A., *The Chemicals We Eat.* New York: McGraw-Hill Book Co., 1975.

Hall, R. L., "Food Additives," *Nutrition Today*, July/August 1973, pp. 20–28. *Toxicants Occurring Naturally in Foods*, 2nd ed. Washington, D.C.: National Academy of Sciences, 1973.

Whelan, E. M., and F. J. Stare, *Panic in the Pantry.* New York: Antheneum Press, 1975.

chapter **5**

To Preserve and Protect

Living in New England in the middle of January, one thinks of how good a vine-ripened tomato would taste and how long it has been since that particular flavor was savored. There is no disagreement from anyone in the field of food science and nutrition that a very fresh vine-ripened tomato would taste better, look better, and probably be more nutritious than any processed or preserved tomato that one could find. Unfortunately, in January we have a problem in New England and in many other parts of America and the world. That problem is snow, cold weather, and, in general, extremely unfavorable conditions for the growth of vine-ripened tomatoes. This is the case with many foods, so in order to have a nourishing, acceptable, safe, and reasonably priced food supply the year round, we must preserve and protect our foods.

We have talked about nutrition, food additives, organic gardening, and other matters that are dear to a consumer's heart. Today, there is a tremendous demand for highly nutritious foods. While demanding highly nutritious foods, the consumer must realize, however, that factors other than nutrition are involved in eating—for instance, quantity, quality, cost, safety, and acceptance. These factors must all be considered; if any one of them is out of line, the consumer will not purchase or will not be able to purchase and therefore will not eat a highly nutritious food. It is extraordinarily difficult to isolate nutrition from these other parameters.

Preservation and processing begin when one prepares the soil for planting. In order to obtain maximum yield, as will be discussed in Part II of this book, Chapters 7 and 10, one must irrigate appropriately, fertilize appropriately, and prepare the soil for the arrival of the plant. The growing plant is subject to insects, rodents, weeds and all other unsavory characters that destroy tremendous amounts of our food prior to the time it is harvested. Surveys indicate that in certain areas of Africa, up to 50 percent of the dried fish harvested is lost as a result of insect infestation. That is, up to 50 percent of a vital source of protein is lost to a country that is in the throes of starvation. This alone indicates the importance of using such substances as insecticides, herbicides, and fertilizers in appropriate and judicious amounts. In order to process a food material, we must be able to harvest it. People who decry the use of chemicals in growing foods are just not aware that spoilage can reduce the total crop yield by up to 50 percent.

Assuming that we can harvest a reasonable supply of food materials from our fields, we must determine what to do with these materials in order to keep them acceptable, reasonably priced, and as highly nutritious as possible for a given period of time. Our problem is to prevent the deterioration and spoilage of foods when they are fresh. We've all seen instances of foods going "bad" when left out of the refrigerator or even going "bad" when left in the refrigerator for too long. Some of this spoilage is due to chemical change, some to biological change, and some, of course, to microbial growth on the food. Many consumers think of spoilage in terms of a threat to their safety. They think of the growth of microorganisms and the possibility of food poisoning. But this is only one part of the picture. The other part is extraordinarily important. It includes the chemical and biological changes that the food undergoes upon storage. These in turn cause changes in flavor, odor, and appearance that may make the food inedible.

Let's look for a moment at the history of food processing. How long has it been going on? Why was it used? Has it been essential? Is it essential now? These are questions we must answer when considering the safety and desirability of food processing.

Food processing has been going on for centuries. Early humans had to rely on growing plants. Animal foods, unfortunately, became inedible fairly quickly because early prehistoric humans did not know how to process or preserve them. In ancient Rome, runners were sent to the Alps to obtain ice with which the Roman aristocracy could keep their foods cold. Spices have been used for centuries. In Europe they were used during the Middle Ages to stretch the inadequate supply of food that was available. During this time, spices were very valuable. For instance, a pound of mace was worth three sheep or half a cow. Pepper, the most valuable spice of all, was measured in terms of human life; it could be used to buy slaves or have men killed. Wars were fought over some of the colonies that produced spice for such countries as Spain, Portugal, France, Holland, and Great Britain. Why were spices used? At that time, most people used spices in order to mask or disguise the flavor of "spoiled" food that was still nutritious but would, because of its flavor, be totally inedible if unspiced. This proves that even our forefathers of long ago were aware that nutrition was not an isolated phenomenon; food had to be acceptable in order for people to enjoy its nutritive value. Some spices were used because of chemicals they contained. For instance, the cloves used in cooking hams contain a chemical called eugenol, which inhibits the growth of bacteria, a fact noted in ancient times. Interestingly, cloves are still used today as a flavor ingredient in cooking hams, but our processing techniques have developed to the point that cloves are no longer required as a means of inhibiting bacteria. Cultural habits have lingered, however, and, today, cloves are desirable mainly for flavor. Those who feel that food processing and preservation is something invented by modern man to poison the public must realize that it has been used through the ages. Another discovery that we found rather unusual is that the first vending machine known to man dispensed holy water in an Egyptian temple about 200 B.C. Processing is not new, and the kind of food-service systems that we have now are obviously not entirely new either.

The type of spoilage that does not endanger the consumer's health should be mentioned, but we should probably spend more time on an understanding of how food is made safe. This is not intended to imply that chemical and biological spoilage is less important than microbial spoilage; rather, you may be more interested in spoilage that presents a danger to you. In order to clarify these two types of spoilage, it might be simpler to call one deterioration and the other spoilage.

Deterioration of food is commonly seen by the consumer, but not always recognized. Consider how many times you have smelled off-flavored milk or bacon, ham, or other fatty meats that have stayed in the refrigerator too long and have acquired a rather sickening odor, and you know what deterioration is. The deterioration, or rancidity, of fatty meats is due to the fat molecules breaking down chemically and forming compounds that cause certain odors and flavors. Milk deterioration is caused by microorganisms that break down the protein in the milk to smaller compounds, which have a very definite flavor and odor. However, such microorganisms are not harmful to the consumer. Among other types of deterioration are the wilting of lettuce, the toughening of beans and peas, the loss of texture in strawberries, and the drying out of oranges. All of these are changes that you can see as your foods mature and finally become inedible.

When you open a can of food, you never worry about such deterioration as long as you eat the food right away. Yet that food has remained in the can much longer than you could hold anything fresh in the refrigerator or in your kitchen. Processing—in this case, canning—has stopped deterioration until the can is opened and exposed to oxygen. Many people feel it is unsafe to leave a food in its can after the can has been opened. This is completely untrue; the can is probably freer of microorganisms than any dish you might put the food in. During the heat process to which it is exposed, the can has been heated to temperatures far higher than those produced by any diswasher or those used in hand-washing dishes. At times, the interior of the can may cause off-flavors in certain acid products if these are left in the container in the refrigerator, but such flavors certainly cannot harm your health. Deterioration is at times prevented by packaging. The next time you buy potato chips, see if the container suggests that the chips not be exposed to sunlight; quite often, the container itself is colored or opaque. This is because the fat in the potato chips, when exposed to sunlight, becomes rancid and forms the odoriferous compounds referred to previously. There is a reason for almost every package or process that is used in modern food processing. Consider natural grains or cereals. These must be stored in the refrigerator and cannot be exposed to room temperatures for long periods of time. If they are so exposed, fat rancidity occurs and they become inedible. Think of this in worldwide terms. If grains were not milled to remove most of the fat, then the flour that is formed from such grains could not be stored in large bins at room temperature as flour may be stored today. This would lessen the likelihood of flour being shipped to developing countries with hot climates, because of the rancidity that might occur. One can see, therefore, that there are technological and scientific reasons for milling grains. The food industry isn't just "making white flour."

Spoilage, the term we are applying to microbiological hazards, cannot be ignored by the consumer. We really don't know just how prevalent the hazards from food-contaminated bacteria and other organisms are. The reasons for this are that the illnesses resulting from such food contamination are not always evaluated by the victims or reported by physicians. Nevertheless, informed estimates indicate that perhaps as many as 20 million Americans suffer the effects of bacteria-contaminated food each year. This does not seem to be an especially great number, but such illnesses are occasionally fatal and only the common cold causes more loss of work. The contamination is due almost entirely to unsanitary handling practices in restaurants, catering establishments, and, alas, in the home. Stomach upsets or worse used to occur so frequently at church picnics, as a result of home handling of foods, that "church picnic" nearly entered the medical lexicon as a descriptive term. It should be stressed that the foods received in the home today are rarely, if ever, the cause of microbial hazards. Only after they are opened and handled do they become hazardous due to microbial growth.

There are three major types of microorganisms that affect foods—bacteria, yeast, and molds. Bacteria are the major health problem. Yeast are not usually considered poisonous, but they do cause foods to decay. A few toxins that are formed from molds have recently been found in certain foods, but this is not true of all molds.

Let's consider bacteria first. We are all familiar with ptomaine poisoning, which results from eating certain foods that have been contaminated by bacteria. However, the term ptomaine poisoning should be ruled out of your vocabulary. It does not exist. This term was developed before we understood bacterial poisons. In reality, there are two types of food poisoning caused by bacteria. The first, food infections, is caused by the presence within food of bacteria that can grow rapidly within the intestinal tract of humans, producing symptoms such as diarrhea and vomiting. That is, the ingested bacteria grow within the intestinal tract of a human and cause the symptoms of food poisoning. The organisms that cause this type of food poisoning are *Salmonella* and *Shigella*. *Clostridium perfringens* was classified as a food infection until very recently, but is now considered a food intoxication, the second type of bacteria-caused food poisoning. As the name implies, food intoxications are due to toxins that are produced by bacteria and then ingested by a human.

In this case, it is not the bacteria themselves that cause the food poisoning but the toxins produced by the bacteria if a food. *Clostridium botulinum, perfringens,* some molds, and *Staphylococcus* produce harmful toxins.

In most cases of food poisoning, whether it be food intoxication or food infection, the symptoms include diarrhea, nausea, vomiting, and related symptoms. However, *Clostridium botulinum* results in death in about 60 percent of all cases. Because of the dehydration and weakening that they cause, other varieties of food poisoning can result in debilitation and death if they attack a young baby or an elderly person. Food poisoning, although not common, is dangerous and of major concern to the modern food-processing industry.

A food that is inedible, for whatever reason, will not be eaten. If a food has a terrible off-odor or off-flavor, the consumer will not accept it and thus, of course, will not obtain any nutrients from it. However, a food that does not exhibit off-flavors or off-odors may still be subject to microbial contamination and, if consumed, may result in sickness and perhaps death. Interestingly, only one out of six cases of food poisoning reported from 1968 to 1973 can be partially blamed on mishandling or processing by the food industry. The other five were due to preparation and handling after the food was purchased.

Clostridium botulinum, though often fatal, is almost never the result of mishandling in the food industry. Nearly every case reported is due to home canning or some other type of food processing in the home. Approximately 800 billion cans of food were produced before 1972, and during that time only five deaths from *commercially* canned foods were reported. In 1973, six deaths from *Clostridium botulinum* were reported, but only one of these was caused by industrially processed food. Several other outbreaks of food poisoning from *Clostridium botulinum* have occurred since 1973 particularly in the canned mushroom industry, but this problem is under control and is of no consequence today.

For the consumer, the handling of food should always be viewed in terms of proper sanitation. Even people who do their own dishes often exhibit extremely unsanitary practices in the use of their dish cloths. How many times in a home have you seen someone drying dishes wipe some dirt off the floor, scrub a child's face, or even wipe a nose with the same dish towel and then blithely go on drying the dishes? Certainly, the contamination from the floor, the face, and the nose could add to the microbial load on the dishes. This contamination could later be transferred to a food on a dish and cause food poisoning.

Cooking food properly is of great help in preventing contamination by *Salmonella*, because the organism is destroyed by heat. In the many households in which people use wooden meat boards, meat may be contaminated by *Salmonella* or some other organism. The organism gets between the fibers in the wooden board and may later on be transferred to another food, even after it is cooked, which is then ingested by the human. We are seeing the demise of wooden cutting boards, which is fortunate because these can be a danger in the home.

Clostridium perfringens, a food intoxication, is usually contracted from meats, eggs, gravies, and other protein foods. This organism consists of a vegetative cell and a spore that is a kind of protective coating for the cell. When ingested, spores may vegetate inside the intestines and produce a toxin, which in turn causes the symptoms of food poisoning in the human.

Staphylococcus, another food intoxication, is a very common form of food poisoning. It's the one that hits us very shortly after eating. Very violent diarrhea and vomiting are the symptoms. The incubation time is only two to four hours after ingestion. *Staphylococcus* contamination is commonly found in cream pastries, tuna, canned chicken salads, and similar mixtures of foods. It is extremely important to refrigerate such foods immediately after handling, because heat will not destroy the toxin that *Staphylococcus* produces. If the bacteria do not grow due to refrigeration, then the toxin is not produced. Therefore, both sanitation and refrigeration are needed in order to prevent the formation of the *Staphylococcus* toxin.

Death from *Clostridium botulinum* is a sure way to make the newspapers, probably because it is so rare and yet so devastating. It is an anaerobic organism, that is, it cannot grow in the presence of oxygen. It is normally found in canned foods, where oxygen does not exist, and in sausage meats, where oxygen is also excluded. Like *Clostridium perfringens*, it has a vegetative cell and a spore. But unlike the *perfringens* spore, the *botulinum* spore has to vegetate within the food material in the absence of oxygen and produce a toxin prior to ingestion. It is the toxin that causes the symptoms of *botulinum* poisoning that often result in death. Adequate processing of foods—in particular, heat processing—will destroy the vegetative cells and the spores of *Clostridium botulinum*. In the home, many people misread the pressure cooker gauge when they are canning foods, or they do not process the food long enough at a high enough temperature to insure the destruction of *Clostridium botulinum*. This is the reason for the larger number of botulinum outbreaks in home-canned foods than in industrially processed foods.

Having mentioned some of the microorganisms that cause spoilage and some of the deteriorations that take place in foods that are not processed, it would now be appropriate to discuss some of the methods whereby foods are processed. Processing is simply a way to maintain safety, acceptability, and nutrition in our food supply for an extended period of time, so that we do not have to rely on the hunt to prevent starvation and malnutrition.

How do we prevent the growth of bacteria in a food material? This is probably the fundamental question in food processing, because the safety of food is of the utmost importance. Once we have established the appropriate process to insure a safe food, we may then consider ways to prevent deterioration and ways to make the food more appealing, in flavor, color, texture, appearance, and so on.

Microorganisms or bacteria are like you and I: they are born, they have a life span in which they must eat food and excrete waste, and they die. The question is, how do we control the life, growth, and death of bacteria? There are several possible ways of doing this:

1. Take away the bacteria's food.
2. Change the temperature in order to kill or prevent the growth of the bacteria.
3. Remove water.
4. Change other environmental conditions.

Let's consider each of these in turn. The first method would take away the food source of the bacteria, which is, of course, the food source for us as well. Thus, we can dispense with this alternative immediately.

Changing the temperature, our second option, is an extraordinarily effective way to kill bacteria and/or prevent their growth, thereby preventing both deterioration and microbial spoilage from occurring. The temperature can be changed in a number of ways. First, we are all used to refrigerators; in North America this is a common method of keeping fresh produce and opened processed foods for a longer period of time than such food would keep at room temperature. The refrigerator's lower temperature slows the growth of bacteria so that they cannot multiply to such an extent that they cause food intoxication or food infection. To some extent, the refrigerator prevents deteriorations such as the wilting of lettuce, the rancidity spoken of previously, the souring of milk, and the generally undesirable changes that take place so much faster in a food if it is left in the sun or at room temperature. A refrigerator adjusted to 40°F can just about quadruple the keeping time of most foods.

Freezing is another method of preservation based on temperature control. Freezing prevents the growth of microorganisms; it does not kill them. It prevents growth in two ways. One, it freezes the available water so that the microorganisms do not have enough water to grow. Second, it lowers the temperature to a point where the microorganisms either cannot grow or grow very slowly. Home freezing has become a very common way to process food, but although it produces a very desirable product, it is uncommon to find home-frozen food of as good quality as industrially frozen food. This is not to cast aspersions on the freezing capabilities of the average consumer or on the average consumer's kitchen. However, one of the major dimensions of processing a high-quality food product is the length of time the process takes. That is, the quicker you can freeze the food the higher in quality it will be. Less tissue damage will occur, and, therefore, the texture will be better and flavor loss, color loss, and nutrient loss will all be lessened. Industrial processes use such techniques as freezing by liquid nitrogen ($-280°$ F) and blast freezing— that is, using a fan along with the freezer to create a wind effect. By now, most of us are used to hearing about the wind-chill factor that is computed for those of us unfortunate enough to live in areas with cold winters. We know that a low temperature coupled with a strong enough wind can result in a wind-chill factor of, say, $-60°$ F or colder. Industrial blast freezers attain the equivalent of very low temperatures and quick-freeze the food. In the home we cannot be as fancy, nor should we be. Instead, we use a normal freezer compartment, which takes longer to freeze food than the industrial freezers.

We should add that it is necessary to blanch a food prior to freezing it. Blanching simply involves subjecting the food to a high temperature (approximately $190°$ F) for a minute or so prior to freezing it. This process destroys the enzymes present in vegetables. Remember from Chapter 2 that an enzyme is a biological catalyst; that is, it hastens reactions. If the enzymes are not destroyed by heat, certain chemical reactions will occur while the food is frozen, and off-odors and off-flavors will result. These chemical reactions constitute a deterioration rather than a spoilage: they do not present a health hazard, but they create a real problem in quality.

The average consumer feels it is unsafe to thaw a food and then refreeze it. A good general rule is this: if you thaw food, use it. If, however, you thaw food slightly in the refrigerator, it is quite safe to refreeze it. Problems arise when one leaves food on a kitchen counter for an extended period of time; the food thaws and then stays at a temperature at which the microorganisms (which were not destroyed by freezing but merely rendered dormant) begin to multiply. The organisms may or may not produce toxins, or they may multiply to the point where they are likely to cause a food infection.

If the food is refrozen, the toxins or the bacteria that were not destroyed may cause food poisoning when the food is ingested at a later time. A good rule of thumb is that it is safe to refreeze a food if ice crystals are still present in it.

The other obvious way of utilizing temperature to control or kill microorganisms is heating. Cooking is the most obvious example of using heat to destroy microorganisms, and we recommended it above in the case of *Salmonella.* We do not normally use cooking as a method of destroying microorganisms; we use it as a method of making food more palatable. However, cooking does destroy microorganisms. The major method used in food processing and preservation is the canning and heating process. This method was originated by a Frenchman named Nicholas Appert during the time of Napoleon. Napoleon needed foods that could be stored for longer periods of time for his armies, and he offered some 12,000 francs to anyone who could discover a way of producing such food. Appert invented a method of sealing foods inside a container and then heating it. He thought that the foods were made safe by the destructive action of heat on the bacteria in the container. Home canning, which is becoming increasingly popular, can be dangerous, as we mentioned previously in this chapter. Anyone wishing to begin home canning should consult their local land-grant state college or university and their extension service to find out the exact time and temperature that apply to a given food in a given size of container. In the food-processing industry, mathematical analyses have been worked out so that a specific time and temperature that are known to destroy hazardous microorganisms can be predicted for any size of container and any type of food. Unfortunately, accidents do occur on occasion, but as we mentioned previously, they are extraordinarily rare. The thing to remember in canning a food is that the higher the temperature used, the shorter the heating time required, and the lower the temperature used, the longer the time required. The modern food-processing industry has been able to achieve higher and higher temperatures and shorter and shorter times. This combination manages to kill the same number of bacteria as an older process but does not destroy as many nutrients. This, of course, contradicts those who would have us believe that processed foods today are not as nutritious as the processed foods of the past—a belief that is untrue and normally held by those who are ignorant of the available technology.

The removal of water is the third way in which we might prevent the growth of microorganisms. Bacteria require, just as you and I do, a certain amount of moisture to grow and survive. The drying process simply removes enough moisture from the food so that the bacteria cannot grow, multiply, and/or produce toxins. Drying is probably one of the oldest methods of food processing. Sun drying, which is used to make raisins from grapes, is a very old method and one of the fundamental ways of drying a food material. The American Indians used to make pemmican, a meat and berry mixture that was pounded together and then dried in the sun. The berries contained sugar and salt, which aided in binding the water so that microorganisms couldn't grow, and the acids from the berries also helped prevent microbial growth during the drying process. At the time pemmican was being made these factors were certainly not known, but the Indianas found that if certain methods were not used in the preparation of this food, people who ate it became sick. As with freezing and heating, the quicker the drying the more nutrients that are retained. It has therefore become a challenge to modern technology to develop methods whereby the drying process can be done much more quickly. In the past few decades, drying has become a finely tuned technology that produces very high-quality, safe foods. From ancient methods of sun drying there evolved other methods, such as tunnel drying, whereby a food is put on a belt moving through a tunnel where a hot-air draft moves in the direction opposite the travel of the food. This decreases the time of drying by a tremendous factor. Spray drying was developed as a means of improving quality further, and this is how most dried milk is produced. In spray drying, fluid milk is fed into an atomizer, which breaks the milk down into fine particles and sends them into a heated chamber. Each tiny particle is then dried very quickly, and the resulting spray is collected to produce our spray-dried milk powder as we know it today. Many of you have probably seen the television advertisements in which the water is sucked out of a cup of frozen coffee. This rather whimsical advertisement is supposed to represent the process of freeze drying. We assure you that the water is not sucked out of a frozen food when it is freeze-dried. In this process a food is frozen and then some heat is applied in order to sublime the ice into water vapor; that is, the ice is transformed directly to vapor without going through the water phase. Most kinds of physical transformation that you are familiar with involve ice to water and water to vapor. In the freeze-drying process the ice changes directly to vapor, and as a result the cellular tissue is not broken down as much and the food maintains more of its physical integrity. This means that when you return the water, the freeze-dried food is more similar to the fresh food than most dried foods would be. Unfortunately, the cost of freeze drying still prohibits the marketing of a complete array of freeze-dried foods.

The amount of water that has to be removed from a food in

the process of drying is not as high as one might think. What is important is not the amount of water present as much as the availability of the water within the food. This "availability" is known as the water activity of a food and has to be below a certain level in order to prevent the formation and growth of microorganisms. For instance, the semi-moist dog foods that are currently on the market today do not feel or look like the completely dry product that we are used to seeing. This is because not all the water has been removed from these foods. Rather, sugar and salt have been added, which binds the available water so that it cannot be utilized for bacterial growth. The so-called. binding effect is achieved by the use of many food additives, which, by lowering the water activity, produce a very acceptable, safe, and nutritious food. Again, we have a trade-off between nutrition and producing a safe, long-lasting food. If we do not remove all the water, we probably will not destory as many nutrients. By using food additives such as sugar and salt or sorbitol and mannitol (simple sugars), we can bind some of the water that's available and thereby prevent it from being used for bacterial growth.

Irradiation is another method of preservation. Currently, it is not legal in this country, but in certain other countries it is used to stop the sprouting of potatoes and onions, thus preventing spoilage and deterioration.

The fourth method of controlling or destroying microorganisms is "changing other environmental factors." Remember that bacteria are single cells that grow just as you and I do, only we're made up of billions of cells. And just as we find certain environments harmful to our growth, such as various forms of pollution, bacteria also find certain environments harmful to their growth. Environmental factors have been manipulated for hundreds of years as a means of controlling the quantity of microorganisms in a food material. For instance, fermentation is a microbial process whereby microorganisms grow and produce an environment that is unsuitable to the growth of other microorganisms. This is how beer, hard liquor, and sauerkraut are made. Fermentation gives nonharmful microorganisms an environment in which they can thrive. These microorganisms grow and excrete acid that inhibits the growth of harmful microorganisms. Another means of producing an unhealthy environment for certain microorganisms is changing the acidity of the food product. Acidity is measured in terms of pH. The lower the pH the higher the acidity, and the higher the pH the lower the acidity. It is known that *Clostridium botulinum* will not grow in a food whose pH value is less than 4.5. Therefore acids are added to certain food products in order to decrease the pH to below 4.5, insuring that *Clostridium botulinum* will not grow. These acids are food additives, and quite often they occur naturally: malic acid comes from apples, citric acid from oranges, and acetic acid from vinegar. Many food additives are simply natural compounds added to a food material to prevent the undesirable formation or growth of microorganisms and the subsequent changes or harm they might cause.

Smoking a food is another method of changing the environment so that it inhibits the formation or growth of microorganisms. Smoking is as old as any of the other processes mentioned above. It has been used for hundreds of years as a means of producing meat that is long-lasting, nutritious, and acceptable. The smoke dries the surface of the meat and thereby prevents the growth of microorganisms to some extent. In addition, some of the compounds produced in the smoke inhibit the growth of particular microorganisms. Certainly, the smoking of meat and the barbecuing of steak that is so widely practiced in this country today produces compounds that may be carcinogenic. This is not to scare anyone away from barbecued steaks but merely to indicate that there is a certain risk as well as a certain benefit to enjoying a barbecued steak. Each person must weigh the benefit and the risk involved and then make the choice. We think the risk is so minimal and the benefits so great that we'll continue to enjoy barbecued steaks. However, there are many more carcinogens in barbecued foods than there are in any of the food additives currently used.

Filtration is another method whereby certain microbes are removed from food materials. In some cases, pasteurization of beer is accomplished by filtering the beer so that the microbes and in particular the yeast are left on the filter and the beer passes through. As a result, the beer does not have to be heated prior to canning. This type of filtration has opened the way for several brands of "real draft beer" in cans.

Another method of manipulating the environment is, of course, packaging. Any home canner knows that the way to prevent mold formation on jams and jellies is to pour some hot wax over the top of the preserve. Upon cooling, this wax prevents the oxygen in the air from coming into contact with the preserve and thereby prevents the formation and growth of molds. Vacuum packing accomplishes the same purpose, removing the oxygen by suction or by some other method prior to packaging. Vacuum packing is simply modern technology's way of placing a wax coating on today's foods.

We hope that this chapter, though incomplete in some ways, has given the reader an understanding and "feel" for the techniques used in modern food processing. We also hope that after reading this chapter you'll realize that processing isn't magic, isn't bad, isn't good; it's just another means of preventing the spoilage and deterioration of foods, and the harm that may come to us through spoiled foods. We must process foods because we do not live in a world in which we can grow foods any time we want to. The elements are against us. The growth cycle of foods is against us. Therefore, we must find a suitable means of providing fairly inexpensive, safe, acceptable, and nutritious foods the year around. Undoubtedly, modern technology is giving us these foods. Modern technology has also provided the consumer with many foods that are very convenient to prepare. Prepackaged foods that are ready to heat and serve have liberated certain segments of our society to engage in activities that they feel are more meaningful than household labor. Convenience foods have in some respects provided us with a different kind of domestic help—a better kind, we feel. Not everyone wants to use convenience foods and not everyone should; many people like to cook from scratch and so they should. On the marketplace today, however, there are a wide variety of convenience foods, admittedly at a fairly high price, that consumers may utilize if they so desire in order to spend their time doing things other than cooking. Cooking is a marvelous art and one that should be worshipped by those who wish to follow its path. However, there are those who do not enjoy this art form, and it would be unfair to deprive them of convenience foods in order to satisfy those who decry the use of such materials as being unhealthy for today's consumer. This claim is simply not true and is an injustice to the food industry.

Food processing is necessary in today's world, and it is up to the industry to maintain its integrity in producing safe, high-quality, nutritious foods and in providing us with an ever increasing supply of more nutritious foods.

BIBLIOGRAPHY

Labuza, T. P., *Food for Thought.* Westport. Conn.: AVI Publishing Co. Inc., 1974.

Paddock, William, and Paul Paddock, *Famine 1975! America's Decision: Who Will Survive?* Boston: Little, Brown and Company, 1967.

Stewart, G. F., and M. A. Amerine, *Introduction to Food Science and Technology.* New York: Academic Press, 1973.

chapter **6**

*Food Fads
and Eating Right*

There is no question that what you eat affects how you feel and is thereby an integral part of your health. Food, however, will not provide cure-alls for anyone. An appropriate diet allows people to live up to their genetic potential and feel a sense of completeness about their body, but particular foods do not affect mental well-being or change genetic potential. A person five feet tall will not grow suddenly to seven feet and become a star in the NBA by eating special foods. Magic is much like witchcraft: there is good and bad magic as well as white and black witchcraft. People who believe in food magic feel that certain foods provide good magic and are good for them whereas other foods bestow bad magic and ill health upon

126

them. This concept is entirely false. As we stated in Chapter 2, the best diet is a widely varied diet, a diet that includes all the foods available to us but that stays within certain caloric limits so that we don't become overweight.

FOOD FADS

The desire for food magic has resulted in many food fads, some of which have existed for thousands of years. These are constantly being replaced by new fads or are being revitalized and revived. Different types of food fads exist. The categories we have decided upon, though not a complete list, provide a broad grouping of the reasons for certain eating habits:

1. Philosophical, religious, and cultural fads.
2. Antiestablishment fads.
3. Chemophobia-related fads.
4. Cure-alls and fads for specific disorders.
5. Fads related to weight loss.

There are other reasons for specific diets or changes from a typical cultural diet, but these five categories cover most of the kinds of fads that currently exist in North America. Certain eating habits have been developed down through the ages in other cultures, and since these habits have a cultural and historical background to prove their safety and nutritive value, they have ceased to be fads and are now an accepted part of life.

Philosophical, Religious, and Cultural Fads

The best example of this kind of faddism in the United States is vegetarianism. There are vegetarians in the United States whom we don't consider faddists. These are religious groups or philosophical orders that have a cultural and historical tradition of vegetarianism. They have existed long enough for their adherents to establish a nutritional basis for their diets. These people understand which vegetables to eat together and which combinations of foods to eat in order to obtain high-quality proteins. They know as well that vegetables are deficient in vitamin B_{12}, and they compensate for this by eating certain animal products or taking vitamin supplements. The diets of these people are not faddish. In addition, we do not consider the vegetarianism of Eastern civilizations to be a fad; it is a way of life and one that has long been established. Vegetarianism becomes a fad, and a dangerous one at times, when people decide that tomorrow they will become vegetarians. This decision is made without any cultural or historical tradition and often without any nutritional knowledge. These people may eat the wrong kinds of foods, and their children may suffer as a result of this ignorance.

Another fad that is included in this category is that of organic or natural foods. The organic movement was covered in Chapter 3, which included some discussion of natural foods and of the belief that foods should be eaten as close to the natural state as possible with a minimum of change in the food material. This belief is pertinent in one respect. As we discovered in our discussion of water-soluble vitamins (Chapter 2), there is good reason for not cutting vegetables too small and then boiling them: if the vegetables are cut very small and then boiled, there is more surface area from which the water-soluble vitamins can be leached during cooking.

The zen macrobiotic diet is another fad that falls under this broad category. This diet is not part of the Zen philosophy or religion, but rather was established by a person named George Ohsawa. It is a diet that begins with a fairly broad group of food materials, from which certain foods are slowly excluded until one is consuming only brown cereal grains and a sparing amount of water. From Chapter 2, you should realize that this diet can be extraordinarily dangerous to one's health. Mr. Ohsawa once stated that "a zen macrobiotic person cannot be killed by an atomic bomb." This kind of thinking should warn those considering such a diet that it is not based on sound logic.

It has been found that children who were fed a zen macrobiotic diet by their overzealous parents suffered critical nutritional deficiencies. *Newsweek*, in its issue of September 18, 1972, reported that two such children were tested for bone development. Normally, a child's "bone age" should be within two months of his actual age, but in these tests a two-and-a-half-year-old child showed a bone age of six months and a one-and-a-half-year-old registered three months. Diagnosis showed that both little boys were suffering from severe cases of rickets and scurvy—and that they had been living for months on the zen macrobiotic diet. Neither child could walk or crawl; the older child had a vocabulary of two words and weighed sixteen pounds; the younger just managed to tip the scales at eleven pounds; their hair was coarse and brittle and they were extremely cranky. Ironically, the parents of these youngsters brought them to the pediatrician not because they were concerned about the state of their health but to show the doctor how well the zen macrobiotic diet worked. Concerned friends had tricked the parents into visiting the clinic with their children by telling them that the doctor was interested in zen macrobiotics. The parents refused to abandon macrobiotics altogether, but they finally agreed to give their sons oranges, meat, fish, eggs, and dairy products. After six months the children no longer showed the painful, fragile bones of rickets or the skin eruptions of scurvy, and the eldest had started to walk. Even so, the future for these youngsters is not promising. What is unfortunate about this incident is that the parents were looking for magic from food and ignored the health of their children. Through their own ignorance they have perhaps caused permanent damage.

As we stated previously, we do not consider the cultural and historical tradition of vegetarianism to be faddism, nor do we believe that any of the ethnic or religious dietary concepts that are held by many groups constitute faddism. These traditions have been tested down through the ages, and through education and practical experience healthy diets have developed and become a part of them.

Antiestablishment Fads

Perhaps this section should be entitled "Establishment and Antiestablishment Fads" because certainly both exist. Establishment fads that are not particularly healthy include the tremendous overuse of alcohol in America and a diet of almost totally refined foods, such as soda and sweets. Do not forget, however that soda and sweets are not unhealthy when eaten as part of a varied diet. They are unhealthy only when they become virtually the whole diet of an individual. Weight lifters or other athletes who drink inordinate quantities of milk to the exclusion of other foods are not observing good nutrition either. Nor would it be healthy to eat inordinate quantities of meat to the exclusion of other foods. Remember, a varied diet is a healthy diet.

One antiestablishment fad is overuse of drugs, which seems to be declining in this country. However, the consumption of alcohol, particularly among the young, seems to be increasing along with this decline. Antiestablishment fads also include the organic and natural foods movement and the movement away from processed foods. This type of faddism seems to exclude certain food groups and depend on others. Here is an interesting list prepared by Dr. Frank Konishi, head of the Department of Food and Nutrition, Southern Illinois University at Carbondale. It describes how the daily requirements of certain key nutrients can be obtained from some rather unusual sources.

Nutrient	*Food to Obtain Daily Requirement*
Protein	30 slices of bread, 82 "protein pills," or 40 servings of gelatine dessert
Vitamin A	22 pounds of sunflower seeds
Vitamin E	60 raw eggs
Vitamin C	10 apples
Niacin	36 glasses of beer
Riboflavin	230 tablespoons of honey and vinegar
Thiamine	25 tablespoons of blackstrap molasses
Calcium	68 raw oysters
Iron	45 doughnuts
Iodine	6½ quarts of seawater

Obviously, none of the foods on this list are good sources of the nutrients mentioned, although some people believe them to be. The point of reproducing this list is that there is no single source that can provide us with all the key nutrients. An example of the antiestablishment faddism that gives virtues to some foods and not to others is the popularity of honey. This food is thought by some to be a panacea, yet refined sugar—that is, white sugar—is thought of as a "bad" food. But as we noted in Chapter 2, these compounds are very similar chemically. It is interesting to note how honey is made. Six-legged creatures fly off to heaven knows where and ingest nectar, to which their stomach adds the nonnutritive enzyme invertase, which converts the nectar to invert sugar. The bees then fly back to the honeycomb, where they vomit this material. The rest of the bees wave their wings and thereby dry the regurgitation until it is about 80 percent solid in which state it is packed and sold as honey. Chapter 5, we would hope, points out better ways to dry foods than the waving of bees' wings. And there are better ways to mix and treat foods chemically than in the stomach of an insect. There is nothing wrong with honey; it is a healthy food. But suppose that a food manufacturer went to the government to have such a process approved as a means of making foods for the population of the United States. Do you honestly believe that this process would be approved? We do not think so. The rationale behind favoring certain foods and downgrading others seems to be that anything that nature does is grand, and anything that man does is bad. A ridiculous idea!

Chemophobia-related Fads

For many reasons, including antiestablishment feelings, the work of consumer activists, mistrust in the American food industry and in federal regulatory agencies, and a general misunderstanding of what chemicals are, "chemophobia" (a fear of chemicals) is developing in our nation. This has led to the belief that any processed food is bad, that any food manipulated by man is bad, and that the addition of any chemical to a food is wrong. It should be evident from the previous chapters that foods are simply chemicals, humans are simply chemicals, and the only really scientific reason for eating is to replace the chemicals in the human body with chemicals from food. One can only conclude, therefore, that the addition of chemicals to foods, as long as such chemicals are safe, is at times necessary. Unfortunately, however, scientists have sometimes proclaimed on the basis of very poor evidence that certain foods are bad for health and that the consumer should therefore not eat them. Generally, such beliefs are held by a minority of the scientific community. Some consumer activists, certainly not all, claim that anything the American food industry does is somehow at fault for world starvation—a statement that escapes logical analysis. Dr. Benjamin Feingold has recently written a book stating that food colorants and many food additives are responsible for hyperactivity in children.[1] This is an extraordinarily serious charge, for Dr. Feingold has very little scientific evidence with which to prove the validity of such a statement. Currently, a large amount of research is investigating this claim. It is very hard to believe that food colorants and additives could be the only cause of hyperactivity. Results of this research have been inconclusive and the most they have shown is that further work needs to be done. The Institute of Food Technologists has recently published a review in this area which is very enlightening and shows the inconclusive nature of the charges.[2] Certainly it must be remembered that Feingold is speaking of total diet and hyperactivity, not just food additives, since he recommends the exclusion of twenty-one fruits and vegetables as well as food additives. Certainly there have been very unusual cases in which some food additives have caused allergies in some people, but the vast majority of the population is helped—not hurt—by additives.

Another chemophobia-related fad has led to the belief by many consumers that the consumption of certain foods, such as eggs, butter, and meat, causes heart disease. Granted, some of these products are high in saturated fat and cholesterol, and if one has the potential,

---

[1] Benjamin Feingold, *Why Your Child Is Hyperactive* (New York : Random House, 1975).

[2] Institute of Food Technologists' Expert Panel on Food Safety and Nutrition, "Diet and Hyperactivity: Any Connection?" *Journal of Food Technology,* April 1976, pp. 29–34.

genetic or otherwise, to develop heart disease, one should lower the amount of cholesterol and saturated fat in one's diet. To state, however, that the whole population should restrict their intake of such foods is, we believe, dangerous and misleading to the public. For example, the American Heart Association has suggested that people restrict their intake of eggs to two a week. This advice is illogical to many consumers because eggs are a good food. In order to combat this kind of publicity, the egg industry came out with a rather ridiculous but somewhat amusing advertisement. An egg was pictured with the caption, "the sexy egg," and at the bottom of the advertisement was the statement, "Remember, cholesterol is the building block of sex hormones." We do not believe in this kind of advertising by the food industry, and yet we do not believe in the kind of publicity generated by the American Heart Association's suggestion regarding eggs. We do believe that rationality might temper both of these kinds of inflated information.

Another striking example of the kind of publicity that can create chemophobia-related fads among consumers appeared in the March 11, 1975 issue of the *National Enquirer*. Kurt Oster, a cardiologist in Bridgeport, Connecticut, stated in this issue that axanthine oxidase (XO), an enzyme found in milk fat, is linked with atherosclerosis and heart disease. Oster maintained that when milk is homogenized, XO passes directly through the digestive system and into the bloodstream, where it damages the arterial walls and thereby leads to hardening of the arteries. He believes that simmering milk before drinking it will inactivate the enzyme. The nation's leading research scientists have rejected this hypothesis as implausible, and have refused to back further investigations of it. Yet the *National Enquirer* accorded this concept the banner headline, "Milk is a Major Cause of Death from Heart Attack." The article claimed that a "Harvard Medical School Chief Backs Top Doctors' Warning," but the man quoted, Dr. Kurt Isselbacher, states he was never contacted by the newspaper, spoke to no reporter, and never spoke to Dr. Oster. He said there is "no scientific evidence to my knowledge that a molecule of molecular weight 300,000 is, in fact, absorbed as compared to other, smaller macromolecules," and that "there are no data that axanthine oxidase is absorbed."[3] The *Enquirer* also quoted researchers at the Rush Medical School in Chicago as backing the hypothesis. It turns out that this institution refused an interview with the *Enquirer* on the basis that no data were available. Furthermore, work being done at Rush involves the nervous system and has nothing to do with milk. As far as the hypothesis itself goes, experts in

[3] Press release from the National Dairy Council, May, 1975.

the fields of enzymology, biochemistry, and medicine do not believe that a large protein molecule such as XO can enter the digestive tract and pass through it into the blood without being broken down by the digestive enzymes. Ongoing research on milk's nutritional components has shown that such enzymes are digested in the stomach's acid environment. There are no published data to support the opinion that XO can reach the circulatory system in its original form. We believe it is unfortunate that a scientist and then a newspaper promoted a story that is totally untrue and very misleading to the consumer.

Cure-alls and Fads for Specific Disorders

This is a very common type of food faddism among our population. Some of us take vitamin C to cure the common cold, in spite of recent tests that have shown that vitamin C neither cures the common cold nor prevents its onset. There are some very slight indications that the length of time one has a cold may be lessened though almost imperceptibly, due to the intake of vitamin C. The idea that vitamin C has this curative value was started by Dr. Linus Pauling, a winner of two Nobel Prizes. Dr. Pauling's status lends credibility to this claim. Since it is different when Dr. Pauling sneezes than when you and I sneeze, I am sure that cures that we think we have for the common cold will not receive the banner headlines that Dr. Pauling's supposed cure has.

How many people take vitamin E to increase sexual potency (a completely unfounded belief)? Vitamin E has also been claimed to reduce heart disease and atherosclerosis, a claim that has very little scientific backing.

The list of such fads goes on and on. It is most unfortunate that people are being bilked into taking extraordinarily large dosages of vitamins or other nutrients in order to prevent or cure certain organic disorders that by and large are not curable by the ingestion of food. Although these fads seem illogical, they are followed by many people. Perhaps the reason for this is that it's easy to ingest a food in an attempt to cure a disease; one thinks, "It's worth a try." Unfortunately this kind of cure-all can be extraordinarily dangerous. We know that certain diseases, such as malignant cancers, are recessive. That is, the pain or other effects of a tumor that are noticed by a person may disappear for a short time, only to return again. This does not mean that the tumor is receding or going away, but just that the symptoms disappear for short periods of time. If a person with such a disease eats a certain food at a time when the symptoms are disappearing naturally, they immediately believe that the food is curing them. If the symptoms and pain return, more of the food may be ingested, and if the symptoms go away naturally again, the belief that the food has curative powers is reinforced. When the pain becomes intolerable after a year or so, the person may then go to a physician and find that he has cancer. The physician might then comment, "I could have cured you had you come to see me a year ago." In such a case, the use of food as a cure-all might take a life or irreparably harm someone's health.

Fads Related to Weight Loss

Probably the biggest fads in this country are connected with weight loss. Weight loss is a national obsession, more so than chemophobia. We discussed weight loss in some detail in Chapter 2, but we should state again that weight loss should not be transitory; one's diet should not change every other month. In order to maintain a healthy weight, people should first review all their eating habits and establish for life a healthy pattern of eating—a whole new pattern, if necessary. For example, people must stop rewarding themselves with food, associating food with love, and consuming food whenever they feel bad or good. Eating is an enjoyable experience, but it should be placed in its proper perspective when it begins to affect health in the form of overweight and obesity.

One pattern of eating is typical of all the fads we have discussed in this chapter: the exclusion of certain foods and the promotion of certain foods. In other words, if you want to maintain a certain weight, you eat more of a certain food. This means that you must exclude other foods. There are very sound, scientific reasons for excluding certain foods from the diet at certain times. For example, people who have a history of heart disease in their family, suffer from high blood pressure, and have high cholesterol and high triglyceride levels in their blood should lower their intake of cholesterol and therefore those foods that contain it. People who suffer from hypertension or heart disease should exclude salt or, at most, use moderate amounts of it in their diet. There is also sound scientific evidence for this. But faddism tends to promote the exclusion, or the adoption, of certain foods on the basis of perhaps one or two cases, which does not constitute sound scientific evidence. A person may state that he has ingested a certain nutrient and has thereby been cured of a certain disease. However, investigations of these claims have turned up very little evidence that such cure-alls exist. The scientific community is always aware of such claims and constantly strives to test them in order to prove or disprove their validity. They want cures for the ills of mankind, and they want to find simple cures if these exist. No one, and no sci-

entist we know, is attempting to hide results from the public. Therefore, if someone tells you that a particular diet cures a particular
disease, find out from your physician whether this diet is acceptable
or not.

We have said many times that a good diet for a normal, healthy
individual is one that contains a wide variety of foods. It should be
evident by now that any diet that promotes the exclusion of certain
foods or food groups is an unhealthy diet. You may ask, "But what
about the claims made by some consumer activists and health faddists that the food we eat is unhealthy?" We would reply that some
people seem to base their charges against certain foods on the assumption that most people eat such foods almost exclusively. But
this assumption is untrue. Most people do not eat the same food item
all day long. If they do, they have a tremendously boring diet and
probably psychological problems that should have been treated prior
to any consideration of nutritional well-being. The amounts we eat
of the foods that are available today couldn't possibly be unhealthy.
It is very annoying to see the amount of space in the press devoted to
claims about the safety of foods such as presweetened cereals, candy
bars, and soda when there are many more important issues to concern ourselves with. For instance, approximately 70 percent of the
women in this country and perhaps one third of the children under
six are iron-deficient unless they are taking an iron supplement. And
in a study in Massachusetts in 1969 in which 80,000 public school
children were surveyed by the Department of Education, Bureau of
Nutrition Education, and School Food Services, it was found that only
one out of twenty children ate a good breakfast. These are the kinds of
issues that we believe should be of concern to the food industry and
the scientist. We would like to see the consumer activists push for
the fortification of foods with iron, after determining for themselves
the safety of iron fortification. We would like to see all children eat a
good breakfast, part of which could be one of the breakfast cereals—
even one of the presweetened cereals, which provide key nutrients to
children in a form that the children will eat. It is strange that someone truly interested in the consumer would be upset about a food
that tastes good, that looks good to a child, and that is fortified with
key nutrients that we know the child might be missing, such as iron.
What is wrong with such a food? Seemingly nothing—yet we hear all
sorts of unfortunate claims about the dangers of such foods. These
are not the issues we should be concerned with. We should be concerned with the clear and present dangers to both the children and
adults of this country and the world. World starvation, malnutrition,
and the lack of key nutrients are problems; refined, fortified foods
are not.

The authors do not promote the use of any one food over another. If you want to eat nothing but unprocessed foods, fine, but eat a wide variety of them. If, however, you want to take advantage of some of the convenience foods on the market, by all means use them. They are safe, and you can use them with a clear conscience. Eat a wide variety of such foods, and be certain to include some fresh foods in your diet. If you wish to have a candy bar or a bottle of soda once in a while, by all means have it. Children need calories; at times they don't need other types of nutrients. It is not unhealthy for a child to have candy bars or sodas as long as these are taken in moderation. Most surveys have revealed that most such foods are consumed in moderation. Why all the concern? There is really no good reason for it. A large segment of our population is healthy, and all of us in this country have at our disposal the best food supply that's been available in the history of the world.

WHAT IS A HEALTHY DIET?

This is not a difficult question to answer; we've done it several times thus far in the book. A healthy diet is a varied diet and, because there is so much overweight in this country, a diet that contains perhaps a little less than what we eat now in America. The problem, then, is to find out if our diet is healthy. Checking the composition of one's diet is not really a difficult chore, and everyone should compare their diet with their nutritional needs.

For those of you who wish a simple method of changing your diet, a few general concepts might be helpful. Perhaps the healthiest way to eat is to consume a wide variety of foods but to cut down on your intake of fats and fat-rich protein foods. The reason for this is that Americans generally consume too much fat and too much protein. Therefore, in order to keep your calories down or at least at the same level, you should cut down on fats and fat-rich protein foods but increase your consumption of carbohydrate foods, such as grains, potatoes, fruits, and vegetables. There is no particular need to cut down on your sugar consumption if it is about one third of your total carbohydrate intake. As we noted in Chapter 2, the diet of many Americans is slightly deficient in fiber. The ingestion of more unrefined carbohydrates, such as grains, fruits, and vegetables, will provide the necessary fiber, along with the calories you will need to replace the ones that are lost. Keep in mind also that some Americans have been found to be deficient in iron, vitamin A, vitamin C, and certain B vitamins. You can use nutritional labeling to your advantage by keying in on foods that are high in iron, vitamin A, and B vitamins. In order to obtain your daily requirement of vitamin C, you merely have to drink four to six ounces of an accepted breakfast drink that is either fortified with vitamin C or contains it naturally.

We hope that these few comments will assure you that your diet is a good diet. Minor modifications, however, will result in a much healthier diet for you. Simply cut back on fats and protein, and increase your intake of carbohydrates. This will provide you with a diet that is perhaps more rational than the one you might currently be following. Radical changes from a varied diet should not be made. There is no reason to exclude any food or certain foods from your diet. Eat in health and enjoy what you eat, but make sure you eat a wide variety of food.

DETERMINING THE COMPOSITION OF YOUR DIET

Readers who wish to determine more precisely the composition of their diet may do so after acquiring these two books:

1. *Composition of Foods: Raw, Processed, Prepared*, Agriculture Handbook No. 8, supplied by the Agricultural Research Service, United States Department of Agriculture, Washington, D.C.
2. *Nutritive Value of Foods*, Home and Garden Bulletin No. 72, United States Department of Agriculture, Washington, D.C.

These books are inexpensive and may be obtained from the extension service of your state university or from the Government Printing Office, Washington, D.C.

The following exercise may sound frightening, but it is really quite manageable and the information obtained is well worth your while. For instance, the exercise stops you from fooling yourself about weight control. It also provides you with a "health check" on the adequacy of your diet by enabling you to determine whether you are deficient in any nutrients.

1. Record the following information.
   a. Record all food eaten, using Table 6-1 as an example.
   b. Using Table 2-2, determine your Recommended Daily Dietary Allowance (RDA) for each of the nutrients shown (pages 61 and 62).
   c. Using one of the two books listed above, determine the nutrients that are provided by the foods recorded in Table 6-1, and enter these results in Table 6-2. .
   d. In Table 6-3, record your physical activities during your working hours. Using Table 6-4, calculate the calories you expended in your activities, and record the results in Table 6-3.
   e. Calculate your calorie expenditure during sleep by multiplying your body weight in kilograms (your weight in kilograms is equal to your weight in pounds divided by 2.2) by the number of hours of sleep.

Table 6-1. Record of Food Intake for One Day

Name: _____

Food	Measure	Amount in Grams

Breakfast

Lunch

Dinner

Snacks

Table 6-2. Intake of Selected Nutrients for One Day

Date _____

Food	Weight or Measure	Food Energy cal	Pro gm	Fat gm	Carbo-hydrates gm	Ca mg	Fe mg	Vit A IU	Thi-amine mg	Ribo-flavin mg	Niacin mg	Ascorbic Acid mg
Total Nutrient Intake												

Table 6-3. Estimate of Total Activity for One Day

Time of Day	Form of Activity	Time Spent Hours	Min.	Calories Expended

Total calories expended while awake

Table 6-4. Metabolic Costs of Various Activities, Including Basal
Metabolism and Specific Dynamic Action

Activity	Cal./kg per min.[1]	Activity	Cal./kg* per min.
Archery	.0754	Mountain climbing	.1470
Bicycling on level roads	.0734	Pick-and-shovel work	.0979
Bowling	.0975	Pitching horseshoes	.0518
Calisthenics	.0734	Playing baseball	
Canoeing, 2.5 mph	.0441	(except pitcher)	.0686
Canoeing, 4.0 mph	.1029	Running long distance	.2203
Carpentry	.0564	Running on grade (treadmill)	
Chopping wood	.1101	8.70 mph on 2.5% grade	.2652
Classwork, lecture	.0245	8.70 mph on 3.8% grade	.2803
Cleaning windows	.0607	Running on level (treadmill)	
Conversing	.0269	7.00 mph	.2045
Cross-country running	.1630	8.70 mph	.2273
Dancing, fox trot	.0650	11.60 mph	.2879
petronella	.0681	Shining shoes	.0437
waltz	.0750	Shooting pool	.0299
rumba	.1014	Showering	.0466
eightsome reel	.1000	Sitting, eating	.0204
moderately	.0612	normally	.0176
vigorously	.0831	playing cards	.0210
Dressing	.0466	reading	.0176
Driving car	.0438	writing	.0268
Driving motorcycle	.0531	Sled pulling (87 lb), 2.27 mph	.1242
Driving truck	.0342	Snowshoeing, 2.27 mph	.0835
Farming, haying, plowing,		Sprinting	.3423
with horse	.0979	Stacking lumber	.0856
Farming, planting, hoeing,		Standing, light activity	.0356
raking	.0686	normally	.0206
Farming chores	.0564	Stonemasonry	.0930
Gardening, digging	.1365	Sweeping floor	.0535
Gardening, weeding	.0862	Swimming (pleasure)	.1454
Golfing	.0794	backstroke, 25 yd per min	.0566
House painting	.0514	backstroke, 30 yd per min	.0778
Ironing clothes	.0627	backstroke, 35 yd per min	.1000
Lying, quietly	.0195	backstroke, 40 yd per min	.1222
Making bed	.0572	breast stroke, 20 yd per min	.0704
Metalworking	.0514	breast stroke, 30 yd per min	.1056
Mopping floors	.0665	breast stroke, 40 yd per min	.1408

*Calories per kilogram of body weight.

141

Table 6-4 *(continued)*

Activity	Cal./kg. per min.	Activity	Cal./kg per min.
Swimming *(continued)*			
crawl, 45 yd per min	.1278	Playing pushball	.1122
crawl, 55 yd per min	.1556	Playing squash	.1522
sidestroke	.1222	Playing tennis	.1014
Truck and automobile repair	.0612	Repaving roads	.0734
Volleyball	.0505	Resting in bed	.0174
Walking on level (treadmill)		Rowing for pleasure	.0734
2.27 mph	.0513	4.60 mph	.1212
3.20 mph	.0690	5.18 mph	.1382
3.50 mph	.0733	5.80 mph	.1667
4.47 mph	.0969	Walking downstairs	.0976
Playing football (American)	.1178	upstairs	.2540
Playing football (association)	.1308	Washing and dressing	.0382
Playing ping-pong	.0566	Washing and shaving	.0419

Wilson, Fisher, and Fugua, *Principles of Nutrition*, 2nd ed. (New York: John Wiley and Sons, 1967).

2. Summarize your results as follows:
   a. Add up the amounts of each of the nutrients listed in Table 6-2.
   b. Compare your actual nutrient intake, obtained from Table 6-2, with the U.S. RDA, which you determined in step 1b. This comparison allows you to determine if your daily diet is adequate and, if not, which nutrients you require.
   c. Add up your calorie expenditure while awake, which is recorded in Table 6-3.
   d. Add the total calories you expended while awake (obtained from Table 6-3) to the calories you expended while sleeping (obtained from step 1e). This provides you with a good approximation of your total calorie expenditure. Compare this figure with your caloric intake (obtained from Table 6-2). This step is very important in weight control, since input should equal output for weight maintenance, and input should be less than output for weight loss. Remember, to lose one pound you must expend 3,500 more calories than take in. If your calculation shows that you expend 1,000 calories more per day than you take in, then you will have a deficit of 7,000 calories per week, which will result in a weight loss of 7000 ÷ 3500 = 2 pounds per week.

part **II**

Food Supply

Part 1 of this book deals with food problems as we have come to know them in the United States, where food supply has never been a real problem. This type of security is a luxury in many countries of the world today, which cannot or will not produce enough food for their population. Prior to World War II, many countries were food exporters; today there are only six: the United States, Canada, France, Australia, New Zealand, and Argentina. Over 70 percent of the world's food exports originates in the United States and Canada. The margin of safety in terms of food surplus to feed the world has been decreasing steadily, and as of 1974 the world had a little over one month's supply of excess food.[1] Chances are that famines will become more frequent and more severe in the future.

The capacity to increase food production is a very complicated technological, sociological, and political mix. Food production has been outstripping population growth for the past twenty years, but this overall statistic does not tell the whole story. The developed countries have been increasing their food production rapidly, largely by raising their yield per acre. The developing countries have also been raising their food production, on a per-capita basis, largely by bringing new land into cultivation. This is fine if one doesn't run out of land. Land area is finite, however, and all the land best suited for food production is already being cultivated. As marginal land has to be utilized, the capital costs to bring land under cultivation increase. Eventually, attempts to farm more land become uneconomic, and at that point future increases in food production have to come mainly from increased yields per acre. Can this be readily accomplished? One has to answer yes! But the problems are far from simple. One can attribute American agricultural success to four broad principles, roughly equal in importance: the use of better varieties of plants and animals, the use of more and better fertilizer, the application of better pesticide and crop-protection

[1] L. R. Brown. "The World Food Prospect," *Science* 190, No. 4219 (1975), pp. 1053-59.

chemicals, and increased mechanization. The developing countries can certainly apply the first three principles, but except for small areas of relatively low population they cannot increase mechanization to the level of the United States. For example, in parts of India where the arable land is about one acre per person or less, the adoption of American-style mechanization would displace so many farm workers that the resulting unemployment would be a sociological nightmare. The political consequences are unthinkable. Obviously, the developing countries can mechanize to a greater degree, but labor-intensive countries are probably destined to remain labor-intensive for some time. The adoption of the first three principles is imperative, but this involves considerable technological resources, including sophisticated knowledge and capital. Progress on all four fronts is being made, but too slowly, we fear, to cope with population growth.

Countries with a high population density are experiencing a unique type of migration pressure. The usual pattern is for workers to leave the land and migrate to the cities, since the life is usually easier there. In times of economic distress, a reverse pattern usually takes place, since one can at least be sure of getting enough to eat by returning to the land. In some areas already, however, the population is such that the capacity of the land to produce has been reached, and there is a population "push" instead of the usual "pull" to the cities. Eventually, the people who are pushed may literally have nowhere to go. Such a situation may be compounded by a deliberate governmental policy of maintaining low food prices in order to benefit the urban population This destroys any motivation by rural dwellers to increase food production. Such a scenario precedes more frequent famines and eventual disaster.

The above trend may lead one to think some situations are hopeless, but such is not the case. There are reasons for real optimism. For example, it is estimated that 200,000,000 acres of potentially arable land exist in the Sudan in Africa. If capital can be supplied for irrigation and land development, this territory could become an important source of food. Similarly, vast areas exist in the Amazon valley in South America, a region which has been called the "future bread basket" of the world. Unfortunately, the technology to exploit this land for optimum food production does not exist today, but surely it can be developed.

One author (F. J. Francis) recently had the privilege of traveling over 7000 miles throughout India on a two-month tour of food production and processing facilities as a guest of the Indian government. It was startling to note the complete dependence of the Indians on the monsoon rains for production of both food and electrical power. Since it was the dry season (February and March, 1976) this connection was even more striking, yet there was a food surplus. The rains in 1975 were excellent, but not every year will be as good. The officials responsible for food supply planning in India recognize the problems and know the solutions. They have a cadre of exceedingly dedicated scientists who are encouraging irrigation projects that will grow three crops a year instead of one, as well as the construction of storage facilities for surplus food. Processing facilities are being developed to reduce the dependence on what is now essentially a fresh food economy. Finally, they are approaching the population question in a realistic manner. Since voluntary family planning programs have not worked, compulsory sterilization is being invoked. In April, 1976, Maharashtra State passed a compulsory sterilization law and several other states will probably follow soon. Before one becomes too outraged at this moral philosophy, it should be realized that the moral outrage is a Western luxury. Let no one be under the illusion that population will not be controlled. It will be—the choice is only whether it will be planned or will occur as famines induced by natural disasters.

Obviously, the assurance of an adequate food supply is dependent on a complex interaction of technology, storage, preservation, distribution, capital availability, nutritional considerations, and population policies. Part 2 of this book attempts to deal only with some of the technological concepts of food supply.

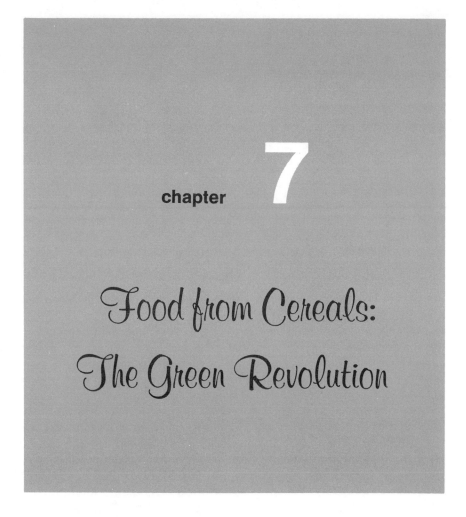

chapter 7

Food from Cereals:
The Green Revolution

The major source of calories for the world's population is the cereal grains. They constitute up to 75 percent of the total calorie intake in some of the lesser-developed countries. There is no question that, directly or indirectly, the cereal grains will continue to supply the major portion of calories in the human diet.

The "Green Revolution" is a general term for a package of technical developments that have doubled or tripled the potential supply of cereal grains. The story reads like a modern miracle, and we need more miracles like this.

WHEAT

Norman Borlaug is known as the father of the Green Revolution. There have been many other contributors, of course, but he was singled out to receive a Nobel Peace Prize in 1970 for his efforts to raise the yield of cereal grains. The story of his life may well inspire other workers who wish to do something significant for mankind.

Borlaug was born on a farm in Iowa in 1914. He attended the University of Minnesota and obtained a B.S. in forestry. He remained at the University of Minnesota to obtain an M.S. and Ph.D. in plant pathology. In 1941, he went to work for the Dupont Company in their fungicide testing laboratory. In 1944, the Rockefeller Foundation asked him to go to Mexico to see what could be done about food production there. To understand just what this charge implied, we should look at the food situation in Mexico in 1944. The country was very poor, with three quarters of the people living on the land. Traditional agriculture was primitive. The land had been worked for over 2,000 years and had received little fertilizer, irrigation, or any other manifestation of what we know as modern agriculture. Farming had a very low social status, and the standard of living for farmers was also very low.

Dr. Borlaug, being funded by the Rockefeller Foundation, was free of any political pressures and of any need to show a profit, or the usual disadvantages of a short-term assignment. Relationships with the Mexican government and the National Agricultural College at Chapingo, near Mexico City, were cordial but distant. If the program was a disaster, this loose association would not discredit the Mexican government. In this unfettered arrangement, Borlaug proceeded to do what he knew best. He surveyed the wheat situation, and decided that wheat rust was probably the limiting factor in holding down the yields per acre. He collected varieties of wheat from all over Mexico and grew them at five locations within the country. Of the many thousands of varieties tested, most were indeed susceptible to the wheat rust diseases, but several were resistant. Painstakingly, Borlaug and his associates made over 30,000 crosses and finally incorporated the resistance to rust into four varieties of wheat that made acceptable flour for bread.

The resistance to rust, important as it was, was overshadowed by another aspect of the wheat-breeding program that Borlaug carried on at the same time: the breeding of wheats that were insensitive to photoperiodism. The photoperiod is the biological clock that tells plants when to bloom and when to produce only leaves.

For example, chrysanthemums grown outdoors bloom only in late fall when the days are short. The blooming process is initiated by the short length of the days. Similarly, poinsettias, a very attractive, red-flowered Christmas plant, will flower only if grown during days that are under nine hours long. If the days are longer, the red "flowers"—actually, they are leaves—will remain green and never turn red. Similarly, a wheat plant with a definite photoperiod will not produce wheat kernels unless the day length is correct. Dr. Borlaug bred the photoperiodism out of his wheat varieties, which meant that a variety could be grown over a latitude of 5,000 miles rather than a belt of 500 miles. It also meant that two or more crops could be grown in the same year.

In 1951 Borlaug had four rust-resistant varieties of wheat, but that same year, race 15B appeared and devastated wheat fields in the United States, Canada, and Mexico. This new race attacked two of Borlaug's rust-resistant varieties. In 1953, a new rust variant appeared and the other two varieties succumbed. The plant breeding research went on, and by 1957, several new varieties had been released and had proved to be rust-resistant. After thirteen years of hard work, the rust problem had been conquered. What had Borlaug accomplished? Seventy percent of the wheat acreage in Mexico had been switched to the cultivation of the new varieties. Borlaug had almost doubled the wheat yield per acre in Mexico, from 11.5 to 20 bushels. Yet the population growth in Mexico was so great that this increase in food production was not enough.

Borlaug began to study wheat production systems in order to determine what was limiting the yield per acre. It was not disease. It was not water. It was not fertilizer. Increased applications of fertilizer to the existing varieties merely made the plant grow tall and spindly, and the wind and rain soon caused the tall plant to collapse into the mud. The increased applications of fertilizer actually reduced the wheat yield. Borlaug decided that the capacity of the plant itself to use fertilizer was the limiting factor. The answer to this problem came from Japan. The Japanese were masters in the art of dwarfing plants, particularly ornamentals known as "bonsai." They had been growing dwarf wheat for seventy-five years. With these dwarf plants, no matter how much fertilizer—or in earlier times "night soil" (a polite term for human waste)—was used, the plants did not grow tall but merely produced bigger yields of kernels. One variety, Norin 10, which had been released to Japanese farmers in 1935, was imported by the United States in 1946 and became part of the ancestry of the famous Gaines variety. Borlaug obtained samples of the Norin wheat in 1953 and proceeded to incorporate its dwarfing genes into his previous selections. The results were amazing.

Borlaug developed varieties that could use three times as much fertilizer (from 40 to 120 pounds of nitrogen per acre) and that yielded two to three times as much wheat per acre.

The new varieties changed the entire concept of growing wheat. In order to exploit the capacity of the new wheats to use fertilizer, a number of other inputs were necessary: an adequate supply of water; pesticide treatments to control insects, weeds, and disease; greater amounts of capital and farm credit; and better equipment for harvesting, cleaning, packaging, and transportation. Probably the most important aspect of the development of high-yielding strains was the motivation it provided the growers. A grower at the subsistence level does not have much latitude for experimentation. One mistake can mean disaster. Developments that promise to raise grain yields by 10 or 20 percent are just not worth the risk. However, a development that promised to double or triple yields certainly provided the motivation for change and it was eagerly accepted. In Mexico, over 90 percent of the total wheat area had been allotted to the high-yielding varieties by 1967, and the average yield was over 30 bushels per acre.

The new varieties were adopted rapidly by other countries. India and Pakistan imported 500 kilograms of the new seeds in 1964 and 600 tons in 1965. During the disastrous famines of 1965/66, they had the cure on their own doorstep and they were quick to capitalize on it. In 1966 these two countries imported 36,000 tons of seed grain, and in 1967 another 40,000 tons. By 1969/70, India and Pakistan had planted over 22,000,000 acres of the new varieties. Both countries had a surplus of wheat in 1971. Never in history had a change of this magnitude been effected so quickly. The story was repeated in Afghanistan, Nepal, Iran, Morocco, Tunisia, Argentina, Chile, Syria, Egypt, Turkey, and many others. In Turkey alone, the acreage devoted to the new wheat varieties rose from 1,500 in 1966/67 to 1,540,000 in 1969/70. In India, the development of the high-yielding wheats started with seed from Mexico, but the early Mexican varieties have nearly all been replaced by varieties that are better adapted to local conditions.[1]

RICE

The development of high-yielding varieties of rice was very similar to that of wheat, except that the time span was longer. The

---

[1] "Imports and Planting of High-Yielding Varieties of Wheat and Rice in the Less Developed Nations," *Foreign Economic Development Report* No. 8, 1971, U.S.D.A., U.S.A.I.D.

story of the development of rice starts in Japan in the late 1800s with experiments to increase the yield of rice by applications of fertilizer. It was found that only the short, erect, stiff-stemmed plants would yield more rice as a result of increased fertilizer. The yield of rice is related directly to the amount of sun the plants are exposed to before they "lodge" or tip over before harvest. When more fertilizer was applied to the conventional varieties of rice, the plants merely grew taller and lodged more quickly, thereby reducing the yield. When Japan turned to occupied Taiwan prior to World War II in order to feed the Japanese homeland, it soon became obvious that the yield of Taiwanese varieties could not be increased by extra fertilizer. The Japanese occupants imported dwarf types from Japan and started to develop varieties that were adapted to conditions in Taiwan. After World War II, when the Chinese regained control of Taiwan, the research continued. By 1956, a variety had been developed that increased the yield by about 50 percent, but few people knew about it.

In the late 1950s, the Rockefeller and Ford Foundations teamed up to share the cost of rice research in Asia. They selected the College of Agriculture at Los Banos in the Philippines as a base of operations, and there they founded the International Rice Research Institute (IRRI) in 1960. The staff started with three Taiwanese semidwarf varieties and by 1966 had produced IR-8, the most famous rice variety of all time. Conventional varieties produced about 1.5 metric tons of rice per hectare (2.47 acres), whereas IR-8 was capable of producing 6 tons under good conditions. The new "miracle" rice, as it was called, could triple the yield, but it was not universally accepted. The chubby, chalky grains tasted different from the conventional rice, and in spite of the promise of instant plenty, consumer resistance developed. Another problem was that IR-8 was susceptible to some diseases. After 1966, however, a number of new varieties were developed that are far superior to IR-8. For instance, they combine disease resistance with acceptable appearance and taste. The stage was set to revolutionize the production of rice in the rice-eating world.

Despite their potential for greatly increased yields, the new varieties of rice have not been accepted as widely as the developers would like. The miracle rice grows best and yields most under ideal conditions, one of which is controlled year-round irrigation. But two thirds of the Asian rice land is dependent on rainfall. Only 25 percent of it is irrigated, and most of that land does not have dependable water supplies. The spread of the new high-yielding rice varieties will depend on the availability of water, fertilizer, and pest-control chemicals. In 1970, the Asian land estimated to be devoted to the new varieties was about 20,000,000 acres. In 1975, it was estimated that about 10 percent of the Asian rice land was devoted to the new varieties.

FUTURE HOPE

The Green Revolution is a striking example of the success of international cooperation and philanthropy. The first truly international research and training institute was the IRRI. It was funded by the Ford and Rockefeller Foundations in collaboration with the Philippine government, and was concerned exclusively with rice. The second such institute was the International Center for Maize and Wheat Improvement (CIMMYT), funded by the Rockefeller and Ford Foundations in collaboration with the Mexican government. Its charge was to improve varieties of wheat, maize, and potatoes. The third center, The International Center of Tropical Agriculture (CIAT), was formed in Colombia. The fourth center, the International Institute of Tropical Agriculture (IITA), was formed in Nigeria. The last two organizations were funded by the Ford, Rockefeller, and W. K. Kellogg Foundations in cooperation with the respective governments. The charge for both institutes was to improve tropical crops and species of animals. More recently, all four institutes have been supported by the U.S. Agency for International Development (AID), the United Nations Development Program, and the Inter-American Development Bank. The first two institutes succeeded so well that six more were founded. Formal leadership of the Green Revolution has now passed from the Rockefeller and Ford Foundations to an international group of nations and foundations known as the Consultative Group on International Agricultural Research. There are now eight international research centers. It remains to be seen whether the most recent six can duplicate the spectacular success of the first two.

Yet in spite of the obvious success of the wheat and rice programs, the Green Revolution has been severely criticized. For example, some say that the rich are getting richer and the poor, poorer. Only the more aggressive, farsighted farmers could take advantage of the potential of the miracle seeds. The cultivation of the new seeds involved irrigation, pesticides, equipment to till the land, farm credit, and so on, so it was only natural that the wealthier and more intelligent farmers would benefit the most. Second, the potential for grain production has made land more valuable, so landowners have attempted to acquire more land and reduce previous owners of marginal land to the status of hired help. Undoubtedly, both claims are true to some extent, but certainly the standard of living has been raised. The tremendous increase in India of tube wells that provide irrigation is evidence that many did share in the increased grain production in that country. Undoubtedly, many farmers, particularly those in the drier areas, are not able to use the new seeds. The third criticism, therefore, is that under these conditions the new seeds may yield even less than the old varieties. This is just not true. Even under poor conditions, including a lack of fertilizer, the new varieties usually outperform the old ones. They do not yield up to their potential, but their ratio of grain to stalk is usually better than that of the old varieties, and this does result in more food. A fourth criticism is that now that three times the quantity of grain can be produced on the same land, it is more economical to grow grain rather than pulses. However, pulses have more and better-quality protein than cereal grains, and if their production goes down, so does the nutritional status of the people.

Some critics of the Green Revolution are even more bitter. They say that the increased use of irrigation water, particularly for rice in the Philippines and wheat in Egypt, has led to an increase in schistosomiasis, sleeping sickness, and other diseases that flourish in water habitats. In Egypt, the Aswan Dam is said to be responsible for a 30 percent increase in schistosomiasis alone. The parasites responsible for this disease use the snail as an intermediate host, and the irrigation water provided by the Aswan Dam is an excellent growth media for snails. The public health aspects of the increased use of irrigation water have probably not been considered as much as the food production aspects, but the health problems mentioned above can be controlled. Even more damning in the eyes of some critics is that population growth has kept pace with food production increases, due to the new technology. We will continue to have population increases, yet do we have another miracle on the horizon? These critics say that it would have been better to allow a smaller number of people to starve without the new technology than to allow the increased population to face inevitable starvation after the Green Revolution has run its course. The authors are not willing to accept this defeatist type of reasoning.

Other critics have said that the stage was set for a disaster such as the world has never seen. In 1970, it was estimated that 44,000,000 acres of the new wheats and nearly 20,000,000 acres of the new varieties of rice were planted. The genetic base for both crops was very narrow. Indeed, the entire acreage for both crops was devoted to a very few varieties, all of which had a common origin. The emergence of a wheat rust or a rice disease that could attack all varieties that contained, for example, the same dwarfing gene could result in a disaster of truly unprecedented scope (see Chapter 13). The scientists responsible for the introduction of new varieties know this, particularly after the devastating corn blight in the United States in 1971, and they have scrambled to broaden the genetic base for both wheat and rice. The supporters of the new varieties have commented that the genetic base of these plants is not as narrow as the critics would have us believe, and that to date there have been no major problems due to a widespread outbreak of plant disease. With each passing year, the danger of famine recedes as more varieties are developed, but the danger can never be really eliminated.

A more compelling criticism of the Green Revolution is that it is a technically sophisticated concept introduced by the developed countries into the developing countries. The technology of irrigation, fertilizer, pesticides, and mechanization requires a great deal of energy and other resources and may eventually be self-defeating for developing countries. They may just be unable to afford it. This may be true if the developing countries attempt to realize the full potential of the Green Revolution, but they can surely use part of the new technology. Full exploitation of the Green Revolution obviously depends on the overall development of the country, and must be accompanied by technological and economic proficiency.

The Green Revolution was never intended to be a panacea. At best, it provided the potential to feed many more people. The yields in most parts of the world are still so low that there is ample opportunity for improvement. The new technology has really been applied only to wheat, rice, and corn. Barley, millet, sorghum, and oats have not been subjected to the same intensive research. Cassava, sweet potatoes, and many other root crops should have the same potential for increased yields. It will be the task of the institutes concerned with tropical agriculture to realize this potential.

BIBLIOGRAPHY

Borlaug, N. E., *The Green Revolution, Peace and Humanity.* Selection No. 35. Washington D.C.: Population Reference Bureau, Inc., 1971.

Paarlberg, D., *Norman Borlaug—Hunger Fighter.* Bulletin PA 969, Foreign Economic Development Service. Washington, D.C.: U.S. Department of Agriculture, 1970.

Sen, Sudhir, *A Richer Harvest—New Horizons for Developing Countries.* New York: Orbis Books, Maryknoll Press, 1970.

——, *Reaping the Green Revolution.* New York: Orbis Books, Maryknoll Press, 1975.

chapter **8**

Food from Animals

Figure 8-1 depicts a rough classification of the world in three ways: population density, areas of hunger, and the green belts. The hunger area is particularly interesting in that it is centered near the equator in an area ranging from 10° south latitude to 30° north latitude. Population is also high in, but not confined to, this area. On the other hand, the "green belt" is a band from 30° to 55° latitude in both the Northern and Southern Hemispheres. Unfortunately, most of this belt in the Southern Hemisphere is ocean. Thus, most of the grain production for human use is grown in the green belt of the Northern Hemisphere.

Why are the hunger areas confined to the warmer parts of the

157

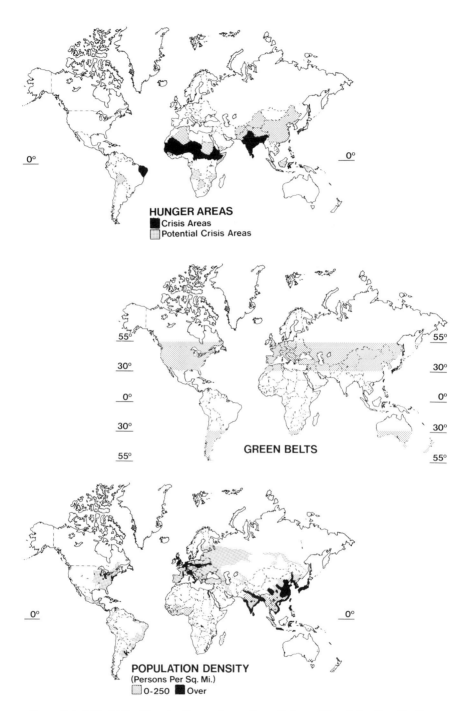

Figure 8-1: A World Plot Showing Hunger Areas, Green Belts, and Population Density. Courtesy Deere and Co., Moline, Ill. From William A. Hewitt, "Famine, 1975," Symposium at Dartmouth College, Feb. 18, 1975.

158

earth north and south of the equator? Is it because these areas do not have an appreciable animal industry, possibly due to an inability to control animal diseases? Perhaps the warmer climate makes the control of plant diseases more difficult. Certainly, it is not a lack of photosynthesis, that creates these hunger areas, since the extra sunshine and temperature make the rate of production of organic matter much greater than in the colder climates. The prevalence of hunger in the warmer climates is not universal, since areas of South America are relatively well fed, but the same areas have low population densities. Whatever the actual reason for the hunger areas, such areas are usually associated with an inefficient animal industry—inefficient because even though seventy developing countries have 60 percent of the world's livestock and poultry, they produce only 22 percent of the world's meat, milk, and eggs. Stated in another way, the developed countries have 21 percent of the cattle numbers, but they produce about 50 percent of the beef and about 50 percent of the milk.[1]

American consumers have developed an insatiable liking for red meat, consuming about 103 pounds per capita in 1971. A liking for red meat is also growing in the developing countries. Apparently, this food preference is related to the level of economic development, at least in countries that do not have religious taboos against red meat. Japan, traditionally considered a fish-eating nation, consumed about 9 pounds of beef per capita in 1974, but the rate of consumption is rising rapidly. In the United States, meat consumption dropped somewhat in the years from 1972 to 1975 primarily as a result of economic constraints, not because of conscious desire. Fortunately, the United States today is able to provide a large supply of meat to its consumers, largely because of a very efficient animal industry. The efficiency of animal protein production has not always existed; it developed during the last fifty years. Table 8-1 shows the improvement in production from 1930 to 1968.

BEEF PRODUCTION

The production of beef in the United States is a highly complex operation. Any efficient high-volume production of beef involves large areas of land. The United States is fortunate in that over ten million acres of land, unsuitable for producing cereal crops, can be used to produce highly desirable animal protein in the form of beef and sheep. Most of this land is too dry for crop production, but even land so unproductive that over twenty-five acres are required to

[1] "The Role of Animals in the World Food Situation." New York: The Rockefeller Foundation. December 1975.

Table 8-1. Improvement in Production of Animal Protein in the United
States from 1930 to 1968

Type of Protein	1930	1968
Annual egg production per hen	121	220
Chicken meat (pounds of chicken/100 pounds of feed)	20	50
Turkey meat (pounds of turkey/100 pounds of feed)	15	28
Annual milk production (pounds/cow)	4,508	9,006
Pork (pounds/100 pounds of feed)	23	32
Beef (pounds/100 pounds of feed)	8	16

W. P. Emslie, *Fifty Years of Livestock Research.* (Hannibal, Mo: Western
Publishing Co., 1970), p. 29.

support one cow can be utilized by efficient range management.
Such management involves maximizing the production of desirable
forage crops and minimizing the growth of brush, weeds, and poisonous plants. Efficient use of the water and shelter available for animals
is highly desirable. Many areas of the world today are so dry that
this is the only feasible type of management for food production.
Problems differ depending on the part of the world. For example,
much of Africa could be used much more efficiently if the dreaded
trypanosomiasis (sleeping sickness) spread by the tsetse fly could be
controlled. In the United States, lands fit only for grazing support
about half of all beef cattle and three quarters of all sheep.

Let us examine the production of the typical steak that we like
to grill on our backyard barbecue. The process starts on the western
plains with the birth of a calf. One cow produces one calf per year. It
would be nice if a way could be found to persuade a cow to produce
more than one calf per year, but so far, no luck. (The fertility pills
show promise, but some problems remain to be solved, particularly
the problem of different sexes among the multiple births.) As of
now, a cow must be maintained on the range for one year to produce
a calf. The calf grows on range forage for six to eight months, at
which time it weighs 400 to 500 pounds. It is then moved to pas-
tures that produce more and better grass than the open range, or it
is shipped directly to the feeding lots. The feeder lots take animals at
400 to 600 pounds and hold them for three to six months, at which
time they weigh 1,000 to 1,200 pounds. The animals are then sent
to the slaughterhouses.

The beef produced in the feeder lots is of top quality and is
usually assigned one of the top three grades (prime, choice, or good).
The main reason for this is that the animal is fed nutritionally balanced rations for optimum growth, such that it reaches slaughtering
size as quickly as possible. Assuming comparable sizes, the younger

the animal, the more tender the meat. In addition, the feeder lots (100 by 200 feet) restrict the movement of the animals to some extent. The animals thereby use less energy in physical activity. Beef from animals that are confined is usually more tender, and the smaller area makes the feeding process less expensive. The feeder-lot operation is usually very large, in order to obtain the economics of large-scale feed purchases. The large amounts of capital involved in such an operation justify utilization of the latest nutrition information, disease control, computerized inventory control, mechanized handling of materials, and so forth. In short, a feeder lot is a very complex agribusiness.

The calves produced for meat production are obviously of both sexes. The female calves are selected to replace the breeding stock, and the surplus are sent to the feeder lots. Nearly all the male calves are used for beef production, since in these days of artificial insemination very few bulls are required to reproduce the species. The male calves are always castrated—by removal of the testes—early in life so that they will be easier to handle. A castrated male animal is called a steer, and nearly all of the beef available on the American market is produced from steers or heifers (female calves). Cows and bulls past their productive years are also slaughtered for meat, but such meat is of lower quality and is not normally found on the retail market, except perhaps as small quantities of hamburger, sausage, and other processed meats.

THE DES STORY

The development of the feeder lot has spurred a great deal of research in optimum animal nutrition, disease control, genetic improvement, and other areas, but one development has backfired in terms of consumer relations. This was the use of sex hormones to produce beef more economically.

The use of sex hormones to improve the efficiency of animal protein production is an interesting story. It starts with the unraveling of the chemistry and physiology of the sex hormones during the 1930s and 1940s. When the structures of the female sex hormone estradiol, the male hormone testosterone, and many similar compounds were determined, it was found that a compound called diethylstilbestrol (DES) could be synthesized and made available at a cost much less than that of estradiol. The compound was very similar in physiological effect to the naturally occurring estradiol, but it was not identical. DES was soon made available in large quantities for physiological research and therapeutic applications. Animal physiologists discovered that DES and many similar compounds, including

Table 8-2. A Comparison of Weight Gain and Feed Efficiency of Bulls and Steers with and without Hormone Treatment

	Steers		Bulls	
	Control	*Treated**	*Control*	*Treated**
Average daily weight gain in pounds	2.25	2.91 (+29%)	6.69	2.73 (+1.5%)
Feed efficiency (pounds of feed/ pounds gained)	6.78	6.26 (+8.3%)	6.14	6.21 (+1.1%)

*The treatment consisted of 10 mg per day of Synovex H in the feed. Synovex H is a trade name for a mixture of the sex hormones, estradiol and testosterone.

R. L. Preston, "Why Hormones for Beef Cattle?," *Ohio Report*, Jan.-Feb. 1972, pp. 8-11.

the naturally occurring estradiol and testosterone, had an effect on the rate of growth of animals and the efficiency of food use (see Tables 8-2 and 8-3). Efficiency in this sense is defined as the weight of food consumed, divided by the gain in weight of the animal. The lower the resulting figure, the more efficient the food use. The poultry producers were the first to exploit sex hormones for feed efficiency. They had been producing "capons" by castrating male chickens in order to make their meat more tender. However, since the testes of a chicken are in their body cavity and not easy to get at, less complex means of castration were obviously desirable. Feeding male chickens a mixture of DES and feed was found to produce a "chemically caponized" bird, which came to be known as a "caponette." In 1947 the FDA approved the use of DES pellets implanted behind the head in the neck of chickens, and the process really worked—it produced tender chickens. Several years later the reactions started. Mink producers who were feeding their animals chicken heads complained that their male minks were no longer breeding adequately. A New York newspaper reported that a restaurant worker who really loved chicken was taking the necks home for his own use. Apparently, some of the DES pellets were inserted too low (we assume he wasn't eating the chicken heads) and were not completely absorbed. At any rate, this man developed female characteristics, including full-sized breasts. With this fascinating instance of public relations, the FDA barred the use of DES in 1959. Actually, this incident was not the reason for the ban; it was due to the Delaney Clause, which prohibited the addition of carcinogens to food. There

Table 8-3. The Effectiveness of DES in Increasing Weight Gain and
Feed Efficiency of Steers

	Control	*Treated* *(20 mg DES per day)*
Average daily weight gain in pounds	2.28	2.86 (+25%)
Feed efficiency (pounds of feed/ pounds gained)	7.24	6.46 (+11%)

R. L. Preston, "Why Hormones for Beef Cattle?" *Ohio Report*, Jan.-Feb., 1972, pp. 8-11.

was evidence that 6.5 parts per billion (ppb) of DES caused tumors in mice. DES was clearly shown to be present in chicken fat and hence was banned.

DES was approved for use with cattle in 1954, but with the proviso that the additive be withdrawn from the feed forty-eight hours prior to slaughter. The rationale for allowing DES to be used in apparent violation of the Delaney Clause was that no residues could be detected in the meat. Analytical methods at that time were sensitive to about 50 ppb of DES. Methods were soon developed that were sensitive to 10 ppb, and then 2 ppb. Finally, a radio-immunology method that could detect DES in parts per trillion was created. In the late 1960s, the USDA laboratories and other laboratories started to find DES in 0.5 to 1 percent of their samples of beef liver, in average amounts of 2 ppb. Some samples were reported to be as high as 37 ppb. The DES was found only in the liver, never in the meat. Two ppb is equivalent to 1½ drops in 25,000 gallons. The FDA extended the withdrawal time for DES from two to seven days, yet minute residues of DES were still detected in livers. This may have been due to the inability of the industry to enforce the withdrawal times.

Public clamor to ban DES developed in the late 1960s, yet the *coup de grâce* was probably due to a completely unrelated event. Three researchers at a Boston hospital reported seven cases of a rare form of vaginal tumor in young women. The only thing the women had in common was that their mothers had participated in an experiment in Chicago from 1950 to 1952. In the 1940s, DES was being prescribed by doctors for women with histories of problems in pregnancy. The Chicago experiment was designed to determine whether DES was of any value in helping women carry a baby to full term. The experiment involved about 1,600 women, of whom half were given 25 to 100 mg per day of DES for their prenatal period and half were given an inactive preparation. Neither the women nor the attending doctors knew who received what. This may seem strange to readers today, but this experiment was conducted before the days of "informed consent." The research did clear up the DES question, since it showed that DES was clearly of no value to high-risk-pregnancy mothers, and physicians stopped prescribing it. Yet thirty years later, a small percentage of the babies born to mothers given massive doses of DES (up to 100 mg per day) developed vaginal tumors. There surely can be no association between the 2 ppb found in 1 percent of beef livers and the massive doses given to the mothers, yet the point was not appreciated in the press at the time. One might also consider that one type of "morning-after" birth-control drug involves two pills per day, each containing 25 mg of DES, for five days—a total of 250 mg. Assuming 2 ppb of DES in liver, these ten pills have as much DES as about 250,000 pounds of liver.

In August, 1972 the FDA banned the use of DES in cattle feed. In April, 1973 the use of DES implants was banned. In January, 1974 the ban was ruled invalid on the basis of a technicality: inadequate hearings had been held. The use of DES is legal today. Very little is being used today because of the likelihood that it will be banned in the near future.

The use of DES is claimed to allow a steer to reach a marketable weight of 1,200 pounds thirty-five days earlier with a saving of about 500 pounds of feed. Other advantages are an increase in the rib-eye area of roasts and steaks, a decrease in the amount of fat developed in the animal, and a decrease in manure production. The savings to the consumer are estimated to be from 3½ to 15 cents a pound for steak at the retail level. Several consumer advocates have asked, "In view of the unknowns, do we really need this saving?" Considering that if one were to eat as a source of protein only the livers that contained 2 ppb of DES, this would be about 1/500 of the amount of hormone produced by a healthy female adult, our answer would be yes!

The use of DES is under a cloud because of the adverse publicity, but other alternatives are open to meat producers. They can use estradiol and testosterone, the naturally occurring sex hormones, and accomplish the same end; but these hormones cost about ten times as much as DES. Yet even with the increased cost, the feeding of natural hormones would result in cheaper meat. However, there is some doubt that a sufficient supply of natural hormones would be available. The beef producers have another alternative. Bulls do not show any increase in growth rate from DES, since they already grow fast and are efficient in feed use. Why not raise bulls instead of steers? An obvious reason for not doing so is that bulls are hard to handle in mixed lots. However, if they are raised in one lot, they are less prone to fighting and can be handled with reasonable care. Another reason is that the American consumers are not accustomed to eating bull meat. Probably the only such meat they have eaten is that of breeding bulls that are slaughtered at an advanced age, a procedure that is guaranteed to produce tough meat. A third reason for not raising bulls is that the meat-grading system has traditionally placed bull meat in a separate category. However, a new class of meat, "bullock beef," became available in 1974. It comprises bulls under two years of age, which are graded in a manner similar to that of steers. Bullock beef is leaner, more variable, and probably tougher than steer beef but otherwise quite desirable.

The production of top-grade beef in feeder lots has been criticized because it requires larger amounts of grain. It is also expensive owing to the recent rise in the price of feed grains. The producers have responded by reducing the time that the animals spend in the feeding lots and increasing the time they spend on the range. In recognition of this decrease in feeding-lot time, the "choice" grade has been changed to include beef with less fat than before. These developments will reduce the cost of beef, produce meat with slightly less fat—which may be good for the American consumer prone to heart disease—and make the beef slightly tougher. There is also a movement to market more cattle that are range-fed according to the European methods of beef production. Beef from range-fed cattle is even leaner and tougher, primarily because these cattle take a much longer time to reach marketable size. In the future, we will probably see more beef in this category marketed in the United States.

The beef industry, and the American consumer as well, have been criticized on the grounds that beef production requires much grain that could be fed to humans. This is partially true but hardly realistic. The grains that are consumed by humans are primarily wheat and rice, very little of which is fed to cattle. Beef cattle are fed primarily corn. Corn is produced on land that could be used to produce food for humans, but there is no assurance that if Americans did reduce their meat consumption, the released corn would in fact be used for human food. A better case could be made for poultry and pigs, since they do compete for food that humans can consume. On the other hand, cattle on the range do not compete with humans. The suggestion is often heard that one pound of meat represents ten pounds of grain, implying that this is all it takes to produce a pound of meat. This simplistic approach is not realistic. A truer picture would be that a one-pound steak represents 300 pounds of grass, 18 pounds of grain, and 3 pounds of protein supplement. This is based on the assumption that a 1,000-pound steer would consume about 10,000 pounds of grass, 2,500 pounds of grain, and 400 pounds of protein supplement, and would produce about 130 pounds of steak. Another 30,000 pounds of grass, or other roughage, would be required to maintain the mother cow for one year. Obviously, a steer produces more meat cuts than just steak. A 1,000-pound steer produces in all, about 420 pounds of retail meat cuts. Thus, the above figures would be reduced if our calculation were based on a "yield" of 420 pounds of retail meat rather than 130 pounds of steak. That is, one pound of retail meat (out of a "yield" of 420 pounds) would represent less grass, grain, and protein supplement than one pound of steak (out of a "yield" of 130 pounds).

The above calculation depends on the time the animal remains on the range or, inversely, the time the animal spends in the feeder lot. Beef animals grow more slowly on the range because of the way they are nourished. The first stomach, or rumen, of a steer or cow is really a big fermentation vat. The microorganisms in the rumen break down the carbohydrates, fats, and proteins ingested by the animal and use the products for their own growth. The steer then digests the microorganisms as its own source of nutrients. This is why it is possible to feed urea to animals. The microorganisms use this nitrogen to synthesize their own protein, which is eventually digested by the animal. Unfortunately, the amount of urea that can be given the animal is limited, because ammonia is readily produced in the rumen by the action of enzymes on the urea, and this is hard on both the animal and the microorganisms. Simple chemical compounds that release nitrogen more slowly than urea does, such as biuret, show promise of becoming inexpensive sources of nitrogen for the synthesis of protein by microorganisms in the rumen.

There is another fascinating aspect to the operation of the rumen of an animal. One major function of the action of microorganisms in the rumen on carbohydrates such as starch and cellulose is to produce large quantities of simple organic acids, such as acetic, propionic, and butyric acids. The animal utilizes these acids as a major source of energy. The FDA has just approved a new additive (monensin sodium) that increases the production of propionic acid in the rumen at the expense of acetic and butyric acids. This focus on propionic acid shows good sense, because the formation of the other two acids in the rumen is inefficient: energy is lost in the form of carbon dioxide and methane, which the animal excretes by belching. The addition of 30 grams of monensin per ton of feed allows the animal to grow at the same rate with 10 percent less feed, thus saving up to 300 pounds of grain per animal. Just how the additive works is not known at the present time.

Despite the considerable progress already made, there would seem to be room for improvement in the efficiency of feed for animals. The ability of the ruminant animals (cattle, goats, sheep, and others) to convert inedible (for humans) organic matter into highly desirable food will ensure the place of these animals in the food chain.

MILK

The cattle industry has one great advantage in the production of protein from grasses and grains, because the production of milk is a very efficient operation. The dairy cow is the most efficient in converting energy to protein, followed by the chicken and hen in the United States, then the pig, and finally the beef cattle. The efficiency of production doesn't necessarily show in the consumption patterns since, in 1975, about 42 percent of the nation's protein consumption was provided by meat, 22 percent by diary products, and 6 percent by eggs.[2] The American consumer just likes meat.

Milk has been important to mankind as far back as recorded history. Apart from its acceptance as a superb food, it has been held responsible for increasing longevity. Indeed, the ten countries with the highest life expectancy, ranging from Sweden (74.2 years), the Netherlands, Norway, Denmark, Canada, France, the United Kingdom, Switzerland, and New Zealand, to Australia (7.10 years), all consume large quantities of dairy products. Whether this is the main reason for the longevity is debatable, but the fact remains that dairy products are a nutritious food.

A modern dairy farm is a complex operation, streamlined to produce milk as efficiently and economically as possible. This involves the selection over hundreds of years for animals which will produce large quantities of milk. The selection has proceeded to the point where a dairy cow will eat four times its food requirement for maintenance of its body and turn the excess into milk. Obviously the efficiency of the conversion depends on the feed ration for the cow (see Table 8-4). Much higher yields of milk can be obtained, if the rations contain concentrated sources of calories and proteins, namely grains and oilseed protein meal, in addition to forage.

The traditional index of efficiency in the dairy industry has been the total yield of milk and the percentage of butterfat. Unfortunately, this concept is obsolete today, since it is much cheaper to

---

[2] "The Role of Animals in the World Food Situation," New York: The Rockefeller Foundation, December 1975, p. 48.

Table 8–4. Production of Milk by Dairy Cows

Feed	Yield of Milk (lbs./year)
Forage (no feed concentrates)	8,000
Forage + 25% feed concentrates	12,000
Forage + 50% feed concentrates	20,000
Forage + 60% feed concentrates	30,000

produce fats and oils for human use directly from plants rather than use a dairy cow. Butter has only one advantage over margarine, in that butter has a better flavor as a spread and in baked goods. Having conceded that, all the other advantages are on the side of margarine. This situation has convinced some dairy scientists that the emphasis in dairy cattle breeding should be on protein production, not fat. This obvious conclusion has been very slow in adoption, and butterfat production still remains the usual basis of payment to producers.

The production of dairy products has yet another advantage in that the operation is associated with the production of beef. About 30 percent of the beef produced in the United States comes from dairy animals. A dairy cow produces one calf per year, which, if not needed for replacement of the dairy herd, can be sold as a feeder calf for beef production. Feeder calves of both sexes from dairy-type animals are just as suitable for beef production as beef-type animals. Dairy-type animals are also marketed as veal. If they are slaughtered when only a few days old, they are called deacon calves or bob veal. In the United States, calves to be marketed as veal are usually fed whole milk or reconstituted milk for six to eight weeks, at which time they weigh approximately 200 to 250 pounds. In Europe, veal calves are usually marketed at 500–600 pounds. Consumption of veal in the United States is very low, approximately 4.1 pounds per person in 1975.

The efficiency of feed conversion plus the almost universal acceptance of dairy products will ensure the place of the dairy cow in the future food supply.

PORK

Meat from pigs has been an important food for man for thousands of years. Except for people whose religious beliefs proscribe its use (Moslems and Jews), pork is an important food throughout the world. The modern pig is believed to be descended from the European wild boar and the East Indian pig. Pigs were domesticated in

China about 4900 B.C. and introduced into the United States on the second voyage of Columbus in 1493. Apparently they thrived, and salt pork became a mainstay of the early colonial diet.

The raising of pigs in the United States has been described essentially as a means of transforming corn into meat. Corn is the primary carbohydrate and protein feed for pigs, but this diet has to be supplemented by high protein supplements, minerals, vitamins, and medicinal preparations. Actually, pigs will eat almost anything, but for optimum growth they require a balanced diet. In some countries, the pig is a true scavenger and is used as such, but obviously, without the benefit of good nutrition they grow much more slowly. Pigs are monogastric—that is, they have one stomach as compared to cattle, sheep, and goats, which have four stomachs. They cannot use plant roughage containing cellulose as efficiently as the animals with multiple stomachs; thus pigs may compete with man for food. This is literally true, but they also consume materials such as waste products of the fish and meat processing industries which humans may not consider to be very appealing. Also, a small proportion of pigs in the United States are fed cooked garbage. Garbage to be fed to hogs must, by law, be cooked to prevent the spread of a virus disease (exanthema) and a parasite (trichinosis).

The great advantage of pigs is their ability to produce large numbers of offspring and their rapid growth. A good sow can produce two litters of ten piglets each in one year. With good rations, the piglets grow to marketable weight (220 pounds) in five to six months. If overfed—and pigs apparently are quite willing to overeat—they will grow quite fat. In earlier times, lard was a valuable commodity and fat pigs were welcome. However, in the 1930s, when vegetable shortenings became popular, the demand for lard decreased. The animal breeders, recognizing that the American consumer wanted leaner pork, converted the pigs from lard to meaty types. In 1955, packers cut 35 pounds of lard from a 220-pound pig, whereas in 1975, it was only 20 pounds. Research to produce pigs with an even thinner layer of fat around the meat is continuing. There is a limit, however, because it is the layer of fat surrounding the meat that is being reduced, not the fat within the meat (the marbling effect). It is considered undesirable to reduce the fat within the meat because the pork would be less juicy and flavorful. Another factor also contributes to the flavor of pork. The meat of male pigs or boars which are kept for breeding purposes has an unpleasant sex odor described by some as "perspiration" odor. It is due to a steroid compound which is a normal metabolite of the male hormones. Male pigs to be used as human food are castrated at an early age to prevent their meat from acquiring this off-flavor. It is curious that women apparently are more sensitive to this odor than men. The odor may make the pork less attractive, but it does not affect the wholesomeness.

The production of pigs in the United States is becoming a specialized agribusiness operation. Some operators specialize in producing young feeder pigs from brood sows. Others specialize in growing the feeder pigs to marketable size. Others specialize in slaughter and merchandizing. The degree of specialization has not progressed as far as in the production of beef but the trends are similar. With more progress in disease control and waste removal, pork production could become much more specialized.

In 1975, Americans consumed about 54.5 pounds of pork per capita, as compared with 120.1 pounds of beef.[3] Even though consumer surveys have shown that pork is not considered to be a particularly desirable form of meat, it is economical and will continue to play an important part in the American diet.

POULTRY

The production of highly desirable protein in the form of poultry and eggs is the food production success story of the century. America has been the leader in this development, and other countries are starting to use our methods. High-quality poultry meat is available at low cost in the United States, and foreign visitors are amazed at the relatively low cost of what is considered a luxury in some countries.

Poultry production involves mainly two types of birds, broilers and roasters. The difference is one of age and hence size. Broilers weigh up to four pounds, and roasters average six pounds. Broilers and roasters are of both sexes. Some male birds, called capons, are castrated and fed to larger sizes, sometimes up to twelve pounds. The castration does not improve the rate of growth but does make meat of much superior quality.

A typical broiler operation is a highly sophisticated vertically integrated agribusiness. A company usually owns a feed supply business, a chick hatchery, and a slaughtering and marketing facility. The integrator provides chicks, feed, medicinals, and some specialized services to the producer, who usually owns the growing facilities and provides the labor. The integrator usually owns the birds at all times and pays the producer for his services. Sometimes, however, the producer owns the birds. In a typical operation, the

[3] *Meat Board Reports*, March 8, 1976, p. 2. Published by the National Meat and Livestock Board, 444 N. Michigan Ave., Chicago, Ill. 60611.

integrator supplies a given number of day-old chicks to the producer, who feeds them for fifty to sixty days and ships them back to the integrator at an agreed-upon weight, up to four pounds. The premises are then completely free of birds for seven to fourteen days, after which another cycle is started. The all in–all out system is desirable as a means of reducing the spread of disease.

The operation is very efficient in terms of labor, since one person can handle up to 100,000 birds at a time. This necessitates automatic feeding, watering, lighting, ventilation, temperature control, and so forth. Some of the operations are very large in order to take advantage of the economics of scale. This makes it possible and indeed essential to utilize the most recent knowledge of poultry nutrition, disease prevention, rates of growth, cost of alternate sources of feed, and so on. The application of modern science has made the chicken a very efficient feed converter. A four-pound broiler can be produced from eight pounds of feed. This efficiency decreases as the bird ages; for example, about nineteen pounds of feed are needed to produce a seven-pound roaster. The production of roasters and broilers is similar, except for the length of feeding. Broilers and roasters are not to be confused with roosters, which are surplus male breeding stock, and fowls, which are hens over one year of age. Hens which are too old for efficient egg production are marketed as "fowl."

Most broilers and roasters are grown in pens on the floor, each of which contains about 2,000 birds. Another system is being developed in which the birds are grown in cages that become the actual containers that are shipped to the slaughtering plant. The catch-and-transfer operation sometimes bruises the birds, a problem that can be eliminated by the new method. This method appears to be the ultimate in automation.

EGGS

Eggs are one commodity which is accepted almost universally throughout the world; consequently they are important as a source of food. The United States produced 68.7 billion eggs in 1969,[4] which works out to about 340 eggs per person per year. This total number of eggs is nearly twice that of the USSR, the next largest producer. Mainland China is thought to have high egg production also, but no reliable data are available. Consumption of eggs about 1950 was approximately 390 per person per year in the United

[4] U.S.D.A. Foreign Agricultural Service, FPE 2-70, October 1970.

States and has declined steadily. In 1973, consumption was 294 per person.[5] The decline in the later years may be partially due to the association of eggs with cholesterol and atherosclerosis.

The production of eggs prior to World War II was largely a farm-flock business, with the majority of flocks having less than 400 laying hens. Today, production is a highly specialized business with many flocks having 30,000 or more hens and some up to 1,000,000. One of the main reasons for the increase is the development of mechanical equipment to aid the caretaker in feeding, watering, ventilation, egg handling, and litter management. One worker can easily care for a flock of up to 30,000 birds.

Modern egg production is divided into a series of specializations. A small number of breeders supply fertile eggs to the hatchery operators. These in turn provide day-old chicks to the firms producing the pullets that are sold to the laying flock managers. Similar specialists produce the rations which are specially compounded for each phase of the hen's life. Other specialists produce the equipment and housing. Still others are marketers of shell eggs which go to the consumer as shell eggs or in various formulated products. Modern research in disease control, sanitary handling, and poultry nutrition has played a very important part in the success of modern egg production systems.

There are some curious beliefs today about the quality of eggs. One has to do with egg color. In New England, brown eggs are preferred, whereas in the rest of America, white eggs command a premium price. There is no detectable difference in taste or nutritive value between eggs with white or brown shells. Some food faddists would have us believe that fertilized eggs are more nutritious. There is no measurable nutritional difference between fertilized and non-fertilized eggs and it is hard to imagine how one little sperm cell could contribute much nutritive value. Actually, if the embryo is allowed to develop, it may indeed contribute some nutrients, but not many of us would wish to eat a visible embryo in an egg. Others say that "organic" eggs are more nutritious, but there is no scientific evidence to back up this claim. However, regardless of the beliefs, eggs are a well-accepted food and provide high quality animal protein at a low price.

SHEEP

Sheep and lambs have been associated with the progress of mankind at least as far back as 4000 B.C. They are popular in many

[5] "National Food Situation," U.S.D.A. Economic Research Service, May 1974, p. 4.

countries, since apparently there are no religious taboos against them. For example, in India, where Hindus do not eat beef and Moslems do not eat pork, sheep and chickens are popular with the non-vegetarian populace.

Sheep, marketed in the form of mutton for mature animals and lamb for younger animals, have been popular in the United States since their introduction by Columbus in 1493. In colonial times, sheep were highly prized as a source of both wool and meat, and they were able to utilize forage in arid areas that were not favorable for cattle. However, their importance is declining. The introduction of synthetic fibers and the importation of wool from other countries with very large herds of sheep (such as Australia and New Zealand) has led to a decreased demand for American wool. American consumption of lamb and mutton (mostly lamb) in 1945 was about seven pounds per year per person. In 1975, it was about two pounds. At this rate, lamb cannot be considered an important part of the diet. Its production in the United States may decline even further, since imports of both lamb and wool will probably increase.

GOATS

Goats were probably the first animal domesticated by man, since they date back to the New Stone Age. According to the Old Testament, they were very helpful to man, furnishing milk and meat for food, fiber for clothing, and skin for bottles. Goats and sheep are very similar in that they can forage in arid or mountainous areas unsuitable for cattle.

The distribution of goats in America is interesting. Texas has over 90 percent of the goat population, and over 95 percent of the Texas goats are of the Angora breed.[6] Angora goats are grown primarily for their fleece, which is known as mohair. Goat meat tastes much like mutton or lamb and is equally nutritious. However, since they are grown primarily for mohair, goats are not usually fattened as well as sheep; hence the yield of meat is lower. Most goat meat is sold under the trade name of Chevon, but consumption is so low that most consumers would not even recognize the name.

Goats are also maintained as a source of milk. A good doe will supply two quarts of milk per day for ten months. Some produce as much as four or five quarts. Actually, more people in the world consume dairy goat products than cow's milk products simply because goats are more widespread. The consumption of goat milk products in the United States is increasing because they are more

[6] M. E. Ensminger, *Animal Science* (Danville, Ill.: The Interstate Printers & Publishers Inc., 1969, p. 779).

adaptable to small towns and suburbs or low income areas where there may not be enough feed for a cow. Goats are not likely to replace cows in the United States because the labor input per quart of milk is twice as much for goats as for cows.

Consumption of goat's milk in the United States is still very low even though it is a good product. When compared with cow's milk, goat's milk has a higher mineral content and smaller fat globules, and it forms a fine soft curd, thereby making it more digestible. Goats seem to be getting more public attention as a source of milk for those interested in the "back-to-nature" movement, but their overall importance in the food supply at the present time is minimal.

CALCULATION OF MEAT CONSUMPTION

The figures quoted for meat consumption are misleading. For example, the figure for beef is 120 pounds per person per year, but this is the raw carcass weight. When the bones, excess fat, etc., are removed, the figure is reduced to 84.4 pounds. After cooking, it is 41.6 pounds (see Table 8–5). The carcass weight is used by the USDA to calculate production, which can be compared with other foods calculated on the basis of the raw commodity.

However, to a consumer, the carcass weight is not important; it is the weight of food as actually consumed that counts. From Table 8–5 it can be seen that the figure 180.7 pounds of red meat consumed per person in 1975 in the United States results in a cooked weight of 62.9 pounds. This works out to 2.8 ounces of cooked meat per person per day. This is less than half of the 3 to 6 ounces of food from the meat group which is the USDA's recommendation for adequate nutrition. The figure 2.8 ounces translates into about 18 grams of protein. This is a little more than 1/3 of the US RDA for protein (45 g). Nutritional surveys have shown that many Americans

Table 8–5. Consumption of Red Meat in the U.S. in 1975

	Carcass Wt. (lbs./year)	Retail Wt. (lbs./year)	Cooked Wt. (lbs./year)	Cooked Wt. (oz./day)
Beef	120.1	84.4	41.6	1.82
Pork	54.5	43.6	19.2	0.84
Veal	4.1	3.4	1.4	0.06
Lamb	2.0	1.7	0.7	0.03
	180.7	133.1	62.9	2.8

Meat Board Reports, Chicago, IX no. 5, March 8, 1976.

eat more protein than they need. The reason for the discrepancy is that there are many more sources of protein in the diet and that protein consumption is not evenly divided. For example, infants and young children require much less than 45 g per day. Other population groups, such as some older people, possibly for economic reasons, consume less that the US RDA for protein.

BIBLIOGRAPHY

Alternative Sources of Protein for Animal Production. Washington, D.C.: National Academy of Sciences, 1973.

Campbell, J. R., and R. T. Marshall, *The Science of Providing Milk for Man.* New York: McGraw-Hill Book Co., 1975.

Emslie, W. P., *Fifty Years of Livestock Research.* Hannibal, Mo.: Western Publishing Co., 1970.

Ensminger, M. E., *Animal Science.* Danville, Ill.: The Interstate Printers & Publishers Inc., 1969.

Hayes, J., ed., *That We May Eat.* Washington, D.C.: Yearbook of Agriculture, U.S.D.A., 1975.

Schneidau, R. E., and L. A. Duewer, eds., "Symposium: Vertical Coordination in the Pork Industry." Westport, Conn.: AVI Publishing Co., 1972.

Stadelman, W. J., and O. J. Cotterill, *Egg Science and Technology.* Westport, Conn.: AVI Publishing Co., 1973.

chapter 9

Food from the Sea

UNLIMITED POTENTIAL?

Man has always looked to the sea as a source of food, and it has served him well. More recently, many countries have increased their capacity to harvest fish as a source of protein, in order to raise their standards of nutrition. The promise of almost unlimited protein from fish has led many countries to invest heavily in ships to catch and process fish for human consumption. Traditionally, the Scandinavian and other European countries have had a long history of commercial fishing. Lately, the Soviet Union, Japan, East Germany, Poland, Spain, Iceland, Korea, and other countries have joined the fishing fleets in almost every fishing ground in the world. Peru has the distinction of landing the greatest annual tonnage of fish, but nearly all of it goes into fish meal for animal consumption.

In the 1950s and 1960s, the prospects for harvesting fish seemed almost unlimited. This led to many popular articles and books proclaiming that the sea alone could support five or even ten times the population of the world at that time. In theory this may be true, but in actuality we do not have the technology to harvest that many living creatures from the sea in a form usable by man. There may have been grounds for optimism in the increasing fish landings of the 1950s, since in 1950, the world landings of table-grade fish, comprising some thirty species, were approximately 21 million tons. In 1970, the take was estimated, perhaps optimistically, at 70 million tons and was increasing at 8 percent per year.[1] Then the results of overfishing became evident, and in 1973 landings were only 62 million tons. Without more stringent conservation measures, it is likely that the take will go even lower in the future. The 1974 conference on sea law in Caracas, Venezuela did not show much cause for optimism. The Caracas Conference was one of the biggest international meetings of its kind ever held. Five thousand delegates from 150 countries labored ten weeks to come to grips with the problem of anarchy on the high seas. The mimeograph operators generated over 250,000 pages of documents per .day in five "working" languages. The only firm decision resulting from this massive effort was to hold more conferences. The fish conservation area was only one of many important issues, but it was evident that the accepted theory was that the fish are there for all to take. It is obvious that this attitude will have to change, and the sooner the better. The need for international agreements for adequate conservation has never been greater.

The development of vast fishing fleets has had profound political impact. For example, the Soviet Union has built very large fleets of vessels to catch and process fish in all parts of the globe. She probably has over 16,000 fishing vessels. Apparently, the Soviet government decided soon after World War II to divert tremendous quantities of capital to the building of ships that would supply the Soviet people with protein from fish. The United States, on the other hand, put its faith in the development of animal husbandry that would supply protein from red meat. The Soviets have not been particularly successful in developing a beef industry, but they are trying now. In 1962, a short grain crop occurred in Russia and not enough feed

---

[1] L. R. Brown, "The World Food Prospect," *Science*, 190, 4219 (1975), 1053-59. (The United Nations estimate of the 1969 catch was 63 million tons. "World Fisheries Catch." *Comm. Fish. Rev.* 33 (1) 45, 1971.)

grains were available to feed the beef herds. The Soviets reacted by slaughtering a portion of their animal population. In 1973, a combination of weather factors resulted in another short crop. This time, the Soviets did not reduce their number of animals but elected instead to purchase 30 million tons of grain from the United States. The resulting decrease in American supplies in a hungry world was alarming. It resulted in world-wide publicity for grain sales and price rises, and a realization that the margin of food supply in the world was dangerously thin. It was suggested that the bleak forecast of the Paddock brothers in the book *Famine 1975* might indeed have come true.[2]

In January 1976, it became apparent that the Soviet feed grain harvest was a disaster once again. The expected crop of 215 million bushels was reduced to 135 million bushels. There was no way to make up for the 80-million-bushel shortfall. The Soviets contracted to purchase about 30 million bushels, mainly from the United States, but they did not have the transportation system in the interior of Russia capable of handling imports over 30 million bushels. The Soviet animal population was reduced because of the lack of feed. The increased slaughterings produced plenty of meat during the winter, but shortages are to be expected in the spring and summer of 1976. This situation has a curious political moral. In 1972, the Soviets diverted two million tons of their 1972 United States purchases directly to India. In 1976, India had a 10-million-ton surplus of grain and, knowing that the Soviets were short, wanted to repay the 1972 loan. The Soviets refused the payment in grain and insisted on manufactured goods. One interpretation of this decision was that it was politically unthinkable for a world power such as the Soviet Union to accept food from a country such as India.

THEORETICAL PRODUCTION

To one who has sailed the Atlantic or the Pacific Ocean, it may seem incredible that one could attempt to calculate theoretically the production of fish in all the oceans of the world. Yet numerous attempts have been made, albeit with a high degree of uncertainty. One of the more credible concepts was developed by J. H. Ryther. His fascinating proposals have been simplified in the following pages.

---

[2] The Paddock brothers wrote a book in 1966 which created quite a stir. It was one of the most pessimistic of the "gloomers and doomers" and predicted widespread famine in 1975. W. Paddock and P. Paddock, *Famine 1975* (Boston: Little Brown & Co., 1967).

The forecasting of ocean productivity started with the development of a method that used radioactive carbon to measure *in situ* the rate of photosynthesis in plankton (marine algae). Surely, in the calculation of fish production the most basic starting point is the uptake of carbon in the open sea. This technique was used by the research vessel *Galatea* from 1950 to 1952 to measure rates of photosynthesis in marine algae in all the oceans of the world. The *Galatea* made only 194 measurements, one for every 2 million square kilometers, but more recent observations, including 7,000 supplied by the Soviets, have not changed the picture appreciably. The data from this research permit the following conclusions:

1. Carbon fixation in the open sea averages about 50 grams of carbon per square meter per year. The open sea accounts for 90 percent of the surface of the world's oceans.
2. The shallow coastal waters (less than 180 meters in depth) average about 100 grams of carbon per square meter per year. They constitute about 9.9 percent of the ocean surface.
3. A few areas of the world are very productive, averaging 300 grams of carbon per square meter per year. They constitute about 0.1 percent of the ocean surface.

The areas in the last-mentioned category are waters off the west coast of lands that experience prevailing offshore winds—Peru, California, Africa, Somalia, and the Arabian coast. Surface waters in these areas are blown offshore, and the deeper, colder waters that replace them generally have a high content of dissolved minerals, which, together with sunlight, allow the marine algae to grow. Waters with extensive upwelling also exist near Antarctica, but they are not well charted.

Table 9–1 and Figure 9–1 depict the food chain in the ocean. Phytoplankton are the primary organisms in the chain. They average about 0.0001 inches in size and use sunlight and mineral salts to fix carbon dioxide by photosynthesis. The next stage in the chain, the herbivores, averaging 0.001 inches in size, feed on the smaller plankton. The next stage, the first carnivores, averaging 0.04 inches, feed on the herbivores. The second-stage carnivores, averaging less than one inch in size, feed on the smaller carnivores, and so it goes until a stage usable by man is reached. The concept of one size of organism feeding on another is called a "trophic" level. There is obviously an efficiency factor here in terms of growth. This can be visualized by, say, a fish that has reached full growth eating one pound of smaller fish. The full-grown fish does not increase in weight at all, so when it eats fish the efficiency is zero. However, a young growing fish weigh-

Table 9-1. Estimate of Potential Yields per Year at Various Trophic Levels in Metric Tons

	Ecological Efficiency Factor					
	10%		*15%*		*20%*	
Trophic Level	*Carbon*	*Total Weight*	*Carbon*	*Total Weight*	*Carbon*	*Total Weight*
	(Millions of Tons)					
0 Phytoplankton	19000	19000	19000		19000	
1 Herbivores	1900	19000	2800	28000	3800	38000
2 1st Carnivores	190	1900	420	4200	760	7600
3 2nd Carnivores	19	190	64	640	152	1520
4 3rd Carnivores	1.9	19	9.6	96	30.4	304

J. H. Ryther, "Photosynthesis and Fish Production in the Sea," *Science*, no. 3901 (1969), p. 73.

Figure 9-1: Diagram Illustrating Nine Trophic Levels in the Ocean

ing one pound may eat one pound of fish and gain one-fifth of a pound in weight. This trophic level would have an efficiency of 20 percent. In fish populations, which, of course, contain both very young and mature individuals, the efficiency ranges from zero percent to 20 percent and perhaps even higher. The 10-, 15-, and 20-percent levels are accepted averages. At the 10 percent efficiency level, for instance, whenever one fish eats a smaller fish—that is, a fish at a lower trophic level—90 percent of the weight of the smaller fish is lost, returning to the sea in the form of nutrients that go through the carbon-fixation cycle again. Or this 90 percent may merely sink to the bottom if the area is very deep.

Table 9-1 lists the amount of carbon (in metric tons) that is fixed at three efficiency levels and five trophic levels. The tons of carbon are converted to tons of living organisms by multiplying by ten. Table 9-2 lists the average productivity and the total productivity, in terms of carbon fixation, of open ocean, coastal zones, and upwelling areas. As you can see, in the open ocean a mind-boggling amount of carbon is fixed in living organisms. Table 9-3 lists the carbon fixation, the trophic levels required, the growth efficiency, and the total fish production for each of the three ocean areas described in Table 9-2. More trophic levels are required in the open ocean because the primary organisms are much smaller there. In the coastal zones and upwelling areas the primary organisms are larger and tend to grow in clumps, and, hence, some carnivores can feed directly on them. Also, growth is much more efficient in these two areas. For these two reasons, a lower number of trophic levels are required in coastal zones and upwelling areas. In spite of the tremendous quantity of carbon fixed in the open ocean, only 1.6 million tons of fish are produced there. The other two areas provide 240 million tons. The open ocean is a biological desert as far as commercial fishing is concerned. Nearly all fish are produced in 10 percent of the ocean's waters.

The above calculations assume about 240 million tons of fish produced yearly in the world's oceans. Yet production is not the same as harvest. Predators such as birds, tunas, squid, and sea lions probably consume as much as man harvests. The guano birds off the coast of Peru alone are estimated to consume 4 million tons of fish. Also, sufficient fish to reproduce the species must remain in the ocean. Predation and reproduction, then, account for an estimated 140 million tons of fish (see Table 9-4). This leaves an estimated 100 million tons for man to harvest. Fish landings in 1970 were an estimated 70 million tons, leaving a theoretical increase of only 30 million tons. This potential increase is unlikely to be realized with existing technology, since landings have been decreasing since 1970.

The theory described above has been tested in two areas. The area between Hudson Canyon and the southern end of the Nova Scotian shelf is approximately 110,000 square miles. It should produce about 1 million tons of fish. This area did in fact produce about 1 million tons in 1963, 1964, and 1965, but since then production has shown a decline that becomes more serious each year. The theory

Table 9-2. Average and Total Production of Organic Carbon in
Three Types of Ocean Waters

Area	% of Ocean	Area (million square kilometers)	Average Productivity (grams of carbon/m^2/yr)	Total Productivity (million tons of carbon/yr)
Open ocean	90	326	50	16,300
Coastal zone	9.9	36	100	3,600
Upwelling areas	0.1	0.36	300	100
Total				20,000

J. H. Ryther, "Photosynthesis and Fish Production in the Sea," *Science*, no. 3901 (1969), p. 73

Table 9-3. Estimated Fish Production in the Three Ocean Areas Listed
in Table 9-2

Area	Carbon Production (million tons)	Trophic Levels	Efficiency %	Fish Production (million tons)
Open ocean	16,300	5	10	1.6
Coastal zone	3,600	3	15	120
Upwelling areas	100	1½	20	120
Total				24×10^7

J. H. Ryther, "Photosynthesis and Fish Production in the Sea," *Science*, no. 3901 (1969), p. 74

is probably optimistic for this area, since the area is clearly over-exploited. The coastal upwelling area associated with the Peru Coastal Current is the most productive fishery in the world. This area, which comprises 24,000 square miles, should produce an estimated 20 million tons of fish annually, according to the theory. Assuming that this total is divided equally between man and preda-tors, the 10 million tons available to man equals the actual landings

Table 9-4. Estimate of Fish Available to Man

Total fish production	240 million tons
Harvest by predators	70 million
Stock for reproduction	70 million
Available for harvest by man	100 million tons

J. H. Ryther, "Photosynthesis and Fish Production in the Sea," *Science*, no. 3901 (1969), p. 76.

in 1971. In December, 1971 an ecological disaster overtook Peru: anchovies disappeared from the fishery. The disappearance was attributed to the warm "El Nino" current displacing the cold, nutrient-rich Humboldt Current offshore. This had happened before to the Peruvian fishery, but prior to the large expansion of the anchovy fishery for the purpose of producing fish meal. Another possible contributing factor is that the fishery was unable to sustain a yield of 10 million tons per year; in other words, it was being overfished. Peru in 1971 exported a record 2,000,900 tons of fish meal. But regardless of the reason for the disappearance, the theory may again have been optimistic in its prediction of the amount of fish an area should produce. The main conclusion to be drawn from these two examples is that the theory is probably over optimistic, and this should lay to rest the hope of greatly expanded fish harvests.

One way to increase the take of "fish" from the sea is to harvest at at a lower level on the production chain. As you can see from Table 9-1, the harvest of phytoplankton, for example, would be ten times as great as the harvest of herbivores. Such a scheme already exists in the form of Soviet and Japanese attempts to harvest krill in the Antarctic. These small crustaceans, up to one inch in size, can be made into a paste that has an appetizing shrimplike flavor. Japanese experts have estimated that as much as 500 million tons of krill are available. Unfortunately, no technology is available to harvest krill economically. Krill form the basic diet of many whales in the Antarctic, and it might be more economical to allow the whales to harvest the krill and for humans to harvest the whales. This presupposes that the whale harvest will be regulated such that an optimum, or at the very least, a replacement, number of whales will be allowed to live, i.e., a "sustained yield" basis. Authorities from the International Whaling Commission say that this is exactly what is happening. Some conservation groups, however, say that the number of whales is decreasing. The next ten years should indicate which group is right.

Another fascinating way of harvesting krill in the Antarctic

Ocean was proposed by scientists at the Northwest Fisheries Center, Seattle, Washington. They suggested that young salmon be released into the currents that circulate around the South Pole. The releases of young salmon from hatcheries near the tip of South America would have to be timed so that the salmon would make one complete circuit around the pole in two years, or two in four years, and would then return to spawn in their release area. Research is necessary to determine the correct age of the fish at time of release and the correct date of release, since these would be critical for the return of the fish. If the biological clock governing the urge to spawn gave a signal to spawn when the fish were 5,000 miles from the tip of South America, the fish would not return. They would have no place to spawn and would be lost in the open sea. Large-scale hatcheries would be necessary, since southern South America has few rivers and therefore few natural spawning grounds. This would seem to be an excellent way of converting Antarctic krill into a highly desirable human food.

Some people believe that fishing technology still reflects the philosophy of the hunter. They compare the fishing industry with agriculture and note that hunting as a means of food production was abandoned thousands of years ago. We may eventually learn mariculture (salt-water farming), but research and technology are proceeding slowly. Mariculture still provides less than 10 percent of the marine food consumed in Japan, probably the most advanced nation in terms of mariculture. Food production by means of mariculture is very small world-wide. The production of fish by aquaculture (fresh-water farming) is well established but nevertheless constitutes only a very small percentage of the total fish harvest.

FISH PROTEIN CONCENTRATE

The dramatic increase in fish landings after World War II led to a surge of interest in fish protein concentrate (FPC). The need for greater supplies of animal protein was being voiced by the Food and Agriculture Organization of the United Nations and many other scientific groups. FPC seemed to be the answer. Fish were apparently available in unlimited quantities, and they could be made into a bland grayish powder with good nutritional properties that could be incorporated into soups, gruels, bread, noodles, and other foods. Almost every ethnic group consumed some form of food in which FPC could be utilized.

Research in FPC technology boomed after 1945, and over fifty methods of making FPC were proposed. Most of these processes involved solvent extraction, acid or alkali treatments, or mechanical approaches. The solvent-extraction approaches—which generally depended on two solvents, dichloroethane and isopropanol—were most successful. The dichloroethane process was developed by Ezra Levin, who probably deserves the title, "Father of FPC." The process that probably has the most scientific support today is the Halifax method. In this process, whole fish are ground up and the slurry is washed with acidified water. The mixture is then treated with isopropanol in countercurrent fashion. This means that the slurry moves in one direction and the isopropanol solvent moves in the opposite direction. The solvent removes oil, water, and some nitrogenous compounds from the mixture. The isopropanol is then removed from the mixture, and the final result is a practically tasteless creamy-colored powder with a very faint fish odor. Many variations of this product are possible, depending on the type of fish, degree of purity required, and so forth.

One of the latest (1970) entries into the FPC trade is the Astra Nutrition Development Corporation in Sweden, who teamed up with Nabisco, Inc. of the United States to make a high-quality FPC. The two groups intended to merchandize FPC in bakery products and perhaps also in the American school lunch program. They converted a 25,000-ton whaler into a floating factory to catch fish on the high seas and process them immediately into FPC. The process used only fish fillets, thereby ensuring a high-quality FPC with a low ash (that is, fluorine) content, and applied a modification of the isopropanol solvent-extraction method. Apparently, the venture was not successful, and the only FPC used in the United States today is imported from Sweden.

FPC appeared to be a real panacea for the world protein shortage, particularly the shortage in developing nations. But for many reasons, it did not work. Perhaps the most important reason was the shortage of fish. The need for sophisticated technology, available only in countries that did not really need FPC, was another factor. The complicated problems of production, packaging, distribution, government regulations, and local preparation for consumption were not easy to solve. Not the least important reason was that the product could not be consumed alone; it had to be added to something, and this involved the complicated concept of consumer acceptance. Whatever the reasons, there is no appreciable production of FPC anywhere in the world today.

The history of FPC in the United States from a regulatory point of view is an interesting story. Serious research on FPC began in the U.S. Bureau of Commercial Fisheries in the Department of the Interior in 1961. In 1962, the Food and Drug Administration ruled informally that FPC could not be made from fish containing viscera or heads. The premise at that time was that no unwholesome material could be added to food, and surely intestinal contents were unwholesome. There may be some question as to the interpretation of this ruling, since the subsequent processing would certainly remove the unwholesome material. However, the consensus at that time was that in order to be economical, FPC would have to be prepared from whole fish. The FDA decision was a major deterrent to the apparent incentive of American industry to invest time, effort, and money in FPC production. The Committee on Marine Protein Resource Development, appointed to study the situation, reported that FPC prepared from whole hake was safe, nutritious, and wholesome. In 1967, the FDA ruled that FPC could be made from whole hake as long as it contained 75 percent protein and as long as the protein was equivalent in quality to the protein in milk. A further regulation permitted domestic distribution only for household use and stipulated that packages of the product must weigh one pound or less. Bulk use of the additive by food processors would not be authorized unless preceded by the presentation of data demonstrating that the proposed use would not be deceptive to customers. The one-pound regulation was another serious deterrent to the commercial development of FPC.

The first attempt to produce commercial quantities of FPC in the United States took the form of a $900,000 contract awarded by the Agency for International Development to Alpine Geophysical Corporation to produce 970 tons of FPC for Biafra and Chile. A plant was to be constructed by Ezra Levin in New Bedford, Mass. Winter storms, a shortage of hake, and technological problems prevented delivery of the FPC. Only 70 of the 265 tons delivered met the specifications, and the contract was cancelled. In 1970, the Astra Corporation launched a publicity campaign urging that their product—which would easily meet the American specifications, particularly the 100-part-per-million limit on fluorine—be used to satisfy one third of the protein component in the school-lunch program. The price of FPC, approximately $.50 a pound at that time, was encouraging, but the program never came to fruition.

One of the problems with FPC was public acceptance. How can nutritionists persuade the younger set to accept it? One waggish suggestion, attributed to Prof. Harold Olcott of the University of California, was, "Just add a little oral contraceptive, put in a pinch of aphrodisiac, pack it in a Coca-Cola bottle—and make it illegal."

BIBLIOGRAPHY

Rothschild, B. J., ed., *World Fisheries Policy*. Seattle: University of Washington Press, 1972.

Ryther, J. H., "Photosynthesis and Fish Production in the Sea," *Science*, no. 3901 (1969), 72–76.

Shapiro, S., ed., *Our Changing Fisheries*. Washington, D.C.: U.S. Govt. Printing Office, 1971.

chapter 10

Potential Sources of Protein

The world's population currently derives about 70 percent of its protein from plant sources. It is unlikely that the proportion of protein from animal sources will increase in the foreseeable future, in view of the increased pressure on the land for total food production.

It may well be that the future will see more emphasis on total food production and less on the relative importance of protein. However, the past generation has seen great importance attached to improved protein supplies, and hundreds of new protein formulations have been developed for infant and child feeding. This emphasis has stimulated much more research and development in the area of protein than in the corresponding area of carbohydrates and fats. In spite of this research, protein in the human diet will probably continue to be derived primarily from conventional plant and animal sources. A description of these phases of agriculture is beyond the scope of this chapter. Our purpose here is to suggest that there may be something additional, and hopefully better, on the horizon.

PROTEIN FROM SOYBEANS

Because it has been publicized as a possible replacement for animal protein, soy protein has captured the imagination of the American public lately. Americans eat too much meat, we are told, and a partial switch to plant protein would be beneficial. We will probably see a gradual switch to plant proteins for economic reasons if nothing else.

Soy products have traditionally been associated with oriental cooking but in recent years America has dominated the soybean market. In 1973, the world production of soy beans was an estimated 58 million tons, of which the United States produced 75 percent, China 11 percent, and Brazil 8 percent. The United States provides over 85 percent of the world's exports of soybeans.

Soybeans were practically unknown in the United States in 1925, but they rapidly became the second largest plant crop in the United States. Today, they are second only to corn in importance. The reason for this amazing increase in production is that soybeans are a good source of both edible oil and protein. In 1940, in the United States, seven times as much butter, as compared with margarine, was consumed. In 1972, margarine was in the lead by two to one, and nearly 85 percent of American margarine was made with soy oil. The protein portion of the soybean has become the mainstay of the meat and poultry industries. Together with fish meal from Peru, it is the major component of the high-protein animal rations.

It should come as no surprise that with such a large investment in soy protein in the animal industries, major efforts were made to introduce more soy products into the human food chain. A number of products are available today, and their consumption is rising slowly.

Food-Grade Soy Products

Food-grade soy products apart from oil can be conveniently divided into four areas: whole beans, flours, concentrates, and isolates.

Whole Beans   These are used in the United States in very small amounts. They are canned in the immature stage as green beans in the pods similar to conventional green beans. The mature beans are also canned in tomato sauce or ground with water to make a beverage. A milklike beverage can be prepared by making a water extract of the whole beans. Such beverages have been very successful in other areas of the world, but not in the United States. A number of soy-based beverages are sold as formulas for infants allergic to cow's milk, but the volume of such beverages is small.

A considerable portion of the soybean crop is used to make traditional oriental seasonings and high protein foods. Soy sauce is made in the Orient by mixing cooked defatted soy flakes with wheat, inoculating this mixture with *Aspergillus oryzae*, and salting and fermenting it for eight to twelve months. In the United States, soy sauce is usually made by acid hydrolysis. Tofu is made by precipitating the curd from soy milk. Tempeh is made from cooked soybeans inoculated with *Rhizopus oligospores* and fermented for twenty-four hours; the resulting cakelike mass is sliced and fried. There are many other soybean-based foods popular in the Orient, such as dried tofu, kinako, miso, and natto.

Soy Flours   Soy flours and grits are important but relatively unknown items in the United States because they are usually incorporated into other products. The only difference between flours and grits is particle size; flours are ground finer. Both are made in a defatted form, a full-fat form, and any combination in between. Full-fat flour is made by cleaning the soybeans, cracking them to remove their hulls, heating them to minimize their beany flavor and to inactivate their enzymes, and drying and grinding them. Defatted flour is prepared in a similar manner except that after dehulling and crushing, a solvent extraction process—usually with hexane—is introduced to remove the fat. A defatted flour is approximately 51 percent protein, 1.5 percent fat, and 34 percent carbohydrate. A full-fat flour is 41 percent, 21 percent, and 25 percent, respectively. An estimated 500,000 pounds were consumed in the United States in 1971.

Protein Concentrates   Protein concentrates are prepared by removing the water-soluble sugars, ash, and other minor low-molecular-weight components from defatted soy flakes. These components are usually extracted with either water or alcohol. The protein content of the resulting product is usually from 66 to 70 percent. The consumption of protein concentrates in the United States in 1971 was an estimated 25 million pounds.

Protein Isolates   These are prepared from defatted soy flour in essentially two steps. Flour is treated with dilute alkali so that the mixture has a pH of 7–9 and the protein dissolves. The insoluble residues are removed, and the liquid is acidified to a pH of 4.5. The protein precipitates and is filtered off as a curd. The protein can be redissolved, and extruded in any shape or passed through fine nozzles to produce threads that are not unlike nylon. Acutally, the protein threads are produced on equipment very similar to that used to produce nylon threads. A dried bundle of soy isolate threads looks like blond hair. The threads can be bundled together, colored, flavored, and packaged to simulate chicken, ham, scallops, beef, and other foods. The protein content of a typical isolate is from 93 to 95 percent. The American consumption of protein isolates in 1971 was an estimated 25 million pounds.

Uses of Soy Protein

Protein that is incorporated into other foods is generally classified as "functional" or "filler" protein. Filler protein contributes to the protein content of the food, and that is all. Functional protein also contributes to the protein content, but in addition it has some functional value, such as emulsification, fat absorption, water absorption, or texture.

Emulsification   Emulsification is a very important property of soy proteins, which can stabilize both oil-in-water and water-in-oil emulsions. Soy flours, concentrates, and isolates are used extensively in ground meat products such as sausages and wieners in order to make them more stable products. They are also used in baked goods and creamed soups for the same reason. In addition, they can be incorporated as effective emulsifiers in whipped toppings, frozen desserts, simulated ice creams, and confections.

Fat Absorption   Soy proteins have the ability to bind fat in products such as hamburger and sausages, thereby reducing the fat that is lost in the cooking process. The flavors are retained in the fat portion; thus, the products are usually juicier and more flavorful. With products such as pancakes and doughnuts, the soy protein decreases fat absorption. The actual phenomena involved in the ability to decrease fat loss and minimize fat absorption are not well understood at this time.

Water Absorption   Soy proteins absorb water and tend to retain it in finished food products. This is a very useful function in baked goods, pet foods, and simulated meats. The addition of soy protein to macaroni, however, decreases water absorption, thereby producing a firmer, more desirable product. Adding soy protein to hamburger patties decreases their drip loss and produces a juicier product.

Texture   Soy proteins can provide desirable textures to many products. The simplest example of this is the thickening of soups and gravies. The gelling properties of soy protein in sausages and luncheon meats is more complicated but nevertheless effective. The tendency of soy protein to gell upon heating is utilized when, for example, pet foods are put into a can in the form of a slurry. The subsequent heat in the canning process imparts the desired texture to the product.

Functional protein in foods has many other uses, such as cohesion, elasticity, film formation, and color-control aeration. With these obvious advantages, soy proteins are being added to many foods. Soy proteins are also being added as filler proteins to a number of products in order to increase their protein content. They can be added conveniently to almost any homogenized product, such as hamburger, luncheon meats, and chili. They can form up to 30 percent of the protein in the school-lunch program.

The major uses of soy proteins in the human food supply are in the form of flours, grits, and concentrates. These are used for functional reasons and constitute up to 3 percent of the food to which they are added. The use of isolates in the form of textured products has received the bulk of the publicity connected with the replacement of meat by soy products. However the manufacture of textured soy products in the form of threads, or whatever, requires considerable sophisticated processing. Consequently, a simulated chicken meat, for example, is relatively expensive. Such products should enjoy a cost advantage over traditional meat, but the price differential and the ultimate quality of the products will probably determine their degree of success in the marketplace.

Soy beans are never eaten raw. All of the recipes and processes employ either a heat treatment, a fermentation process, or a physical process to purify the product. There are good reasons for this. Raw soybeans contain at least twelve toxic components, which have to be broken down or removed prior to human consumption.

PROTEIN FROM PETROLEUM

The prospect of creating protein by growing microorganisms on petroleum products has captured the imagination of researchers in the past fifteen years. The prospect of obtaining high-quality protein from a factory instead of an animal farm is exciting indeed, and a great deal of research and development effort has gone into this area. It is one of the most promising ideas for food production available at this time.

The concept of making usable protein from microorganisms is not new, but large-scale commercial trials have been attempted only in the past ten years. The researchers at the Massachusetts Institute of Technology coined the term "single cell protein" (SCP) as a general term for protein from microorganisms. The story of SCP began in 1970 when the British Petroleum Company built a 4000-ton-per-year plant in Grangemouth, Scotland and a 20,000-ton-per-year plant in Lavera, France. The Grangemouth plant used simple chemicals from petroleum (specially purified C_{10} to C_{18} alkanes) as food for a yeast, *Candida lipolytica*. The Lavera plant used a petroleum fraction to grow the same yeast but did not include the special purification of the feedstock. Both processes are continuous and require the addition of mineral nutrients, air as a source of oxygen, and mechanisms for removing heat, centrifuging off the cells, and so forth. The Japanese developed an interest in these processes, and at least three firms announced plans to build plants with annual production of up to 250,000 tons per year. The rapid Japanese developments were brought to a halt in 1973 when the spectre of trace residues of carcinogenic compounds was raised by the consumer groups. Nearly all hydrocarbon sources contain very small quantities of carcinogens, such as 3,4, benzpyrene, and about 1 part per billion of these compounds were detected in yeast grown on petroleum fractions. The large-scale programs were delayed until adequate systems could be developed for monitoring public health.

The potential market for SCP was too big to be abandoned, and research shifted to other sources of feed for yeast and also other microorganisms. Practically any source of carbon can be used as a feedstuff for microorganisms. This includes natural gas, methanol, ethanol, acetic acid, sugar, and cellulose. In view of the recent rise in price of petroleum, development emphasis in the production of yeast has shifted to methanol and ethanol. Both are products of petroleum refining, but ethanol can be and is produced in large quantities by fermentation in the beverage industries. Present indications in the United States, Japan, and Europe are that ethanol may be the feedstock of choice. It is apparently preferable to methanol even though it is much more expensive, because traces of methanol are toxic and ethanol is already well established as a human beverage. The use of methanol as a carbon source may receive a real boost if the jumbo plants proposed for the production of methanol for addition to gasoline become a reality. Methanol would then become available in very large quantities at very low prices. The price in 1974 was estimated at 3.34 cents per pound. The use of either methanol or ethanol would eliminate the possible purification processes involved with direct petroleum stocks. The processes based on petroleum were the first-generation pilot plants; the alcohol processes are described as second-generation plants. Economics will determine the third-generation processes.

There is no question that protein from microorganisms will become much more important in the near future. The stakes are big.

It will first be introduced as a major animal food source in most of Europe and Japan, and later as a human food source. A commercial plant for SCP has to produce at least 100,000 tons per year to be economical. The market for fish meal in Europe is estimated at 1,000,000 tons. The United States could use up to the same quantity. Obviously, this quantity of fish meal is not likely to be available, and the difference will be made up from United States soybean meal. The estimate of the market for competitively priced SCP is about 400,000 tons for Europe and the same quantity for Japan. Other countries—for instance, Italy, West Germany and the Soviet Union—have a great need for a high protein animal feed and are building plants. This may be the answer to the Soviet fishing dilemma (see Chapter 9). Obviously, the share of the animal food market being filled by soy meal, fish meal, and SCP meal will be determined by the economics involved, and these may well be to the advantage of SCP. SCP has the advantage of not being subject to the vagaries of nature. The developing countries may build many large pilot plants, but large-scale commercialization in these countries will depend at least in the first stages, on their development of the animal industries. However, with the existing potential to produce animal feed, it is a small step forward to produce protein products for direct human consumption.

The introduction of SCP into the human diet will have to be by way of established foods. It is unlikely that entirely new foods based on SCP will be introduced in the near future. Many studies on the acceptability and nutritional implications of SCP have been performed, and the consensus is that SCP is quite acceptable at levels up to 20 percent of the diet. The incorporation of higher levels will probably require processing that reduces the level of nitrogenous compounds produced by yeast nucleus (nucleic acids). These compounds have a tendency to cause gout in humans. Certainly, the concept of adding SCP to human diets is perfectly feasible.

Criticism has been directed towards the protein-from-petroleum idea on the basis that the world is running out of petroleum. This fear is groundless in the foreseable future, since 2 percent of the current crude oil production would provide enough protein for the world's needs. The time is rapidly approaching when we will not be able to afford burning petroleum.

PROTEIN FROM CARBOHYDRATES

The production of SCP from yeast grown on carbohydrates is a major industry around the world. Nearly all of the SCP produced in this way is used in the animal feed industry, but small quantities are incorporated into the human food chain. There are three major types of SCP produced from yeast: molasses, spent sulphite liquor, and whey.

The production of SCP from molasses, using the yeast *Saccharomyces cereviseae*, is the largest of the three types. Beet-sugar molasses is preferred to cane-sugar molasses because it contains more nutrients, but both are used in large quantities. A conventional fermentation in large tanks, which are optimized for the growth of yeast rather than the production of alcohol, is used. The product is called Primary Dried Yeast.

SCP may also be produced from spent sulphite liquor from the pulp and paper industries. The composition of the sulphite liquor varies with the source of wood and type of process but may average 2 to 3 percent sugar. The sugars are fermented by the yeast *Candida utilis*, which is then recovered as a source of SCP. Considerable sulphite liquor is being dumped at present, and since it is a source of pollution it may become economical to use it instead as a source of food for yeast. Yeast from this source is called Torula Dried Yeast.

SCP may also be produced from whey, a by-product of the production of cheese. The lactose sugar in whey can be fermented by the yeast *Saccharomyces fragilis*, which produces a product called Dried Fragiles Yeast. Much of the whey currently being produced is dumped, again creating a pollution problem. Considerable research has been devoted recently to methods of treating whey to recover high quality milk proteins present in low concentrations in the whey and to use the sugar for fermentation. The problem with this concept is that the cheese plants are usually small and scattered, making collection a problem for large-scale yeast plants. Since less than half of the available whey is now being recovered, there is no doubt that both production of yeast protein and milk protein from this source will increase.

Brewers' yeast is another potential source of SCP. An estimated 100 million barrels of beer would provide as a by-product 25,000 tons of dry brewers' yeast. Less than half of this is currently being recovered.

The production of SCP from yeast by fermentation would be very large if all the existing raw materials were used. For example, an estimated 1,000,000 tons could be made from molasses, 500,000 tons from sulphite liquor, and 400,000 tons from whey. Obviously, this potential is not likely to be realized fully, but these estimates are five times the existing production.

PROTEIN FROM LEAVES

Among novel sources of protein, green leaves have the most potential for production. However, the technology of leaf protein concentrate (LPC) has been slow to develop, and production at the present time is very small.

The basic technology for extracting protein from leaves was developed in Europe, particularly Hungary, in the 1930s and was pursued vigorously by England's N. W. Pirie, who well deserves the title, "Father of LPC." The concept of protein production from leaves received considerable support in England in the early 1940s as a result of the possibility of a food supply blockade during World War II. The International Biological Program from 1964 to 1974 also provided considerable encouragement.

The techniques developed by Dr. Pirie and his supporters were deliberately simple. The assumption was that LPC was needed more in the developing countries, and that sophisticated technology would therefore be inappropriate. The LPC program was divided into production, processing, nutrition, and acceptability. Many types of plants were tested for their ability to produce protein under a wide variety of horticultural and agricultural conditions. Suitable plants were chosen for processing studies.

The plants are pulped and pressed in one operation, which separates the fibrous matter from the green slurry. The green slurry containing the protein is heat-treated, which coagulates the protein, and is then pressed. The final product is a green curd, which can be dried and added to other food products. The curd contains approximately 40 percent protein of good biological value and has become a successful high-protein component of animal feed.

Unfortunately for human purposes, the green crude protein has a bitter taste and an unattractive color. Dr. Pirie, particularly, has developed a series of human food dishes, such as soups and baked goods, that use LPC. It is obvious that they all have to be highly flavored and very dark in color. A safe conclusion is that they have not been particularly well received.

Another approach has been developed in the United States. On the assumption that a dark green, bitter protein preparation has limited appeal, the approach has been to purify the protein. One example of this approach is a process, developed at the USDA laboratories to handle alfalfa leaves. Alfalfa was chosen because alfalfa meal was already well established in the United States primarily as a source of yellow pigment for poultry. In this process, fresh leaves are ground and pressed. The liquid is heated to 60°C; this coagulates the chloroplast proteins, which are filtered off as a green curd. The liquid is then heated to 80°C; this coagulates the cytoplasm proteins, which are filtered off as a gray curd. The resulting liquid, known as "alfalfa solubles," can be dried and, together with the original press cake, sold as animal feed. The protein curd resulting from both pressings is obviously rich in protein and has been developed as a feed for nonruminant animals. The next phase is to purify the protein concentrate from the second pressing even further, in order to create a source of protein for humans. The process described above was commercialized under the trade name Pro-Xan.

Another purification added to the processes described above would introduce a degree of sophistication that might be inappropriate for developing countries, but such a purification would be essential for human acceptability in the United States. There is at present only pilot-plant production of food-grade LPC. Harvesting aquatic weeds, now considered a major nuisance in the South, and processing them as a source of protein is a fascinating idea, but the economics are something else. In spite of its vast potential, LPC is unlikely to make much of an impact as human food in the near future. There may be one important exception. In countries like India where vegetarian diets are common, many foods are greenish brown in color and very highly spiced. Neither the green color nor the bitter taste of LPC would be a disadvantage with these types of foods.

PROTEIN FROM ALGAE

As a source of SCP, algae (*Chlorella*) has received considerable publicity in the press and in the scientific community as another "factory" for protein. Algae can be grown from a very simple inorganic source of minerals plus carbon dioxide from the air and sunlight. Many countries have grown algae in large-scale laboratory setups, but the need for sunlight as an energy source has limited the development of large plants. The use of artificial light in a "factory" to grow algae is far too expensive.

An interesting development in pollution control may make the production of algae economically feasible. In California, considerable research has been done to optimize the growth of algae so that it produces oxygen and removes minerals from sewage effluents. In effect, the algae are being used to clean up the effluent from sewage and other waste disposal plants before this liquid is released into rivers. Ponds ten feet wide, six inches deep, and hundreds of yards long are employed for this purpose, and they are very effective. Sewage is an excellent source of nutrients for algae, and it is one commodity in plentiful supply. The algae are at present being produced as a by-product and are not being utilized. Apparently, the production of SCP from algae is uneconomical at the present time due to the cost of recovery and purification. If the economics change, SCP from algae may be available in large quantities.

Consumption of algae by humans is not new. The Chinese and Japanese have eaten algae as seaweed (*Porphyra, Chondrus,* and several other varieties) for centuries. The natives around Lake Chad in Africa have eaten *Spirulina maxima* since ancient times. *Spirulina maxima* is also produced in large quantities in Lake Texcoco in Mexico. The ocean has been estimated to produce a mind-boggling 20 trillion tons of algae annually—more than 5 tons for each person on the earth today. Unfortunately, the maximum concentration of algae in seawater is about 3 mg per litre, and the minimum considered feasible for harvesting is about 250 mg per litre. Also, some algae are toxic to humans. The red tide (*Gonyaulax*), which periodically causes large fish kills on the Atlantic coast, is a good example. There is currently no known technology for the economical harvesting of algae from seawater. We will have to let the fishes do it for us.

PROTEIN FROM FUNGI

We do not normally consider fungi a source of protein, and probably rightly so. For example, the 120,000 tons of mushrooms consumed yearly in the United States provide about 0.05 percent of the required protein. Fungi are important in the United States, but primarily as flavor enhancers in cheese and condiments. This is not the case in the Orient, where large quantities of fermented products from soybeans, wheat, rice, copra, peanuts, fish, and other foods are produced by inoculation with fungi. Fungi do increase the protein content of foods, particularly high-carbohydrate foods. It is possible to exploit this capability with almost any type of carbohydrate food. For example, the protein content of rice can be doubled by inoculation with a fungus (*Trichoderma sp.*). Manioc roots (cassava or tapioca) have a protein content of about 0.7 percent; after inoculation with a fungus and four days growth, this figure can be increased to 5.7 percent. Sugar cane is probably the most efficient user of sunlight in the plant kingdom. Its photosynthetic apparatus is capable of producing large quantities of carbohydrates (sugar), yet, ironically, some strains actually produce more protein per amount of land than soybeans. The protein in sugar cane is so dilute as to be unusable. However, the carbohydrate in the cane can be the substrate for a fungus capable of producing nearly 3 tons of protein, compared with the 800 pounds produced by an acre of soybeans. White potatoes, sweet potatoes, corn, sorghum, millet, and many other foods are good candidates for this method of increasing a food's protein content. W. D. Gray has proposed that "vastly greater contributions to the world protein supply could be made if the carbohydrate-synthesizing capabilities of the green plants were combined with the protein-synthesizing capabilities of the non-green plants."

Undoubtedly, protein supply can be increased by the above methods, but there is much to be done before the resulting products are likely to be accepted by the Western world. We are not used to eating fungi, except in the form of mushrooms and in cheese, so the flavors would be quite different. There is also a problem of contamination with fungi, which produce toxins. However, existing technology can handle both of these problems.

MISCELLANEOUS SOURCES

Many suggestions have been proposed for the production of proteins for human consumption. For example, cottonseed meal contains high-quality protein, yet it has not been used to any extent in the human diet. The reason for this is that cottonseeds contain a toxic yellow pigment called gossypol. The heat treatment required to degrade the gossypol lowers the quality of the protein. Nearly all the cottonseed meal currently available is fed to cattle, who apparently can tolerate the gossypol content. Animals with one stomach are fed the heat-treated meal. There are two potential solutions to the gossypol problem. First, a new variety of cotton that contains little or no gossypol in its seeds has been developed. Unfortunately, the cotton fibers in this variety are not quite as good as those in the regular varieties, so this important development needs some refining. Second, the USDA laboratories have developed a process (the liquid cyclone process) that removes the pigment glands that contain the gossypol. The final flour contains about 65 percent protein of good biological value. A pilot plant producing 25 tons per day is now in operation. The potential of protein from oil seed is very large, since the current world-wide production of cottonseeds is estimated to be over 100 million tons.

Protein from peanut meal is a good possibility in countries such as India, where peanut meal is in good supply but is used mainly for fertilizers. Animal protein from herds of antelope-like animals in Africa is said to be underutilized. We should develop a type of animal husbandry more suited to them. Insects have been used as a source of food for man for a long time. The giant African snail, a creature about eight inches long, is reputed to be quite tasty and a good source of edible protein. Fried termites, caterpillars, ants, rats, lizards, locusts, bird nests, and, indeed, almost every conceivable type of organic matter containing protein has been utilized by some culture as a source of protein. Our only comment on some of these is that we don't think people are quite ready for them yet.

BIBLIOGRAPHY

Gray, W. D., *The Use of Fungi as Food and in Food Processing.* Cleveland: Chemical Rubber Co., 1970.

Kumar, H. D., and H. N. Singh, *A Textbook on Algae.* New Delhi: Affiliated East-West Press, 1971.

Mateles, R. I., and S. R. Tannenbaum, *Single Cell Protein.* Cambridge, Mass.: The M. I. T. Press, 1968.

Pirie, N. W., *Leaf Protein: Its Agronomy, Preparation, Quality and Use.* IBP Handbook No. 20. Oxford: Blackwell Scientific Publications, 1971.

de Pontanel, G., *Proteins from Hydrocarbons.* New York: Academic Press, 1972.

Wolf, W. J., and J. C. Cowan, *Soybeans as a Food Source.* Cleveland: CRS Press, 1971.

chapter **11**

Improvement of Food by Nutrification

In earlier generations, mankind relied on a varied diet to obtain an optimum nutritional state. This is still a worthy goal, but for several reasons it may not always be feasible. Pressure on the land to produce calories may reduce the choices available in some of the more densely populated countries. In some of the affluent countries, people may choose not to eat a varied diet for religious or personal reasons. In any case, it is of overriding importance that we make the existing food as nutritious as possible. Nature did not make a wheat kernel to nourish man; the primary purpose of the kernel is to create another wheat plant. The nutrients in the kernel necessary to produce a wheat plant are not necessarily the substances that produce optimum human nutrition. It is up to human ingenuity to discover the combinations of wheat kernels and other foods or synthetic nutrients that provide optimum nutrition. This is true for all staple foods.

COMBINATIONS OF FOODS

Combinations of foods for optimum nutrition have been known for thousands of years. Trial and error has probably resulted in desirable combinations of food in every culture. The rice-eating nations combined rice and fish as a source of protein. The fermented fish dishes such as "nuoc mam" and soy sauce in many Asiatic cultures added protein to a largely carbohydrate diet. The addition of milk to oatmeal and cheese to apple pie had the same effect. The combinations of vegetables, starchy roots, and meat in many cultures were balanced for protein and carbohydrates. In modern times the concept of blending one source of food with another has received great impetus from the development of balanced high-protein formulations for infants and children. It is a short step from this to balance the diet with protein, carbohydrates, fat, minerals, and vitamins from many sources. The United States at least is moving rapidly in this direction.

ADDITION OF VITAMINS AND MINERALS

The addition of nutrients to the diet involves four terms:

1. *Enrichment:* addition of one or more nutrients (naturally present in the food in lesser amounts) in order to increase consumption of these nutrients.
2. *Restoration:* addition of nutrients to a processed food to replace nutrients lost during processing.
3. *Fortification:* addition of nutrients that may or may not be naturally present in the food in order to increase consumption of those nutrients by the general population or a segment of the population.
4. *Nutrification:* a general term for the addition of nutrients to food.

The first three are legal terms as clarified in the proposed FDA regulations on nutrition-quality guidelines.[1]

The addition of vitamins to foods became possible after the exciting research in the 1930s, during which nearly all of the vitamins were discovered and synthesized. Today, all of the vitamins necessary for human nutrition can be synthesized except vitamin B_{12}, which

[1] *Federal Register,* June 14, 1974.

has a particularly complex chemical structure. Fortunately, this vitamin can be extracted as an inexpensive by-product of the mold used in the preparation of the antibiotic streptomycin. Most of the vitamins can be produced very inexpensively. For example, vitamin C costs less than a cent a gram. This paved the way for the addition of vitamins to many foods. Since minerals have always been relatively cheap, they were also added as human biochemical needs became evident.

The earliest addition of vitamins to food was probably the retoration of thiamine and riboflavin to white bread in the 1930s. Calcium and sometimes iron were also added. In 1941, legislation in the United States required the addition of thiamine, riboflavin, niacin, and iron to white flour and bread. The discovery by Steenbock in 1924 that vitamin D could be made by irradiating ergosterol from yeast was a nutritional milestone. It obsoleted the foul-smelling and even worse tasting cod liver oil that every schoolboy of that age hated. It became feasible to add vitamin D to milk, which already had a good supply of calcium and phosphorus. This one development practically eliminated rickets as a childhood disease. The addition of vitamin D and vitamin A to milk became widespread in the 1930s and 1940s.

The low cost and easy availability of vitamins led to another development, one that may not be quite as desirable. The widespread promotion of vitamin pills and vitamin and mineral tonics became a fixture of American life. Undoubtedly, they have helped the nutritional status of the nation, but their promotion may have been overdone. Many people have consumed more vitamins then they can possibly use. Except in the case of vitamins A and D, which can be toxic if taken in excess, probably the only harm involved is an economic loss. Perhaps even this is compensated for by the psychological importance of thinking that one is actually doing something for one's health.

The availability of low-cost vitamins and minerals has led to another interesting phase of American life. We have seen the development of a large number of specialized formulations designed primarily for infants. The social movement against breast feeding in past generations led to a sizable market for milk substitutes. These were balanced for protein, carbohydrate, fat, mineral, and vitamin content according to the best nutritional information available. Some experts in infant nutrition think that the complexity of the formulation and the modification of the nutrients has perhaps been overdone, but on balance the infants have unquestionably been better nourished. The variety of infant formulations may be startling to the uninitiated, but if anyone doubts their effectiveness, they should compare them with the infant diets available in the 1920s. One can obviously make a case for the nutritional advantages of breast feeding, but in these days of freedom of choice for women there will always be a place for human milk substitutes. By the same reasoning, there will always be a market for prepared baby food, in spite of some fanatics who urge women to prepare their own baby food from raw materials in the marketplace. Some women aren't quite ready for that yet.

The nutrification of baby food led to the next logical step in nutrification—formulated complete breakfasts for calorie-conscious adults. By drinking one can of liquid, one can be assured of a food intake of known calorie content and a balanced content of all required minerals and vitamins. The protein and fat content can be adjusted to any desired level and, in the case of fat, to any desired ratio of saturated to unsaturated. Another example of this type of formulation is the cakelike preparations that can be consumed at any meal. They have the same nutritional characteristics as the liquid breakfast preparations. The cakelike preparations have not yet received widespread acceptance, perhaps because their satiety value may be too high; one just cannot eat much of them. It is too early to assess their acceptance yet, but they may be a preview of things to come.

ADDITION OF PROTEIN

The nutrification of food by the addition of protein received considerable impetus from the intense effort to develop and introduce high-protein foods for infant and child nutrition in the era from 1950 to 1970. Protein malnutrition had been touted as the primary nutritional problem in many of the developing countries, particularly those in the warmer climates. Efforts to develop high-protein foods were not aimed at the adult population, since it was obvious that many adults ate cereal grains with practically no extra source of protein and were healthy. An adult can subsist on the protein obtained from an adequate supply of cereal grains, but infants and children cannot. They need food with a higher ratio of protein to calories in order to enjoy optimum growth. This is not to say that adults cannot also profit from protein beyond that obtained from cereal grains. Their nutritional state will be better for it.

The improvement of protein in cereal foods can be accomplished in several ways. One can add synthetic amino acids to increase the amount of the essential amino acids that are limiting[2] in the particular cereal. One can also add a small quantity of a food rich in protein, such as milk powder, fish protein concentrate, soy protein concentrate, yeast preparations, and many others. One can also judiciously blend one cereal product with another, such as a legume preparation, making a mixture in which the protein in one food helps balance the protein in the other. A classic example of this technique, adapted from research at the Institute for Nutrition for Central America and Panama, is illustrated in Figure 11-1. This shows the results of blending corn flour with soybean flour. The left side of the bottom line shows a mixture of 100 percent corn and zero percent soy, the right side represents zero percent corn and 100 percent soy, and the points in between represent blends of the two. The left-hand scale represents the rate of weight gain of rats fed mixtures of corn and soy. The right-hand scale represents the PER (protein equivalent ratio; see Chapter 12) value for the same mixtures of corn and soy. Corn meal alone promotes a low rate of weight gain and has a low PER because it is low in lysine. On the other hand, soy meal alone, although better than corn, is not optimum because it is deficient in methionine. A mixture of 40 percent corn and 60 percent soy provides the optimum growth rate and the highest PER obtainable with these materials. This mixture is better than either corn or soy alone because the amino-acid makeup of the two supplement each other. If the amino-acid makeup of any type of cereal grain and any type of legume is known, it is possible to calculate which mixtures will be superior to either one alone. If the ingredients are correct, this can be a very good way of using the existing protein supplies more efficiently. All cereals are low in lysine. Corn is also low in tryptophan. Wheat and rice are low in threonine as well as lysine. Legumes and oil-seed proteins generally, but not always, complement the cereal grains. This is probably an oversimplification; any prospective combinations should be checked by animal feeding studies. But the theory is appropriate. This concept has been used very effectively in the development of a wide variety of food formulations for infants and children in the developing countries, since it has the major advantage of utilizing foodstuffs available locally.

It is possible to improve the nutritional value of food mixtures such as the above, or for that matter of any carbohydrate source, by

---

[2] An amino acid is said to be limiting when it is present in amounts below the optimum for human growth. In this case, humans cannot use the remaining amino acids to synthesize protein. If the limiting amino acid is supplied, protein synthesis can go on until another amino acid becomes limiting. Amino acids not used for protein synthesis are used as a source of calories.

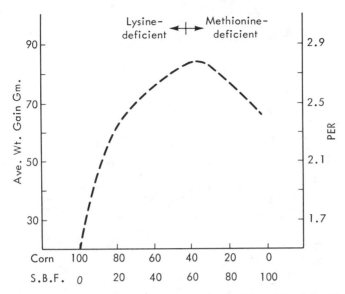

Figure 11–1: From M. Milner, ed., Protein Enriched Cereal Foods for World Needs *(St. Paul: American Association of Cereal Chemicals, 1969), p. 57.*

adding synthetic amino acids or high-protein supplements. Table 11-1 compares the cost of fortifying cereal grains such that the protein in the final mixture has a biological value equal to that of casein. For example, the addition of 0.45 percent lysine and 0.18 percent threonine at a cost of 0.12 cents per pound would raise the protein value of millet and sorghum to that of casein. The addition of 4.65 percent fish protein concentrate at a cost of 1.16 cents per pound would accomplish the same thing. The addition of 7.0 percent soy-meal protein at 1.05 cents per pound would do the same. Obviously, in this last case it would be cheaper to add lysine and threonine. Similarly, it would be cheaper to add lysine and threonine to wheat, or lysine and tryptophan to maize, to accomplish the same aim.

Another example of fortification is shown in Table 11-2. Lysine is the limiting amino acid in wheat flour, and the addition of 0.2 percent lysine markedly improves the flour's biological value and hence the utilization of the protein in it. This is strictly true only if there is no other source of protein in the diet, but in marginal diets the protein would undoubtedly be better utilized. The same effect could be obtained by adding fish flour, and the increase in protein utilization would be more than the mere addition of the fish protein.

Table 11-1. Cost of Fortifying Cereals Such That Their Protein Content Will Have a Biological Value Equal to That of Casein

Cereal	Amino Acids Required	Amount Required (%)	Cost (¢/lb)	Fish Protein Concentrate (%)	Cost (¢/lb)	Soy Protein Concentrate (%)	Cost (¢/lb)
Millet or Sorghum	lysine threonine	0.45 0.18	0.12	4.65	1.16	7.0	1.05
Wheat	lysine threonine	0.30 0.15	0.53	3.10	0.77	4.7	0.71
Maize	lysine tryptophan	0.20 0.35	0.27	2.05	0.51	3.1	0.47
Rice or Barley	lysine threonine	0.20 0.10	0.35	2.05	0.51	3.1	0.47

M. Milner, ed., *Protein Enriched Cereal Foods for World Needs* (St. Paul: American Association of Cereal Chemicals, 1969), p. 200.

Table 11-2. Improvement in Nutrition Value When Lysine and Fish
Flour Are Added to Wheat Flour

Product	Protein (%)	Relative Nutritional Value of Protein (%)	Utilizable Protein (%)
White flour	14	24	3
White flour + 0.2% lysine	14	38	5
White flour + 5% fish flour	17	42	7

M. Milner, ed., *Protein Enriched Cereal Foods for World Needs* (St. Paul: American Association of Cereal Chemicals, 1969), p. 42.

The addition of synthetic amino acids or protein concentrates is undoubtedly effective in raising the biological value of cereal proteins, but it is not without some technical problems. For example, the addition of methionine in excess creates an undesirable flavor in some products. Some protein concentrates are not completely bland, and consumers may not like the flavor. These problems are not too serious, however, and can be solved by appropriate formulations. A more serious drawback is that both synthetic amino acids and protein concentrates are usually products of sophisticated technology, which may not be available where it is needed. The alternative is to import these additives, but this, of course, requires capital and foreign exchange.

Unfortunately, a large proportion of the world's population has to rely on protein from plants rather than animals, simply because of the finite supply of animal protein. The concept of animal versus plant protein for human use is complex. Perhaps a simple albeit macabre example will help. The best protein supply available for a young growing boy is his twin brother. However, eating one's twin is not socially acceptable. The next best alternative for the boy is to eat his brothers or sisters. Again, this is hardly acceptable. The next best source is from animals. If these are not available, the boy must rely on plants as a source of protein. However, the further one moves away from humans and toward plants, the less similar and therefore the less appropriate the source of protein for human nutrition will be. It is up to the ingenuity of man to seek new protein sources, to devise processes for extracting protein from various sources, and to calculate the optimum combinations of protein—in other words, to make the best possible use of the available protein for human consumption.

GENETIC ENGINEERING

The improvement in the biological value of the protein in cereal grains may be accomplished more effectively by changing the genetic makeup of the plant. This is not usually referred to as nutrification, but the result is the same.

The corn plant in the United States is probably the outstanding example of genetic engineering, for many reasons. Not the least of these is the development of hybrid corn. As a cereal, corn, or maize, is very old. Corn cobs have been found in caves in Mexico that date back 5,600 years. Corn pollen has been found in drill cores dated over 80,000 years old. The early varieties of corn were all open-pollinated, and the changeover to hybrid corn had profound effects on American corn production. From 1936 to 1966, the yield per acre increased 300 percent and acreage decreased 25 percent. Corn became the major cereal crop in the United States, with three times the production and twice the dollar value of wheat. It also became a major factor in the production of red meat and poultry.

The protein content of corn and the possibilities for increasing its protein content yield some startling figures if one realizes the volume involved. For example, the 1974 corn crop in the United States was 4,651 million bushels. At fifty pounds to the bushel, this is about 116 million tons. Assuming that corn is 11 percent protein, this represents 12 million tons of protein. If one could develop varieties of corn with even 1 percent more protein, over one million tons of protein per year would be added to the American supply. This occurred to a group of researchers at Urbana, Illinois in 1896, and they started to select corn varieties with a higher protein content. In 1961, after sixty-five years, they had indeed increased the protein content of one variety (Illinois High Protein) from 11 percent to 25 percent. However, this variety was never accepted in commercial quantities because the biological value of its protein was inferior to that of regular corn. What they had done was to increase the zein content. Zein is one of four types of proteins found in corn, but it has a very low biological value, being very deficient in both lysine and tryptophan. If a corn could be produced with less zein in the kernel and more of the other three types of proteins, its biological value would be superior to that of conventional varieties.

A genetic breakthrough occurred in 1964 when Dr. Edwin T. Mertz at Purdue discovered the "opaque-2" gene. This gene was so named because the corn kernels that contained it looked opaque rather than translucent and flinty like normal kernels. It was fortunate that the kernels did look different, because this provided a simple visual marker with which to follow the subsequent development of the opaque-2 characteristics in corn varieties. It was soon discovered that the opaque-2 kernels had twice as much lysine and twice as much tryptophan as normal kernels. The nutritional potential of this finding was obvious. Research on incorporating this gene into commercial corn production was given a high priority, but commercialization was not easy. The opaque-2 gene is recessive, and yields of opaque-2 corn were 8 to 10 percent lower than the yields of conventional varieties. The gene also produced grain with a 20 percent higher water content. Commercial production of opaque-2 started in the United States in 1969.

Another genetic breakthrough occurred in 1965, when Dr. Oliver E. Nelson at Purdue discovered another gene which also increased the proportion of lysine and tryptophan. He called this gene "floury-2." It was distinct from the opaque-2 gene because it was carried on another chromosome. Research designed to incorporate both genes into one variety has been partially successful. The lysine and tryptophan content in the new variety is higher than that in either opaque-2 or floury-2. No commercial varieties of this hybrid have been released to date, but it is only a matter of time until this is done.

The potential of high-lysine corn as an animal feed is shown in Table 11-3. The pigs fed high-lysine corn grew three-and-a-half times as fast and were twice as efficient in feed utilization. A dramatic advantage such as this is obvious only if corn is the only source of protein in the animals' diet. This is usually not the case. It may be more efficient to reduce the other sources of protein, such as fish meal or soybean meal, and increase the corn. The fattening of animals by grain feeding is a sophisticated computer-controlled operation accompanied by careful cost analysis in many large agri-businesses in the United States. If an overall benefit can be demonstrated, high-lysine corn will be used, in spite of its higher cost.

High-lysine corn is currently being used to feed animals in the United States. However, the acceptance of high-lysine corn in human nutrition is encountering much more difficulty. Nutritionally, it is obviously better. But in many communities corn is corn, so why should one pay a higher price for a new variety? Probably the only ways that high-lysine corn will be introduced in many corn-consuming cultures is through government subsidies of school lunches, infant formulations, or national legislation. The recent experiments in which South American children were fed high-lysine corn are very

Table 11-3. Rate of Growth of Young Pigs Fed Normal
and High-Lysine Corn

Feed Efficiency	Normal Corn	High-Lysine Corn
Pounds of feed/pounds gained	7/1	3.3/1
Rate of growth*	1	3.5
Weight gain of 35-day-old pigs after 130 days	7 lbs.	73 lbs.

*The rate of growth on normal corn is arbitrarily given a value of one, and other treatments are referred to this control.

D. D. Harpstead, "High-Lysine Corn," *Scientific American*, 225 (1971), p. 38.

promising. It would be a real triumph for nutrition education if high-lysine corn were to replace conventional corn in the human diet. In the United States perhaps we should make high-lysine popcorn.

FUTURE POSSIBILITIES FOR GENETIC IMPROVEMENT

The discovery of genes that improved the protein quality in corn for human nutrition set off a research race to do the same thing for other crops. In 1973, scientists at Purdue announced the discovery of a gene in sorghum that increased the total protein content in that plant by 30 to 40 percent and doubled the lysine content. Sorghum is the "poor man's corn," in that it will grow on land that is too dry for corn. Sorghum is the principal cereal for over 300 million people, and the new discovery is of great potential benefit to them. This type of genetic breakthrough has not been found yet in the other major cereal crops, such as wheat, rice, rye, barley, and millet. Wheat and rice have been the subject of intense genetic research, but this research has been concerned primarily with yield and resistance to disease. The other grains have lagged behind. The major carbohydrate crops, such as cassava in the tropics, have been virtually untouched by this type of research. The benefits of genetically improving such crops are great, but cassava, for example, is such a poor protein source that it may be more efficient to grow it only as a source of carbohydrates. Perhaps we should explore both avenues.

One may well ask why the emphasis in genetic improvement is on protein. The answer is probably that protein has been judged to be the most important nutrient. Cereal grains are already excellent sources of carbohydrate, so the genetic research there has been to change the type of carbohydrate. One gene in corn called "waxy" produces a corn with a high content of amylopectin. Amylopectin is a type of starch with a highly branched structure, which makes the starch more easily digested or fermented. Another gene in corn produces amylose, a starch with a long straight-chain structure. Amylose is ideal for spinning into fibers or forming into cellophane-like sheets. It can be made water-soluble, or insoluble, permeable to oxygen, and even with great shock resistance. The film that is made from it is superior to many films on the market. And it is edible: one could eat an amylose package as well as the food in it if one wanted to overlook the sanitary problems.

Corn has also been subjected to genetic research on oil type and content. For example, the Illinois experiment on the original Burr White variety, which lasted sixty-five years for research on protein content, was also used for oil research. After sixty-five years of selection, the oil content had been raised from 4.7 to 16.5 percent, and a variety called Illinois High Oil was produced. However, as the oil content went up, the yield went down, so this variety was never accepted commercially.

The composition of the oil in corn seeds would seem to be very important because of the association of saturated fats with heart disease. Apparently, it was purely a matter of chance that corn with a high content of the desirable linoleic and oleic fatty acids and less of the less desirable linolenic acid was developed. There has been little research on changing the chemical composition of the oil by genetic means. This is probably because there has been little reason to do so, since the present makeup is considered good—that is, high in "polyunsaturates." If a more solid fat was desired, it could easily be produced from corn oil by the chemical process of hydrogenation.

There is plenty of room for genetic research designed to improve the nutritive value and other characteristics of many of the world's food crops, but such research is slow and difficult. The scientists who discovered high-lysine sorghum estimate that it may take eight to ten years to develop appropriate commercial varieties. Genetic research may represent many man-years of sophisticated effort, often for meager returns. But the stakes are high, and once achieved, the results—except, of course, for disease resistance—are usually permanent. There is also much room for genetic selection. Man uses very few of the 250,000 known species of higher plants. There has been only one new cereal grain introduced in recent history. This man-made grain, triticale, is a cross between wheat and rye. Triticale produces higher yields than either wheat or rye and it also has a high content of protein. Research on producing an acceptable bread from triticale has been slow, but the pace has increased in the past ten years. Undoubtedly, triticale will take its place among the major cereal grains of the world.

BIBLIOGRAPHY

High-Quality Protein Maize. New York: John Wiley & Sons (Halstead Press, 1975).

Inglett, G. E., *Corn: Culture, Processing, Products.* Westport, Conn.: AVI Publishing Co., 1970.

Scrimshaw, N. S., and A. M. Altschul, *Amino Acid Fortification of Protein Foods.* Cambridge, Mass.: The MIT Press, 1971.

chapter **12**

Nutritional Labeling

Impact

on Nutrification

The food nutrification program received a real stimulus in 1973 with the passage of the nutritional labeling laws in the United States. This is an indirect effect, since these laws were passed for other reasons.

The nutritional labeling legislation is an outgrowth of efforts to make information on nutrition and food composition more available to the consumer. This in itself is a worthy aim, since it really was difficult for the average consumer to judge just what nutrients a food does contain. It was even more difficult to interpret the significance of some of these nutrients. This situation was not helped by the wealth of misinformation being promoted by a series of popular periodicals and books. Some of these have a very wide circulation and cater to popular interest by being sensational without having to be accurate. With this background, it was very difficult for a consumer to judge food content and nutritive value. The nutritional labeling laws were designed to help with at least part of this dilemma—the determination of nutrients in a food.

The nutritional labeling laws in the United States became effective on July 1, 1975, and they are very specific as to the information that must be stated on the label:

1. The serving size and the number of servings per container.
2. The calorie content to the nearest ten calories per serving.
3. The protein content to the nearest gram per serving, and also as a percentage of the RDA (Recommended Daily Allowance; see page 217).
4. The carbohydrate content to the nearest gram per serving.
5. The fat content to the nearest gram per serving.

The serving size is determined by agreement between the manufacturer and the FDA authorities. Some examples are obvious—for instance, one muffin—but others such as catsup, are less so. The concept of serving size has generated considerable discussion but no real problems. The calorie and carbohydrate content can be determined by standard analytical methods.

PROTEIN CONTENT

The protein content is a real problem, in view of the difficulties in describing protein quality. The final compromise was to allow an RDA of 45 for protein if the PER of the protein was equal to or greater than that of casein, a high-quality milk protein. If the protein quality of the food was lower than that of casein, the RDA was 65 grams. If the PER of the protein was 20 percent, or less of the PER than that of casein, no label declaration could be made. The PER (protein equivalent ratio) is a simple measure of protein value. It is determined by feeding food containing the protein in question to a group of young growing rats. The weight gain (in grams) and the protein fed (in grams) are determined, and the ratio—weight gain divided by grams of protein—is the PER. A similar group of rats is fed casein and a PER is determined. This value for casein is arbitrarily set at 2.8, and the PER for the protein under question is adjusted accordingly. The PER is the simplest but not necessarily the best method of establishing protein quality. The overall solution to the problem of labeling protein as a percentage of the RDA is a compromise of many complex considerations, but it is probably one of the best compromises available.

FAT CONTENT

The fat content was the subject of considerable discussion, in view of the importance of the quantity and type of fat in diseases involving the circulatory system. If a manufacturer wishes to make a nutritional claim for fat—i.e., concerning saturated and unsaturated fat—the amount of saturated fatty acids (no double bonds) must be stated in grams per serving. The amount of unsaturated fatty acids in grams per serving must also be stated. These two statements cannot be used if the food contains less than 10 percent fat or 2 grams per serving. This seems reasonable, because if nutritional claims for fat are to be made, the food should have a reasonable content of fat. The cholesterol content may also be stated in grams per serving. If either fatty acids or cholesterol, or both, are stated, the label must have the following disclaimer: "Information on fat (and/or cholesterol, where appropriate) is provided for individuals who on the advice of a physician, are modifying their total dietary intake of fat (and/or cholesterol, where appropriate)." This disclaimer may have about the same degree of success as the medical disclaimer on packages of cigarettes ("Warning: The surgeon general has determined that cigarette smoking is dangerous to your health"). Another concession with health implications is that the sodium content in milligrams per serving may also be stated on the label. Excessive sodium intake in the form of table salt (sodium chloride), or in any other form, has been implicated in high blood pressure.

VITAMINS AND MINERALS

The listing of fat, protein, and carbohydrate in terms of grams per serving is easy to understand but the method of stating vitamin and mineral content was more difficult. In the early discussions, several methods were examined in great detail and with some emotion. The decision was to use the United States Recommended Daily Allowance (U.S. RDA). These units were based on the National Academy of Sciences–National Research Council Recommended Dietary Allowances (NAS/NRC RDA). The latter units were first determined in 1941 and have been revised seven times. The latest revision appeared in 1974 (see Table 2-2, pp. 61-63). The NAS/NRC RDA values represent the best nutritional information available on the daily intake of vitamins and minerals needed to maintain good health. The NAS/NRC RDA replaced the older and obsolete Minimum Daily Requirements (MDR), which were based on the minimum intake necessary to prevent deficiencies and related illnesses. The NAS/NRC RDA recommendations were broken down into a number of categories, such as age, sex, lactation, and pregnancy, and obviously involved too much detail to be declared in the limited space available on a label. Consequently, the U.S. RDA values (see Table 12-1) represent a selection (usually the highest of the NAS/NRC RDAs). The choice of U.S. RDA units for label declaration is a good one, even though the reader cannot determine the actual content of vitamins and minerals from the label. However, reference to Table 12-1 will easily enable one to calculate this information.

The FDA regulations require that the content of seven vitamins and minerals be stated. These are the vitamins A, C, thiamine, riboflavin, and niacin, and the minerals iron and calcium. Twelve others (vitamin D, vitamin E, folacin, vitamin B_6, vitamin B_{12}, pantothenic acid, biotin, zinc, copper, magnesium, phosphorus, and iodine) may be declared if the manufacturer so wishes. All nineteen shall be stated as the percentage of the U.S. RDA that is contained in one serving. No other vitamins or minerals can be claimed on the label. This limitation is to prevent manufacturers from claiming nutrients that the scientific community believes to be unnecessary in the human diet.

FOODS, SUPPLEMENTS, AND DRUGS

The labeling laws as originally presented were very specific about the classification of products. Foods with added nutrients that represent up to 50 percent of the U.S. RDA are considered ordinary foods. Products with added nutrients that represent between 50 and 150 percent of the RDA are considered "dietary supplements" and must be labeled as such. Products with nutrients over 150 percent of the RDA are considered "drugs" and must be so labeled. It is unlikely that many food manufacturers will choose to label their foods as drugs, because the regulations governing the sale of drugs are more stringent than those for food. Interestingly, several of the breakfast cereals that contain 100 percent of the RDA of a number of nutrients are now labeled as dietary supplements. One exception to the drug ruling is that if the nutrient occurs naturally in the food at levels above 150 percent of the RDA, the food need not be labeled as a drug. The FDA has recently relaxed the proposed ruling that preparations with over 150 percent of the RDA be called drugs. They can now be marketed as dietary supplements.

Table 12-1. The U.S. RDA Values for Human Nutrition

Nutrients	Units
Vitamin A	5,000 international units
Vitamin C (ascorbic acid)	60 milligrams
Thiamine (Vitamin B_1)	1.5 milligrams
Riboflavin (Vitamin B_2)	1.7 milligrams
Niacin	20 milligrams
Calcium	1.0 gram
Iron	18 milligrams
Vitamin D	400 international units
Vitamin E	30 international units
Vitamin B_6	2.0 milligrams
Folic acid (folacin)	0.4 milligrams
Vitamin B_{12}	6 micrograms
Phosphorus	1.0 gram
Iodine	150 micrograms
Magnesium	400 milligrams
Zinc	15 milligrams
Copper	2 milligrams
Biotin	0.3 milligrams
Pantothenic acid	10 milligrams

Federal Register, 38, no. 13 (January 19, 1973), 2124; 38, no. 49 (March 14, 1973), 6950; 38, no. 148 (August 2, 1973), 20702.

THE VOLUNTARY ASPECT

The nutritional labeling laws are voluntary, with two exceptions. If a manufacturer adds nutrients or makes nutritional claims, the labels must state the amounts of the five vitamins and two minerals. If a manufacturer does not add nutrients and does not make nutrient claims, then he does not have to label the product in this manner. The concept of voluntary labeling makes good sense because it will allow a manufacturer to label or not to label some food products and may soften the economic impact for complete, mandatory nutritional labeling, which may come later. Proponents of the present legislation are betting that pressure from competition in the marketplace will persuade most manufacturers to comply with the new labeling laws even if they do not add nutrients.

The nutritional labeling laws will have an indirect effect on nutrient content. Marketing managers will not like to see the asterisks that denote "contains less than 2 percent of the U.S. RDA of these nutrients" and will bring pressure on the producers to make their products appear better nutritionally. This has been referred to as "the horsepower race," and it might well be that. However, current legislation is sufficient to curb abuses in this area. Modest additions of nutrients would probably be an advantage from a marketing point of view and marketing managers may encourage this development.

Purveyors of organic and health foods may be hurt by the nutritional labeling laws. They sell food to the public and as such should comply with the food laws. They usually make nutritional claims and thus will have to label the nutrient content of their products. For the first time, the consumer will have the opportunity to compare the nutrient content of health foods, natural foods, and commercial foods. Some of the comparisons are fascinating. For example, read the labels on some of the nonfortified natural breakfast cereals and compare them with the labels on the fortified cereals.

The nutritional claims for some foods will be modified by the new laws, since any nutritional claim should be capable of substantiation by good nutrition data. For example, the following claims will not be allowed.

1. That the food, because of the presence or absence of certain dietary properties, is adequate or effective in the prevention, cure, mitigation or treatment of any disease or symptom.

2. That a balanced diet of ordinary foods cannot supply adequate amounts of nutrients.

3. That the lack of optimum nutritive quality of a food by reason of the soil on which the food was grown, is or may be responsible for an inadequacy or deficiency in the quality of the daily diet.

4. That the storage, transportation, processing or cooking of a food is or may be responsible for an inadequacy or deficiency in the quality of the daily diet.

5. That the food has dietary properties when such properties are of no significant value or need in human nutrition.[1]

The elimination of claims such as these will help considerably to prevent the spread of misinformation on human nutrition. At the same time, it will not prevent the use of legitimate nutrition claims.

[1] *Federal Register*, March 11, 1973.

Some people have suggested that the amounts of nutrients on a label be obtained from tables of nutritional data. This idea was not adopted because the existing tables are not adequate for the purpose and a much greater data bank is needed. Others have objected to the inclusion of only seven mandatory nutrients. What about the other thirty-three or so that are known to be required for optimum human nutrition? The answer is that if the seven are supplied, there is every likelihood that the other thirty-three will be present also. If situations occur where this is not true, then the laws can be modified.

THE OUTLOOK

The nutritional labeling laws are a very complex package of regulations. They deal with an exceedingly wide array of food products and are open to many interpretations, most of which are beyond the scope of this chapter. In the area of enforcement, for example, one FDA spokesman was asked how one should obtain the data for the content of nutrients in a food. He answered facetiously, "Use a table of random numbers—but be sure you are correct." He really meant that the methods of analysis are up to the manufacturer, but the results should agree with the official methods accepted by the FDA and the USDA.

The implementation of the nutritional labeling laws will unquestionably add to the cost of food to the consumer. There will be a large cost to the manufacturer for the initial data, and a much smaller continuing cost entailed by making sure the data are current. Hopefully, the overall cost to the consumer per unit of food will be very small. It will take a tremendous educational campaign to enable consumers to take optimum advantage of the labeling laws. The cost of compliance and the cost of education will have to be balanced against the advantages to consumers. Yet the expenditures are inevitable because the United States is tending to include more processed foods in its food supply. For example, in 1941 an estimated 10 percent of our food was highly processed. The figure was about 50 percent in 1975, and will undoubtedly increase in the future.

Against this background, the old concept of the "basic four" food groups (dairy products, fruits and vegetables, cereal products, and meats) has become inadequate for nutritional guidance. We will have to superimpose more sophisticated yardsticks on top of the basic four. One step in this direction is the declaration of nutrient content on the labels of foods. If the educational goal is beyond the capacity of the American public, then the food fortification program should progress to the point where it would be very difficult to maintain an unbalanced diet. Perhaps we should proceed along this route in any event. Federal legislation is moving toward national nutritional-quality guidelines,[2] and the net effect is to encourage nutrification. There will always be individuals who prefer to eat only one or two foods. One cannot legislate against this belief, but one can educate.

BIBLIOGRAPHY

Deutsch, Ronald M., *Nutrition Labeling: How It Can Work for You*, 1975. National Nutrition Consortium, 9650 Rockville Pike, Bethesda, Md. 20014.

Nutrition Labeling: Tools for Its Use. Agriculture Information Bulletin 382. Washington, D.C.: U.S.D.A., 1975.

---

[2] See the *Federal Register*, June 14, 1974.

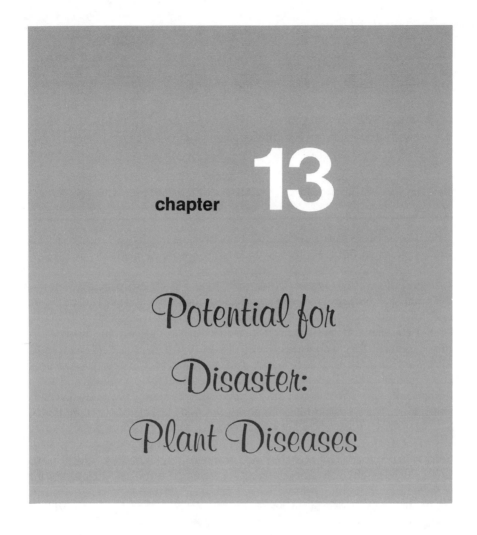

chapter **13**

Potential for Disaster: Plant Diseases

Every person born on this earth has one aspiration in common—to have enough to eat. Let us assume that food means calories and that 2,500 calories per day per person is a good aim. The calories have to come from agricultural production—there are no other significant sources on the world scene. A further narrowing is possible: calories means primarily cereal grains. If we broaden the concept to mean plant products, it is obvious that nearly all the food available to man comes from plant products. Plants have been subject to diseases throughout recorded history, and a number of well-documented disasters have taken place. The potential for disaster may be even greater today, in spite of humans ingenuity, because of the pressure on the land for increased yield and because of the increase in monoculture. The never ending battle between plant pests and agricultural production will grow more intense. It will require all the resources of sophisticated agricultural technology to maintain a favorable balance. This is no area for reduced support of research and human resources.

Every food crop has its own spectrum of pests. A few examples are described in the following pages.

THE POTATO BLIGHT

The Irish potato famine has the dubious honor of being perhaps the worst crop failure in history. It caused untold hardship in Ireland and triggered large waves of emigration.

Ireland in the eighteenth century was a poor country dominated by English absentee landlords who exacted a toll from the villagers and allowed them very small plots (a half-acre) of land to live on. The Irish learned that white potatoes could be grown in "lazybeds" raised several feet above the bogs. These beds, 6 to 8 feet wide and 100 feet long, could be located out of sight of the English soldiers and provided an excellent supply of food. The populace came to depend on the potato as a staple and sometimes as the only food in their diet. This dependence increased until disaster struck in 1845.

The spring of 1845 was warm and pleasant, but in the summer the temperature dropped as much as seven degrees below normal and cold rains began. The weather was ideal for the spread of the potato blight. The blight was caused by the growth of a fungus, *Phytophtora infestans*, which had overwintered on cull potatoes in piles around the houses. A spore germinates on leaves of potato plants and immediately spreads within the plant. In a matter of days, each germinating spore produces millions of additional spores and the disease spreads like wildfire. Most plants are killed, and any that escape with a mild infection may rot in storage or serve as sources of infection for the next year.

The availability of the potato in Ireland as a source of food enabled the population to increase from 4 million in 1800 to 8 million in 1845. With the failure of the potato crop in 1845, the land could not support that many people and the populace became desperate. Food aid from England enabled the Irish to survive the winter of 1845, and the planting season of 1846 came. The rains returned, along with optimum conditions for the growth of the fungus, and again the potato crop was destroyed. This time, the reserves had been used up and famine struck in earnest. The folklore of Ireland is filled with tales of horror of this period. The populace, weakened by starvation, fell easy prey to dysentery, typhus, and many other diseases. In ten years, Ireland lost 3 million people; 1 million died and 2 million emigrated. They came to the United States, Canada, and other parts of the British Empire.

The early emigrants in 1845 and 1846 arrived in the New World prior to the outbreaks of disease. Later emigrants were not as fortunate, and the conditions aboard the ships for people already weakened with disease were awful. The conditions were similar to those on the slave ships with no place to cook, improper latrines, and certainly no place to heal the sick. On the journey across the Atlantic Ocean, one of every twenty Irish refugees was buried at sea. One can imagine their condition when they arrived in the United States and Canada. Local residents were not happy to see the new arrivals in the disease-ridden ships. One monument to the Irish refugees still stands in Montreal—a mound containing the bodies of 6,000 Irish. In spite of the problems, a tremendous number of Irish were absorbed by the United States and Canada. They have left their mark. The railroads across Canada in the 1800s were built by gangs of Irish "navvies." Two families, the Fitzgeralds and the Kennedys, produced an American president.

Ireland was not the only land to suffer the effects of the potato blight. The failure of the potato crop in 1916 in Germany was a decisive factor in the inability of Germany to win World War I. Seven hundred thousand Germans starved to death during the winter of 1916-17. In 1928, an outbreak of the fungus in the eastern United States caused the loss of many millions of bushels of potatoes.

Losses due to potato blight are not widespread today, owing to the development of resistant varieties of potatoes and the constant application of chemical sprays. In some areas, as many as fifteen sprays are required. The crop protection experts tell us that there will never be another disaster with potatoes such as the 1846 famine. Let us hope they are right!

ERGOT IN RYE

Rye cereal grain is attacked by a fungus, *Claviceps purpurea*, which germinates in the spring to produce slender reddish-blue stalks with a pink globe at the top. The fungus produces millions of spores, which find their way by wind to rye flowers. Once there, they grow and produce a sweet secretion containing millions of a second type of spore. The exudation attracts insects, which spread the fungus very quickly. With cool, moist weather, the stage is set for a very rapid spread of infection. The infected kernels produce large purple cockspurs which are harvested along with the rye. The spores contain over twenty very potent alkaloids, which are very toxic to humans. The symptoms are frightening: intense pain in the abdomen, hallucinations, wild babbling, insanity, and finally death by convulsions. The ancients called the disease "holy fire" or "Heilige fever."

Ergotism has changed the course of history. The first major outbreak occurred in 857 A.D. in the Rhine valley and killed thousands of people. France, with a weakened population, could not resist the invasion from the north by the Scandinavians, who did not eat rye bread. This led to the establishment of what is now known as Normandy. Peter the Great, in 1722, led his forces against the Turks at Astrakhan and, like all armies at that time, lived off the land. The bounty included rye, again with ergot, and 20,000 soliders died. Horses are also susceptible, and the Cossack cavalry was destroyed. The Russians never did capture the Dardanelles, even though they have tried six times since 1722. Ergotism continues to develop in all areas where rye is grown. In 1926 and 1927 an outbreak in Russia resulted in 10,000 casualties. The latest outbreak of any size occurred in Pont-St-Esprit, France in 1951. It was caused by ergot-infested rye flour that was added to wheat flour. The outbreak resulted in 200 cases of severe and damaging illness, 32 cases of insanity, and 4 deaths.

The story of ergot in rye is spectacular because the effect of the toxins is so visible. The decrease in yield of rye grain due to ergot infestation becomes minor. Adequate control methods are available to clean the grain so that the spores are not planted along with the grain. A simple flotation process involving a 30-percent salt solution will remove nearly all the spores from grain intended for seed or consumption. There are now very rigid government regulations concerning the content of ergot in rye.

The story of ergotism has a happy ending. The powerful toxins produced by the fungus have been isolated and found to have important medical applications. Some of them have been used to induce childbirth and abortion, and to prevent bleeding, high blood pressure, and headaches. One of the alkaloids has received much publicity lately as a hallucinogen. One ergot alkaloid, discovered in 1938 by a chemist in Switzerland, turned out to be lysergic acid diethylamide (LSD). The chemist tested it on himself and was terrified, apparently, by the sensation that he was floating outside his own body. LSD has since been used to treat schizophrenia and other mental disorders. For these purposes, LSD is synthesized rather than being obtained from ergot. However, ergot is still the main source for many of the other alkaloids.

THE WHEAT RUSTS

The wheat plant probably originated thousands of years ago in the hills of Asia Minor, and wheat rust came soon after. Theophrastus of Greece, the "Father of Botany," described the rusts twenty-two centuries ago, and they are no less important today.

Wheat rust is a fungus disease that receives its name from the brown or rusty appearance of an infected field. Three main types of wheat rust are known—stem, leaf, and stripe rust—and many strains of each exist. The infection starts in the spring when, under warm, moist conditions, a spore carried on the wind reaches a wheat plant. The spore soon produces a fungus growth, which feeds on the wheat plant, and in a week or so the fungus produces thousands of spores. Each spore germinates upon reaching a wheat plant, and the cycle is repeated with frightening rapidity. As the wheat plant matures (with greatly reduced yields of grain), the rust parasite forms a different type of spore, called a teliospore. These can remain dormant all winter and germinate in the spring, producing yet another type of spore, the basidiospore. These spores fall on the young leaves of the barberry plant and produce male and female forms. These mate and produce aeciospores, which are distributed in the wind and infect the young wheat plants. And so the cycle goes.

The alternate host for stem rust is the barberry plant. Leaf rust has two alternate hosts, the basilick plant and the meadow rue. Stripe rust has no known alternate host as yet. The existence of a sexual stage on the alternate host has awesome implications for wheat production. The millions of chance matings makes it possible for new races of wheat rust to develop at a rate that taxes the ability of the cereal breeder. Almost every new variety of rust-resistant wheat that has been developed painstakingly by the plant breeder in the past half century has been successfully parasitized by some virulent new form of rust.

Wheat is the most important cereal grain of commerce. It is grown around the world wherever the climate is appropriate, and specific varieties have been developed for each climatic area. The famed Marquis variety was introduced in the United States around 1900. It was immediately planted widely because of its yield and quality. Unfortunately, a rust race developed in 1916 and doomed the Marquis variety. The Marquis was replaced by a cross of Marquis and Kota called Ceres, but in 1935 the black stem rust (race 56) emerged and millions of acres of Ceres wheat were severely damaged. The Thatcher variety was developed but eventually had to be replaced by varieties that were more rust-resistant. In 1953, race 15B appeared, producing losses of up to 75 percent in durum wheat and 35 percent in bread wheat. Again, the geneticists developed new varieties, and they have since been able to keep one step ahead of the development of new rust strains. How long can this be expected to continue? There are no other established methods of control to date.

Other methods of control of wheat rust have been suggested. An obvious one is to eliminate the barberry plant. The first barberry eradication law was passed in France in 1660, and the first such law in the United States was enacted in 1726, but the barberry plant is still with us. The uprooting of millions of barberry bushes helped, but was no solution. Chemical sprays would certainly be effective in reducing the extent of rust damage, but fungicide treatment is not practical; it is simply too expensive. In 1938 the United States lost an estimated 100 million bushels of wheat to leaf rust. In 1953-54, strain 15B cost the United States and Canada about 200 million bushels.

THE GRAIN SMUTS

The grain smuts are a group of fungi that attack wheat, corn, oats, and barley—in that order of importance. The flour made from infected grain looks dirty—hence the name. The fungus propagates by germinating in the soil in the spring. The fungus filaments enter the cereal plant and grow inside it, finally reaching the seeds. These seeds then become small containers, each holding millions of smut spores. With earlier agricultural methods, the smut spores were sown together with the grain and always took a percentage of the harvest. In order to sow cleaner grain, a series of chemical treatments was developed, starting with copper solutions around 1850 and progressing to formaldehyde and mercury salts, and, since 1950, hexachlorobenzene. These applications applied directly to the grain kernels were effective and have saved billions of tons of food.

Chemical treatment of the seeds is effective for smut spores on the outside of the seeds, but some fungi infect the plant at the time of flowering and become embedded within the kernels themselves. These fungi germinate when the seed is planted. Chemical treatments strong enough to kill the embedded fungi would probably kill the seed as well. The new systemic chemicals that travel through the plant show promise of controlling this type of infestaton, but conventional control is to rotate the crops. With increasing pressure for monoculture and continuous use of land, crop rotation and fallowing (leaving the land idle for one or more crop seasons) is becoming more difficult.

Plant pathologists have identified over 2,000 types of smut, and the number will undoubtedly increase. Scientific methods of control are making them less destructive than in prior years. Losses to smut in the winter-wheat belts in the United States are estimated at 3 percent. Fortunately, to date the bread wheats seem to be less susceptible. Before World War I, losses of wheat due to smut ran as high as 85 percent in some fields. At threshing time, the clouds of black smut were a real explosive hazard to the threshing machines and very unpleasant for the workers. Smutty flour was not uncommon, but if it was too badly contaminated, bread made from the flour had a disgusting smell. An enterprising English miller attempted to utilize smutty flour by baking little cakes with molasses added to mask the color. He added a pungent spice to mask the unpleasant smell, and, lo and behold—gingerbread was discovered. Today, ginger snaps and gingerbread are not made from smutty flour, since there are very rigorous controls on the amount of smut allowed in commercial flour.

Smut consumes about 2 percent of the world's harvest of grain today. It has been kept to that low figure by chemical control and the development of resistant varieties. Apparently, smuts mutate very readily, and as we noted above, there are already over 2,000 of them. So the race goes on!

CORN BLIGHT

In 1970, the United States lost 15 percent of its entire corn crop to an infestation of blight. The stage was set for a modern day disaster. Panic reigned behind the scenes, but the technology that caused the disaster reacted so successfully and so quickly that the problem disappeared. The speed and extent of the successful reaction has no counterpart in history.

The corn blight was caused by a quirk in the production of hybrid corn. Hybrid corn is a source of pride in American agriculture, for it has been heralded as the greatest single breakthrough in agricultural science in this century. The story of hybrid corn began in 1917 in Connecticut when Donald F. Jones discovered the concept of hybrid vigor. He crossed an inbred line A with an inbred B to form an AB selection. Similarly, a line C was crossed with a line D to form CD. When the AB line was crossed with the CD line, the resultant ABCD progeny showed an increase in yield of 25 percent. It took twenty-five years to realize the commercial potential of this concept, but by World War II nearly all the field corn grown in the United States was hybrid corn.

Hybrid corn seed is produced by alternately planting six rows of AB and two rows of CD in the fields. The male pollen on the tassels of the AB rows was removed by taking off the tassels at the top of the plant by hand. The ears of AB corn thus had to be fertilized by the CD pollen, thereby ensuring the cross-pollination. The hand operation provided work for thousands of high school students but it was expensive. A cheaper way would be very welcome.

In 1931, Marcus M. Rhoades discovered a corn plant with sterile tassels. The genetic factor for male sterility could be incorporated into the AB corn, and presto—no need for hand detasseling! Unfortunately, the progeny were also sterile. However, another male-sterile gene was discovered in Texas. In 1948, Jones reasoned that there must be a gene that restored fertility. He did, in fact, find such a gene, and he incorporated it into the CD corn. This meant that he could use a male sterility factor in the AB corn and a restorer gene in the CD corn and obtain fertile seed in the ABCD generation. The stage was set to produce hybrid corn without hand detasseling. The factor that caused male sterility was located in the cytoplasm of the cell, not the nucleus, and since it was found in Texas it was called the T strain. The T strain was soon widely incorporated into hybrid corn seed.

The use of T-cytoplasm also brought a liability. The fungus *Helminthosporium maydis* had always been present in corn fields but was considered a very minor pest. A report appeared in the Philippines in 1962 that T-cytoplasm corn was susceptible to *H. maydis*. The corn was tested in the United States with negative results, and the threat was dismissed as being due to different growing conditions in the Philippines. Unfortunately, a new race of *H. maydis* (race T) appeared in 1970, and all corn with T-cytoplasm was susceptible. The blight appeared first in 1970 in Florida and then moved north and west with frightening rapidity. Over 500 million bushels of corn were lost. Worried corn specialists feared that in 1971 the United States might lose almost its entire corn crop. It didn't happen!

The scientists soon located the problem, and a crash program was started to eliminate seed corn carrying the T-factor. Seed grain was produced in the off-season in Mexico, and in as many other areas as possible, so that enough resistant seed would be available for the 1971 season. It was not possible to shift such a large industry so fast, so resistant seed was allocated to the more susceptible southern areas and T-strain corn was, of necessity, diverted north. Fortunately, the weather in 1971 was unfavorable to the spread of the blight and disaster was averted. In 1971, sufficient resistant seed was produced for the whole 1972 crop and the disaster was eliminated.

Hybrid corn is again being produced in the United States by hand detasseling. This was the first time that cytoplasm had been shown to be an important aspect of diversity. A new dimension had appeared in plant breeding. The technology that produced the potential for disaster removed it. With an interesting form of hindsight, it was perhaps fortunate that the near disaster occurred with hybrid corn. The ability of the breeders to form new combinations enabled them to eliminate the problem in one year. If the susceptibility was due to a factor in an open-pollinated variety, the solution may have been much more difficult.

COFFEE RUST

The story of the coffee rust is a fascinating example of how a disease can change a country's way of life. The coffee plant probably originated over a thousand years ago in Ethiopia. Turkish coffeehouses existed in the fifteenth century. The Europeans became very interested in this new drink and attempted to smuggle out seeds for many years, but with no success. However, by 1600 an Indian on a holy pilgrimage had already taken some seeds back to India. When the Dutch came to India as traders, they found coffee trees in the hill country. The Dutch planted coffee trees in Ceylon and Java, and the coffee tree then spread through the Caribbean islands, Brazil, and Mexico.

Britain took over Ceylon in 1797 and in 1825 reestablished the coffee plantations there. Coffeehouses had been established in Britain in 1652 and were very popular for over a century. It was to cater to the coffeehouse trade that Britain restablished the coffee plantings in Ceylon. The boom was on! Exports of coffee increased from almost zero in 1830 to 100 million pounds in 1870. Planters grew rich beyond their wildest dreams, and then disaster struck. The coffee rust *Hemileia vastatrix*, which was similar to the grain rust, spread through the coffee plantations. The spores germinate on the coffee leaves in warm, humid weather and produce more spores in a matter of weeks. The wind-blown spores soon devastated the coffee plantations. The weakened trees withered and died. In 1892, coffee exports from Ceylon, the world's leading exporter, had dwindled to zero. There was no cure for the coffee rust in Ceylon, and there was only one alternative—switch to tea. Starting in 1875, the dying coffee plantations were replanted with tea. This was a stupendous operation, one that has no parallel in history. In the meantime the British had been importing tea, since it was cheaper than coffee. Britain promoted its tea trade throughout the Empire and became a tea-drinking country. Ceylon switched from a coffee to a tea economy.

Control of the coffee rusts centers around growing the trees in the shade. Indifferent success was obtained with a number of chemical sprays. The real answer is the development of resistant varieties. Fortunately, such attempts have been partially successful and at least one variety of *Coffee arabica* seems to have some resistance. Other hardy varieties are derived from *Coffee robusta*, which has quite a different taste. Nearly all of the *robusta* in commerce today is grown in Africa. Most experts consider *robusta* to be much inferior to *arabica*.

The Western Hemisphere grows 90 percent of the world's coffee. The rust spores have spread east to the Philippines and to the west coast of Africa. If they do jump the 2,000 miles of ocean to the New World, either by ship or airplane, they will surely devastate the plantations of *arabica* in Brazil and Colombia. The fungus spores did reach Puerto Rico once in 1903, but an alert inspector destroyed the plant before the spores could become established. If the disease does spread to the New World, *robusta* may be the only type of coffee available. Tea, anyone?

BANANA DISEASES

The banana trade in the United States offers an interesting tale of agriculture, science, and politics. The banana fruit itself is estimated to be a million years old; some even say that the "apple" in the Garden of Eden was a banana.

It became apparent to entrepreneurs after the American Civil War that opportunities existed in the banana trade. Hundreds of companies were established during the nineteenth century to produce and ship bananas to the United States. Business was so good that around 1900, over 800,000 tons of bananas were being shipped annually to the United States. The United Fruit Company emerged as the giant in the trade and in the 1950s shipped over 2 million tons of bananas per year to the United States and Europe.

In Central America, the pressure on the land to produce bananas and the subsequent monoculture led to the first serious outbreak of Panama wilt in 1915, and production dropped. Panama wilt is a fungus disease (*Fusarium oxysporum cubesse*) that remains in the soil until it reaches a banana plant. It grows within the plant and soon kills the plant. Enough virgin land was brought into production to restore the crop. However, in 1930 a second wave of Panama wilt reduced production by about 50 percent. Flooding the land for six months was found to be a remedy, but it works only if one has enough land and enough water.

Around 1935, a new scourge attacked the banana plants—sigatoka disease, caused by the fungus *Cercospora musae*. This fungus germinates from spores on the banana leaf and soon destroys the plant. It appeared in the Caribbean, first in Trinidad, and then spread rapidly to Jamaica, Honduras, and Guatemala. Production dropped rapidly, and a feverish search for a cure began. A cure of sorts was found in the form of sprays of a well-known chemical containing copper sulphate—Bordeaux mixture. Another type of mineral oil spray gives some protection. These two banana-plant diseases have been kept under partial control in recent years by a combination of chemical sprays and land flooding, but it is an uneasy truce. A more virulent form of either disease could reappear at any time. Eventual control will probably depend on the production of resistant varieties, but progress in this area is very slow.

MISCELLANEOUS

The diseases discussed above were chosen because of their spectacular effect or sheer magnitude, but there have been many other, lesser-known plant diseases. The bacterium causing the fire blight of pears devastated the pear orchards around 1900, and even today, pears cannot be grown in some areas. A bacterium causes crown gall (a type of cancer in trees), for which no control other than eradication is known. The citrus canker threatened to eliminate the citrus industry of the United States, and a frantic total eradication program was started in Florida and Mississippi. If a single infected tree was found, the entire orchard was destroyed. The operation succeeded and the disease never reached Arizona and California. The invasion of the Mediterranean fruit fly threatened to destroy the entire Florida citrus industry in the 1930s. A large-scale spraying program eliminated the insect. These are two of the few battles man has won.

If we study the history of trees, we may be glad that we do not eat them. I write this chapter in a study paneled with "wormy chestnut" wood. The American chestnut was a wonderful tree with a trunk diameter up to 4 feet and a height of 100 feet. It provided superb lumber as well as chestnuts for the wild turkeys. It grew from Maine to Michigan and south to Louisiana, constituting over 25 percent of the total tree population in this country. In 1904, a tree in the New York Botanical Gardens began to die of a fungus disease. The disease blocked the tracheae of the tree and spread very rapidly. By 1935, there were no living chestnut trees. After death, the trees are usually invaded by wood borers, which produce the characteristic pattern of wormy chestnut now available only for picture frames. The panels in my study were milled from trees that were dead but still standing in 1935. The disease crossed the ocean and is now eliminating the chestnut trees of Italy and southern Europe.

The American elm is a gracious and imposing shade tree. In 1930, two sick trees were discovered in Cleveland and Cincinnati. A fungus disease was imported from Holland in elm logs destined for furniture veneer, and it spread rapidly. There is no cure to date, and the American elms are doomed. The total cost of removal of the infected trees is estimated at many billions of dollars. Oak trees are also being infected by a newly discovered fungus disease, but the rate of spread is much slower. Maple trees showed a mysterious decline during the drought in the 1950s, but, fortunately, this malady seems to be slowing down. Let us hope that some of our important food crops do not go the way of the chestnut and the elm.

THEORETICAL APPROACHES

The spectacular successes of the Green Revolution with wheat and rice have been criticized on the grounds that the many millions of acres planted to genetically similar varieties represented potential disaster. However, modern plant breeders realize this and have labored to broaden the genetic base. With every passing year, the potential for disaster decreases as new varieties are introduced. The oat crop in the Midwest is a good example of the hazards of genetic uniformity. In 1942, the Victoria variety, which was resistant to almost every disease, was introduced. It soon replaced all other varieties of oats. In 1946 the fungus *Helminthosporium victoriae* developed, and the whole crop was susceptible.

The National Academy of Sciences in the United States has surveyed all the major American crops to determine the degree of uniformity and vulnerability among them.[1] For example, 96 percent of the pea crop is planted to only two types, and 95 percent of the peanut crop is composed of nine varieties. But in the case of wheat, the largest two varieties constitute only 25 percent of the crop. The degree of uniformity desired in the American food supply is contributing to a narrow genetic base. The genetic uniformity may even extend to several varieties. For example, the same dwarfing gene is used for several varieties of wheat. Similarly, with rice. The stringless gene in beans is similar in several varieties. The gene in tomatoes that makes the plant set all its fruit at the same time is incorporated into a number of varieties. This type of genetic character may or may not make the plant susceptible to a new race of parasites. As

[1] *Genetic Vulnerability of Major Crops* (Washington, D.C.: National Academy of Sciences, 1972).

we move from chemical control to genetic resistance, this becomes an interesting question.

BIBLIOGRAPHY

Carefoot, G. L., and E. R. Sprott, *Famine on the Wind*. New York: Rand McNally and Co., 1967.

Genetic Vulnerability of Major Crops. Washington, D.C.: National Academy of Sciences, 1972.

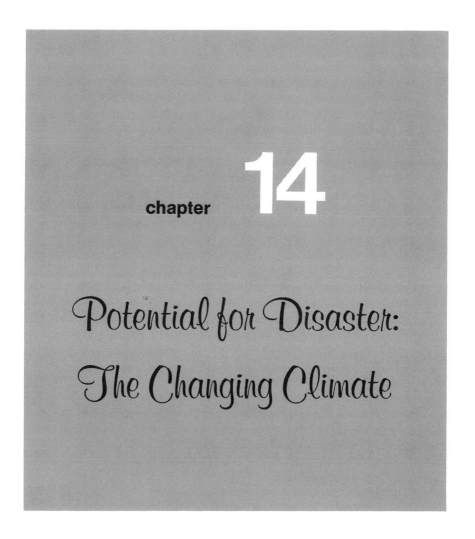

chapter **14**

Potential for Disaster: The Changing Climate

Recent increases in population have triggered a great deal of discussion, both scientific and emotional, on the capacity of the earth to provide enough food. We are not yet in an era in which significant quantities of synthetic food are being produced, so we have to depend on agriculture. Conventional agriculture is tuned so closely to climate that any change in climate could have devastating effects on food production. Changes as small as a drop of 1°C in average temperature can have a large effect on food production. A drop in average temperature of 2°C would eliminate wheat production above the thirty-eighth parallel—that is, wheat production in all of Canada and all of the United States north of Kansas. An average drop of 3°C could produce another ice age. Conversely, an average rise of 3°C would melt polar ice and flood most of our coastal cities.

Most long-range climatologists agree that the earth's temperature is a delicate equilibrium between energy received from the sun and energy dissipated by the earth into space. Many complex forces operate to maintain this equilibrium, and the role of modern long-range climatologists is to attempt to understand these complex phenomena. Progress in this field is vital if we are to develop climate forecasting systems that will enable agriculturalists to respond to changing patterns in order to avert future famines.

Famines are not new to this planet. Historians have clearly identified forty-nine famines between the years 975 and 1804. Famines have been correlated with cold periods in the earth's history. However, the influence of the colder climate was less important in the past because there was less pressure on the land to produce food then. With our greatly increased population and consequent greater dependence on the available land, future cold periods become much more important. The forecasters tell us that we have now entered another cold period.

METHODS OF FORECASTING

The methods used by the long-range forecasters make a fascinating tale. They include analyses of the type and quantity of pollen in bogs, the deposition of lead as dust in glaciers, the variations in tree growth rings, the changing ratios of isotopes of oxygen in earth cores, and the settling of atmospheric dust. Dr. Reid Bryson at the University of Wisconsin is probably one of the better-known long-range climatologists and the following discussion is based primarily on his publications.[1]

It is possible to estimate the average temperature of Iceland by measuring the duration and extent of the ice floes covering the land and surrounding water. The position of the ice and the average temperature have been measured since 1890. The Vikings kept excellent records of the duration and extent of the ice for the last thousand years. Thus, by calculating the relation between average temperature and ice position and projecting backward in time, the average temperature could be calculated back to 900 A.D.

[1] R. A. Bryson, "A Perspective on Climatic Change," *Science*, 184, no. 4138 (1974), pp. 753–59.

THE CHANGE IN TEMPERATURE

In Figure 14-1, an arbitrary base line for temperature was chosen and average temperatures above and below were plotted. The black line starting at 1890 is the measured mean temperature for the whole Northern Hemisphere. It correlates well with the mean temperature of Iceland. Interpreting Figure 14-1 is both fascinating and scary. The Vikings colonized Greenland in the tenth century, and apparently that land was aptly named. But by the fifteenth century, the colonies had been frozen out. There was a brief warm spell around 1400 A.D. and a "little ice age" between 1550 and 1900. The earth started to warm up about 1890, and this trend continued until 1945. Since 1945 the earth has been cooling rapidly. Grandfather was right when he said winters were colder in the late 1800s.

The change in temperature from 1890 to 1945 was only $3°C$, but the effects of this change on agriculture were dramatic.[2] The total drop in temperature since 1945 is only $2.7°C$ to date, but this decrease has reduced hay yields in Iceland by 25 percent.[3] The growing season in England is two weeks shorter. Icelandic fishing fleets can only fish to the south now because of the drifting ice. The drop in temperature since 1945 is believed to be the longest unbroken trend downward in hundreds of years.

The 300-to-400-year cycles, important as they may be in themselves, become even more ominous when superimposed on a 100,000-year cycle. Researchers have been able to plot the average temperature of the earth over the long periods by studying the ratio of oxygen isotopes in shells from sea-bed cores in the Caribbean. Apparently, the oxygen ratio is affected by the water temperature. When the temperature is plotted against time for 700,000 years (Figure 14-2), a 100,000-year cycle emerges. Apparently, we are now at the temperature peak of one cycle; that is, we are experiencing the warmest temperatures that have occurred in the last 100,000 years. If we superimposed the 300-to-400-year cycle described above and the 100,000-year-cycle, it is obvious that the greatest increase in population has occurred at a time when we are enjoying the most advantageous climate in the last 100,000 years. If we are concerned about the food supply in this period, how can we hope to feed the world when the climate gets worse? Yet the population growth rolls along!

[2] W. L. Decker, "Unsettled and Variable Climate—Uncertain Food Supply," *Indus. Res.*, November 1974, pp. 51-56.

[3] J. E. Newman and R. C. Pickett, "World Climate and Food Supply Variations," *Science*, 186, no. 4167 (1974), 877-81.

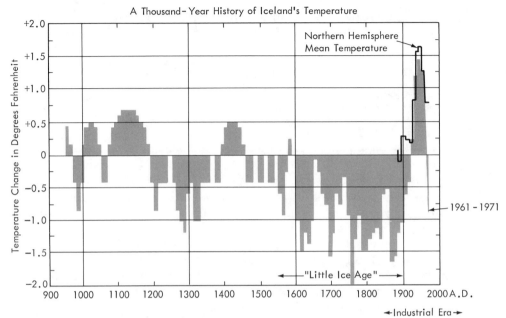

Figure 14-1: From T. Alexander, "Ominous Changes in the World's Weather," Fortune,
February 1974, p. 91. Parios Studios for Fortune Magazine © 1974 Time, Inc.
Reprinted by permission.

Broader Implications

The above prospect is chilling enough but the cooling trend has
many other implications. The cooling of the earth results in an increase in the polar ice caps. The cold air above the ice caps interferes
with the air currents moving around the globe. The large-scale circulation in the atmosphere is influenced by the temperature difference
between the equator and the poles. In simplified terms, warm air
rises at the equator and dumps much of its moisture on equatorial
rainy belts. The dry air moves up and out toward each pole, then
descends to form the world's major deserts. Some of the air moves
back toward the equator and forms the trade winds. The remainder
moves further north or south and forms the westerlies at low altitudes and the jet stream at higher altitudes. The cold air over the
poles pushes both types of winds further south, and this is probably
one reason why the Sahara Desert is moving south.

The six-year drought in the Sahel, a band south of the Sahara
Desert comprising parts of the countries of Senegal, Mali, Mauritania,
Upper Volta, Niger, and Chad, has caused untold misery and famine
to the people of that area. The climate change may be only one fac-

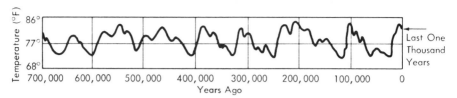

Figure 14-2: Temperature Through Geological Time. From T. Alexander, "Ominous Changes in the World's Weather," Fortune, *February 1974, p. 94. Reprinted by permission.*

tor in the enlargement of the desert in the Sahel area.[4] This enlargement may also be a classic example of "The Tragedy of the Commons."[5] When the French colonial era ended, the old tribal systems began to break down and the nomadic population doubled. More important, since animals were considered a source of wealth, the cattle population tripled. In times of plentiful rainfall, adequate fodder was available, but when the drought started the land could not support the animal population and the system collapsed. The Sahara Desert started to move south at a much faster rate. This movement could be slowed down even in drought years by appropriate land management. This was pointed out by American observers who, while studying satellite photos, noticed a green pentagon-shaped area in the desert. A team of investigators found that it was a 250,000-acre ranch partitioned into five areas. Each area was grazed once in five years. The ranch had been started in 1968 after the onset of the drought, and the only difference between the green area and the desert was a barbed wire fence. The reclamation of the desert is a tremendous task, but some progress is being made. For example, Algeria has started the most ambitious project of the century—the building of a 950-mile tree barrier across the entire country, approximately 200 miles south of the Mediterranean Sea. Composed of eucalyptus and Aleppo pine, the green belt will vary from 3½ to 15 miles wide and is expected to take twenty years to complete at a minimum cost of 100 million dollars. Hopefully, it will help return Algeria to its agricultural productivity of 3,000 years ago. Yet Algeria is a small part of the land menaced by the Sahara Desert.

[4] A discussion of the humanitarian problems in the Sahel can be found in *Disaster in the Desert* by H. Sheets and R. Morris. Carnegie Endowment for International Peace, 1717 Mass. Ave. N.W., Washington D.C., 1974.

[5] *The Tragedy of the Commons* is a classic environment film in which a town common was shown to be able to support, for grazing purposes, a given number of cattle. Since the town common belonged to all the townspeople, some insisted on attempting to graze more cattle. This resulted in destruction of the grass cover and the town common could not support any cattle.

The winds that are pushed south by the polar air masses have important implications for other areas. They form the monsoons that bring life-giving rains to India. Part of this rain has been falling in the ocean, and drought is increasing in India. The same conditions are affecting the grain producing steppes in part of the USSR. In North America, the West is becoming colder and wetter and parts of Kansas have had rainfalls more severe than any of the inhabitants can remember. Part of the grain-growing area in Canada's northwest had a snowfall in August. The cooler air from the west that is moving east and being warmed on the way has contributed to warmer winters in the eastern United States.

A drop in temperature usually, but not always, signifies a drop in agricultural production. It depends on whether or not temperature is the factor which is limiting growth. Apparently, with corn in Missouri it is not, because a drop in summer temperature of $1°C$ and a 10 percent increase in rainfall is estimated to increase corn production by 20 percent. The increased rainfall in the West might well increase grain production in areas where rainfall is the limiting factor. This will mean a return to the situation occurring at the time of the "forty-niner" gold rush in the sense that a hazard of crossing the plains was the height of the grass; it was head-high, and one could lose sight of the main party. These areas of the plains are practically desert today. The decrease in grass alone could have accounted for a 50 to 75 percent drop in the numbers of buffalo, aside from the overhunting. The cooling trend combined with the increase in rainfall might not harm the United States but it could be disastrous for areas further north around the world.

The Greenhouse Effect

One may well ask, "Why is the earth cooling off?" Apparently, the earth's climate is a balance between the "greenhouse effect" and the "particle effect." The greenhouse effect refers to the trapping of the sun's energy by carbon dioxide. The energy from the sun is in the form of short, visible, wavelengths which can pass freely through carbon dioxide. When this energy reaches the earth's surface, it is converted into heat and reradiated back as infrared rays. Carbon dioxide molecules absorb a portion of the infrared rays, thereby trapping the energy and producing a rise in temperature. The concentration of carbon dioxide in the atmosphere from volcanoes and fossil fuels is currently about 320 parts per million and is increasing by about 1 part per million annually. The rate of increase of carbon dioxide in the atmosphere is also increasing as a result of the increasing consumption of fossil fuels. The estimated rate of increase in temperature caused by the increase in carbon dioxide is about $0.01°C$ for each part per million of carbon dioxide. Water vapor also contributes to the greenhouse effect but is controlled by the climate in a feedback system. Carbon dioxide, on the other hand, is continually increasing.

The Particle Effect

This effect refers to the accumulation of particles in the upper atmosphere that reflect the sun's rays back into space. This reduces the energy reaching the earth's surface and thereby produces a cooling effect. It is possible to estimate the concentration of particles in the atmosphere back through history by studying the dust deposits in the ice in the polar areas. Historically, the greatest contributor has been volcanic activity. Volcanoes can produce tremendous quantities of dust in a very short time. The eruption of Tamboro in the Philippines in 1815 produced so much dust that as far as 500 kilometers away there was total darkness for three days. The world temperature fell about $1.1°C$ below normal, and 1816 became known as the "poverty year" and the "year without a summer." The eruption of Laki in Iceland and Asama in Japan, both in 1783, combined to make the following three years among the coldest on record in the Northern Hemisphere. Volcanic activity was very low from 1920 to 1955 but seems to be increasing lately. Volcanic eruptions produce spectacularly colored sunsets around the world, but they bode ill for agricultural production.

Another natural source of dust in the atmosphere is salt particles produced by the evaporation of salt water. Another may be the natural smog produced by forests. It is assumed that natural forces are the major contributors of the particles in the atmosphere, but there is evidence that man's activities are contributing more and more. The dust pall resulting from overgrazing by nomadic tribes may have contributed to the spread of the Thar Desert in northwest India and Pakistan. The dust from barren land increases the turbidity of the lower atmosphere, thereby reducing the upward currents. This reduces the cloudiness and increases the aridity. This, of course, is a local effect, but the dust from extensive agriculture probably does increase the number of particles in the air. The "slash and burn" methods of land clearance in the tropics undoubtedly contribute a great deal of smoke. The increased industrialization certainly produces more smoke particles. More recently, atomic explosions have contributed their share of dust. In the future, the possible increase in supersonic transports may contribute their share. Whatever the source of particles, there is solid evidence that the intensity of

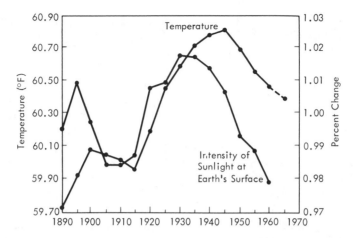

Figure 14-3: From T. Alexander, "Ominous Changes in the World's Weather," Fortune, *February 1974, p. 94. Reprinted by permission.*

sunlight reaching the earth's surface increased from 1910 to 1930 and then started down (see Figure 14-3). The temperature in the Northern Hemisphere increased from 1915 to 1945 and then started down. The lag from 1930 to 1945 was probably due to the greenhouse effect. Some workers have attempted to correlate the intensity of sunlight reaching the earth to sunspot activity on the sun. Presumably, sunspot activity is beyond human control. It seems to us that the particle and greenhouse effects are more logical explanations of climate and are open to some modification.

The prospect of attempting to feed a burgeoning world population in a less favorable agricultural environment is ominous indeed. Can we expect a reversal in temperature trends? On the basis of Figure 14-1, would you expect an immediate return to a warmer climate? A study of past trends would more likely indicate a cooler period. If indeed this is to be the case, it is vital that agricultural practices be adjusted accordingly.

OTHER APPROACHES TO CLIMATE CHANGE

The increasing concern of the world's governments with greater food supplies has led to many schemes—some grandiose, others quite practical. The Aswan Dam in Egypt, which provides power and irrigation to 2½ million acres is an accomplished and practical feat of engineering. It has probably modified the climate of the Nile valley to some extent, probably for the good. The large dams currently being planned for India, Pakistan, China, Russia, Africa, South America, and many other areas fall in this category. If the large dams involve a change in direction of flow of the rivers, we can anticipate other climate changes. For example, it is difficult to forecast the effect of the current project in Quebec in which waters from three rivers that normally flow into James Bay are being diverted south into the St. Lawrence system. Another example is the suggested southward diversion of the MacKenzie River in Canada; it normally flows into the Arctic Ocean. The diverted water would flow east to the Atlantic Coast and south as far as Mexico. The project was estimated to cost over 100 billion dollars and would involve a mind-boggling degree of international cooperation. The proposal to dam the Straits of Siberia to prevent the cold Arctic waters from flowing south would probably warm the climate of Siberia. It might change other areas as well. If indeed the world is entering another mini–ice age, the Russians may well decide that they have nothing to lose. The proposal to extract heat from the Gulf Stream as a source of energy has implications for changes in climate if an appreciable amount (10 percent?) of the energy of the Gulf Stream is removed. The current status of cloud seeding has implications for climate change—to whose advantage, one might ask. We can summarize some of the more grandiose schemes by saying that the world is not quite ready for them yet.

BIBLIOGRAPHY

Alexander, T., "Ominous Changes in the World's Weather," *Fortune*, February 1974.

Kellogg, W. W., and S. H. Schneider, "Climate Stabilization: For Better or for Worse," *Science*, 186, no. 4170 (1974), 1163-72.

"The Weather Machine," Champion International Corporation, New York, 1975.

$\mathcal{I}$ndex